THE
ENDTIME
FAMILY

THE
ENDTIME
FAMILY

Children of God

William Sims Bainbridge

STATE UNIVERSITY OF NEW YORK PRESS

Published by
State University of New York Press, Albany

For information, address State University of New York Press,
90 State Street, Suite 700, Albany, NY 12207

Production by Cathleen Collins
Marketing by Michael Campochiaro

Library of Congress Cataloging in Publication Date

Bainbridge, William Sims.
    The endtime family : Children of God / William Sims Bainbridge.
        p.   cm.
    Includes bibliographical references (p.   ) and index.
    ISBN 0-7914-5263-8 (alk. paper) — ISBN 0-7914-5264-6 (pbk. : alk. paper)
    1. Children of God (Movement)   I. Title

    BP605.C38 B35 2002
    289.9—dc21
                                                                    2001031125

10   9   8   7   6   5   4   3   2   1

Contents

Figures

Tables

Introduction

How are we to understand radical religious movements that depart from the traditions of the ordinary churches and challenge the spiritual deadness of secular society? Are they, as their opponents would have us believe, pathological collections of abnormal individuals and conspiracies based on fraud and deception? Or are they shining examples of honest religious dissent and beneficial revival of faith?

The Family, or Children of God, is among the most vilified religious movements to arise in twentieth-century America. It is also among the most innovative, and thus it has attracted great interest among journalists and scholars alike. Born in California in the late 1960s, the movement burst out of the United States to send missionaries across the entire world. For a decade, it experimented with a sexual ministry and still today practices sexual sharing among committed adult members. They believe they are in contact with the spirit world, and the majority of them think they have channeled messages from the beyond. Surviving without regular jobs, educating their children outside of schools, they live in hundreds of small communes in dozens of nations.

From the perspective of social science, the Family is a religious movement that exists in high tension with the surrounding sociocultural environment. In our comprehensive theoretical treatise, Rodney Stark and I explained: "Tension is equivalent to broad subcultural deviance. The high tension group is *different* from the socio-cultural standard, mutually *antagonistic* toward the dominant groups that set that standard, and socially *separate* from them."[1] Through close examination of the Family, we can learn much about the phenomenon of sectarian tension.

This book seeks to understand the Family through a research technique seldom applied to radical religious movements, and never previously employed with such rigor: comparative survey analysis. More than a thousand members completed a long questionnaire that had drawn its items from the General

Social Survey, a standard research instrument that has measured American opinion and social life for nearly three decades. In the following pages, we will learn the ways in which members of the Family differ from the general public, and the ways in which they may be surprisingly similar.

This project could not begin with the survey, however, because a long process was required to build rapport with the group so they would trust the researcher to be fair-minded and objective. At the same time, repeated field observation ethnography, many in-depth interviews, and extensive reading of the Family's own literature were necessary to provide a basis for designing the survey and interpreting its results. This preliminary research led to publication of a chapter about the Family in my book, *The Sociology of Religious Movements.*[2]

This book begins with a vivid narrative illustrating the high degree of sectarian tension of the Family, through the persecutions members have experienced and the history by which they broke away from American society. The second chapter outlines the survey methodology and reports initial results that describe the lifestyle of the group's communes. The next three chapters consider three aspects of sectarian tension: supernatural beliefs, religious practices, and feelings of alienation. The final pair of chapters examines the Family's revolutionary approach to sexuality and children.

Scientifically, the Family is a mystery. Strewn across dozens of nations, in tiny autonomous communes, it nonetheless sustains a unified subculture. Twenty years ago, social scientists were already asserting that it had begun to reduce its tension with the surrounding sociocultural environment, yet it seems to be just as high in tension today as it ever was.[3] In the years after second-generation members reached adulthood, and the charismatic founder passed away, we would expect The Family to have settled into a static culture, yet it continues to innovate at a rapid pace.

In bureaucratic terms, the Family is a policy challenge. It demands the right to educate its children within the movement, yet it is active in many nations that forbid home schooling. Although it maintains a very effective public relations campaign, it does not fit into the categories and interfaith organizations that governments are used to dealing with. Many nations that guard their borders against alien influences may feel threatened by the tendency of members to enter whatever mission field calls them. When disgruntled former members or relatives of members bring cases to the courts, officials seem perplexed by the group's freedom from bureaucratic formalities.

If we approach the Family without a strict scientific or policy agenda, we see that it is an extremely fascinating part of the contemporary religious world. In an era when business and government leaders urge themselves to "think out-

side the box," here is a group that lives its entire life outside the formal structures that constrain most people. Yet it has found a coherent and apparently
satisfying way of life for its members. More than a mere counterculture, the
Family is an alternative society. Even if we are unprepared to embrace the faith
of the Family, we can be inspired by it.

CHAPTER 1

Persecution

Near the end of the second millennium of Christianity, grave doubts existed about the future of faith in Jesus. Materialism in America and atheistic ideologies in Europe eroded religion. Science was claiming ever more of the territory of knowledge for its own, leaving little scope for faith. Fundamentalists and Evangelicals fought the good fight but failed to offer a distinctly new vision of God capable of conquering the brave new world of secularism. A few tiny religious movements challenged the status quo, notably the controversial "Family" or "Children of God." About the size Christianity was at the time of the crucifixion, it promises religious innovation as well as revival, if only it can survive the persecutions.

This chapter will document the high tension with the surrounding sociocultural environment experienced by this remarkable religious movement, based on interviews with many of the participants and on documents provided by the group. The massive repression it has suffered in several nations testifies to the hostility that some outsiders feel toward the Family. Its countercultural history reveals its own opposition to some conventional institutions. The terrible shock of the Argentine raids introduces us quickly to the human beings who suffered them, then a flashback scans the quarter century of development that brought the movement to this crisis. The goal of this chapter is an understanding of the human meaning that sectarian tension has for the members of the Endtime Family.

Assault

At 2 o'clock in the morning of September 1, 1993, eleven-year-old Steven awoke suddenly in his Buenos Aires commune, as heavily armed police burst

1

into the bedroom he shared with a half dozen other boys of the Family. They grabbed him out of bed, and without a word of explanation a doctor began checking him all over. Soon a psychologist was bombarding him with questions but giving no answers in return. In the cold rain, the police moved the boys between the converted garage and the house, and then back again to get a change of clothing. The raiders threw all their possessions in heaps scattered across the floor, as if they were frantically looking for something. Except for muttering about lawyers and saying the children would be allowed to say good-bye to their parents, they refused to respond to any questions. Then, breaking their promise, they pushed the children on a bus without letting them see their mothers and fathers, and rushed them off into the gloomy night as the littlest ones cried and the bigger ones stared anxiously into the darkness.

Across town in the Media Home reserved for those who had responsibility for communicating with officials and the press, Steven's mother, Claire, awoke at the same moment as her son to yells and pounding on the door. As the police burst in, they commanded the stunned Family members to raise their hands or be shot, and they waved a search warrant that gave no clue about the purpose of the raid. Within moments, fifty officials and social workers had invaded the home, herded the three children into the living room where one of the parents prayed with them, and began confiscating written material and tape recordings. Police vehicles carried most residents of the home away in a short time, but Claire and some of the men were kept under house arrest for sixteen hours while the officers cataloged all their possessions. One asked Claire where the safe was, and when she told him there was none he angrily threatened to tear the place apart until he found it. Later she refused to sign a statement agreeing that the material confiscated was sufficient evidence to justify her arrest. Surrounded by four policewomen, she was hauled off and held incommunicado, told she had no right to know the charges against her or to see her son.

At the Flare, a home for seventeen young adults, Sunny was still half asleep when a camera flashed in his face and men in bulletproof vests with semi-automatic weapons stormed into his room. They took his passport and told him he was under arrest, as guards stood by the telephone to prevent them from warning other Family homes and from calling their lawyer. The teenagers gave the raiders Christian witness, telling them they were unwittingly involved in religious persecution and projecting a confidence during this horrible episode that could only have come from profound faith in God. Most residents of the home legally were minors, and before long the police had lined them up, taken away many of the possessions they wanted to bring with them, and carted them off. They kept Sunny behind until they had completed ransacking the house. As they finally took him away, an officer whose heart had been opened by the dignified demeanor of his prisoners advised him to bring blankets and let him stop to buy food, because where he was going neither would be provided.

That night, the Argentine police seized nearly 140 children and dozens of adults at five communes of a millenarian group that called itself the Family but was better known to the world as The Children of God. The formal charges centered on sexual abuse of children, but the raid was an unrestrained outpouring of moral outrage by officials who had neither sympathy nor understanding for minority religions. The raiders had received special training from self-appointed experts of the international anticult movement, and the attack was merely the most violent action in a worldwide attempt to destroy the Family. From their earliest days a generation before, the Children of God had been the target of professional deprogrammers who physically seized members in order to brainwash them on behalf of their parents. Of all the groups in the Jesus movement that followed the collapse of the hippie and psychedelic movements of the 1960s, none was more feared and despised than the Children of God.

Genesis

One evening in April 1966, the family of David Brandt Berg clustered around a Texas campfire, wondering what fate the future held. For some years, David had worked for evangelist Fred Jordan, helping him set up a missionary school called the Texas Soul Clinic and traveling the country to promote his television program. But the job had ended in an argument, and the family had neither savings nor immediate prospects of income. In the darkness, David listened to the joyous music of his children, as Aaron played his guitar while Hosea and Faith sang. "It seemed like the hairs stood upright on the back of my neck, and I was so thrilled and the Spirit of the Lord came upon me. I saw a picture of these young folks singing out before other young folks these same songs." Three months later, still penniless, they went on the road to spread the gospel, in an old Rambler and a Dodge camper.

David came from a family of evangelists. His grandfather, John Lincoln Brandt, was a very successful preacher, author and leader in the Disciples of Christ.[1] His mother, Virginia Brandt Berg, was a popular radio evangelist for the Christian and Missionary Alliance.[2] In 1965, while visiting Jordan's ranch in Texas, she had received the Warning Prophecy: "Even now, the skies are RED, RED with WARNING, and BLACK, BLACK with clouds gathering for the GREAT CONFUSION which is ALMOST UPON YOU!"[3] David studied the books of Daniel and Revelation, the parts of the Bible that described the Endtime that would usher in the Millennium, and their traveling ministry set out to proclaim this apocalyptic vision. The Endtime must be close, because never before had mankind possessed the means to destroy itself. Fifty million people died during the seven years of the Second World War, and by the late 1960s, intercontinental ballistic missiles with nuclear warheads could kill ten times that number in a single night.

Often they sang and gave testimony in churches along their way, receiving a little money but not much encouragement. Their ministry had no name until a minister introducing them to his congregation picked up the phrase "Teens for Christ" from their handbill. One at a time they recruited other young people, starting with Josh, who had met Aaron and Hosea at the New York World's Fair, Josh's brother Caleb, and Serena whom they found in Florida. In February 1967, David united Faith and Josh in marriage and ordained them ministers along with Hosea, Aaron, and Caleb. Then followed nearly a year on the road, often splitting into two teams, from the snows of Wisconsin to the sands of the West Indies. From California, Grandmother Virginia wrote saying they should come minister to the young "hippies" who had turned on to drugs and dropped out of society. Toward Christmas they obeyed her prophecy: "Thou shalt go to the Land of the Setting Sun and there it shall be shown thee what thou shalt do."[4]

The first month at Huntington Beach, California, they were "flat broke," surviving with the help of grandmother's modest pension, and they sank into desperation that climaxed when grandmother died in March. For David, this was a turning point that demanded either surrender or swift triumph. "One dark night, penniless and in despair, I walked the streets with the drugged and despairing hippies as discouraged as myself who were wandering around as sheep having no shepherd, when God suddenly spoke, 'Art thou willing to go to these lost sheep to become king of these poor, lost beggars? They need a voice to speak for them; they need a shepherd to lead them and guide them, and they need the ROD of My Word to guide them to the Light!'"[5]

For the food, they learned to "provision," as when Hosea would collect unsold sandwiches at day's end from lunch truck drivers. For the light, they borrowed the Light Club beach-front coffee house in the hours of the week when its sponsor, Teen Challenge, could not operate it. The children and the earliest recruits would do most of the work with the hippies, build personal relationships with a few and draw them into the group. David realized now his mission, to fulfill for these hippies the prophecy of Ezekiel 34:23, "And I will set up one shepherd over them, and he shall feed them, even my servant David; he shall feed them, and he shall be their shepherd."

Called "Dad" by his children and by intimate followers, he became "Moses David" to the world, proclaiming a revolution that embraced the hippie counterculture while rejecting the drugs that had been its center and its curse. In many respects, the hippies were already members of a millenarian movement. Their gurus, like renegade Harvard professor Timothy Leary, had proclaimed that "psychedelic" drugs would expand consciousness, revealing the innate pathology of ordinary American society and ushering in a new age of free love. But like lemmings swarming to a cliff overlooking the sea, the hippies of California had crashed on the beach, and Moses David was now laboring to salvage a few from the wreckage of their dreams.

Father David and his family visited churches now as much to shout challenges at the ministers as to seek help, and after being thrown out a few times they began to picket the houses of conventional worship. They grew in numbers and in infamy, soon arousing the hostility of the establishment that hounded them out of California. On the road again, they picketed the national Baptist convention in New Orleans and marched through Chicago in red robes pounding their staves on the ground. A newsman in Camden, New Jersey, called them "the Children of God," so for the second time an outsider had bestowed a name on them. Briefly after 1978 they called themselves "the Family of Love," and today they prefer simply "the Family," but they are still widely known by the name this reporter gave them. And at the beginning of the 1970s, as the Children of God led by Moses David, they denounced the hypocrisy of the established churches and prophesied that the End was at hand.

Hippies, religious seekers, and disaffected wanderers joined by the hundreds, as Family teams crisscrossed the continent. A few horrified parents hired Ted "Black Lightning" Patrick and other deprogrammers to steal back their sons and daughters, and a national "anticult" movement arose with the Children of God high on its hit list.[6]

Part Jewish in ancestry, Father David felt high anticipation when he flew to Israel in 1970, and his flock began spreading out across the globe. He communicated with them through frequent publications, called "MO (Moses) Letters," some of which were distributed on the streets as tracts. Family groups entered Britain, Holland, Germany, and Scandinavia during 1971, and by the end of 1972 the balance of the membership was outside the United States. A sense that the Endtime was approaching energized their witnessing, and Father David suggested that the appearance of the comet Kohoutek heralded the beginning of the end in 1973. He was not the only one to give it great significance, and drug guru Timothy Leary blessed it as the "Starseed" that would bring the Golden Age. Ironically, professional astronomers were wrong, too, when they prophesied that Kohoutek would be the comet of the century, and it passed Earth without incident.

A new era was indeed beginning for members of the Family. They no longer disrupted conventional churches, but made positive efforts to bring Jesus to everyone they met. Literature distribution on the streets, called "litnessing," became a chief source of funds to augment the food and other things the groups were able to provision. Their music blossomed, opening the hearts of strangers as they spread into Latin America and Asia. Soon their recordings were bringing in money and transmitting a message of love. When the Family was growing rapidly back in the United States, there had been a strong emphasis on celibacy, but now marriages were encouraged and thus babies began to be born in increasing numbers. The hippie free love ethic returned in a new, spiritualized form. Through visions and experiments, Father David developed a new form of witnessing, called "flirty-fishing" or "FFing," in which women of the Family would offer their love to emotionally needy men, as a sample of God's love.[7]

Early in 1974, Father David moved to Tenerife in the Canary Islands, accompanied by a young convert named Maria who had become his wife. Tried first on a large scale in Tenerife, FFing was soon adopted in many branches of the Family around the world. For a long time, perhaps beginning with a MO Letter titled "Scriptural, Revolutionary Love-Making" in August 1969, Father David's writings had stressed that sex was a gift of God, as holy as any church sacrament if performed out of love. Journalists hungry for a story, and activists of the anticult movement, soon took renewed notice of the Children of God, painting lurid images of cultic prostitutes.

Mexico

One of the first violent reactions came in Mexico in 1978. The Family was becoming quite popular there, appearing on TV, making phonograph records, and converting some children of influential people. Then vicious publicity about flirty-fishing spread from Spain and unleashed a persecution, even though the three homes around Mexico City had not experimented with this controversial form of ministry. Family members went on a TV talk show that previously had been very friendly but were shocked to see that the commentator had turned against them, and the telephone calls from viewers were extremely hostile. At the time, the Family was registered with the Mexican government as a nonprofit organization, so the authorities knew exactly where the homes were located when they launched a surprise attack.

In the dark of night, police teams broke open the doors of the two homes inside the city, tore off the bed covers, and arrested the stunned Family members. A third home was situated just over a state line, so it took longer to get the necessary warrant, and the raid came in the middle of the next day, when hardly anybody was there. The three-year-old daughter of Phil and Sandy had accidentally cut her lip, so Sandy had taken her out for medical attention, and others were on various errands. But soon the authorities had gathered them up and carted them off to an immigration facility. They were allowed only a single phone call among them, but they fortunately were able to contact a friendly nonmember who found them an attorney and volunteered to make arrangements for their children.

Phil says the authorities tricked them easily, because they were young and inexperienced, falsifying their testimonies. An official wrote out an affidavit for each prisoner, leaving much empty space, then told them to sign along the sides of the paper. Afterward, the corrupt police added terrible confessions at the bottom, which the prisoners knew nothing about, justifying the charge of abuse of public morality. Other prisoners told them they would be locked up for at least six months even if they were found innocent, because justice moved so slowly in Mexico. If found guilty, they were told, they might be incarcerated for as much as five or even ten years. Officials from the American embassy were very unfriendly. Phil recalled, "They didn't want anything to do with us. To fulfill their obligation they came and visited us, but that was it. They didn't intercede at all or try to do anything on our behalf."

Altogether twenty-five were arrested, including two bewildered men who merely worked at the commercial print shop that produced the Family's literature. After the first weekend, the thirteen men were taken to a brand-new prison with decent food. But the twelve women were locked in an old, dilapidated institution, that reminded Sandy of a dark and dirty dungeon. One blessing was that members of the family were kept together in the same cells at both prisons, although they also mixed with ordinary convicts.

True to the religious principles that gave the Family strength, the members in both prisons immediately set about being model prisoners and ministering to the other inmates. Sandy exclaims, "We witnessed! And we put on shows! We helped organize, and we cleaned."

Phil recalls, "We decided to turn the place upside down. We sang every day. We decided we were going to clean that place from morning to night and do the best job we could." Every night before going to bed the men would sing the hundred and third psalm, "Bless the Lord, O my soul: and all that is within me, bless his holy name. . . . The Lord is merciful and gracious, slow to anger, and plenteous in mercy." The sound would ring through the halls, like a chorus of angels. Phil said, "It was beautiful to see that if we kept our faith, even in prison, the Lord was with us."

Every Sunday, Phil's and Sandy's daughter would visit one of her parents, and it was always very painful to let her go afterward. She was being cared for by friends, but they did not speak English so the little girl could not really communicate with them. Thinking back on those terrible days of separation from his daughter, Phil doubts he could tolerate such abuse of one of his children by the authorities again. But with faith and fellowship to sustain them, the two dozen religious prisoners survived week on week of persecution.

After nearly two months, a day dawned unusually clear. Mexico City's constant air pollution lifted and the sun beamed down the promise of hope. Opening a Bible at random, the men received a verse from the thirty-seventh psalm, "Commit thy way unto the Lord; trust also in him; and he shall bring it to pass. And he shall bring forth thy righteousness as the light, and thy judgment as the noonday." They joyously told incredulous ordinary prisoners they knew they would be released this day, and miraculously the prophecy came true.

The Family believed powerful enemies did not want them freed, whatever the validity of the formal charges against them, and American publicity made the case an embarrassment for the officials. Therefore, when all but one minor charge was dropped, they were held until the middle of the following night to avoid media coverage of their release, then placed in a rented bus. Just an instant before the bus pulled away, friends ran up and put the tiny daughter of Sandy and Phil in through the window. Under cover of darkness, the bus rushed north to the border and dumped them in Laredo, Texas, where another Family home took them in.

Argentina I

Brazil also deported members of the Family, and some left that country only to start homes in Argentina. Among them was Claire, a Canadian who had originally gone to Brazil for a year as an exchange student. Initially, the dozen adults in Buenos Aires took regular jobs. Claire first taught English to the owner of a big amusement park, who then hired her to manage the payroll for his hundred and fifty employees, while her husband oversaw the personnel and the maintenance of the park's machinery. One member drove a taxi and did odd jobs, while a couple made a good living teaching English. Some American members had a successful musical band, doing television commercials as well as regular performances, and Argentine members had a band that played in famous night clubs.

During Argentina's dirty civil war, the military government was extremely repressive, and thousands of citizens disappeared without a trace, most of them murdered. Therefore the Family was very cautious in its ministry, aware that their literature might be branded subversive. In the early 1980s, however, they began quitting their jobs and doing full-time missionary work, which at first consisted of provisioning and music shows. Gradually they became more adventurous, selling Spanish-language color posters of Jesus and the Endtime, and distributing music cassettes and eventually videos.

Typical posters are twelve inches by sixteen and have action-filled, cartoon-like color pictures on one side and a story on the other. "Martyrs of the End" shows a voluptuous, scantily clad woman being blasted by one of the Antichrist's storm troopers, as she tries to distribute Family posters on the streets of a futuristic city, and her spirit rising ecstatically from the grave. "Crowns of Life" depicts Jesus giving a saintly halo to a faithful Christian woman, also voluptuous and scantily clad, as she arrives in God's great Heavenly Space City.

The 1980s were a time of consolidation for the Family around the world. Several thousand children had been born to members and were now growing up and requiring regular home schooling and stable environments. Many communes coalesced and a new structure of communication and leadership emerged. While The Family's missionaries was spreading Father David's message throughout the nations, enemies conspired against them. Some were angry ex-members or the bitter parents of members. Others were professional deprogrammers who made their livings saving supposed victims of brainwashing from the cults. And others were journalists or petty public officials who saw career advantages to be gained by demonizing small religious groups that were different from the majority. The Family had often suffered mild persecution, but now the tempo increased as if in fulfillment of their Endtime prophecies. Police raided one of the homes in Argentina, not the immense persecution that would strike them four years later, but a terrifying shock for those involved and a warning of dire events in the future.

One morning in November 1989, the children of a Family home near Buenos Aires were waiting in their living room for the bus that always took them to school at a bigger home, called the Heritage. This was to be a special day at school, and the children had dressed up in fine clothes, but the bus had broken down so they were passing time by reading a story. One of the girls looked out the window, saw several news photographers, and exclaimed, "Oh, how nice, a wedding!" But five minutes later, seventy police from three different units assaulted the house, some leaping over the fence while clutching automatic weapons, and burst through the door. The jeweler who had rented the house to the Family had been robbed some time earlier, so he had installed bulletproof windows and a television surveillance system that only stimulated the attackers' wild imaginations.

The surprise raid had been triggered by a dispute between a husband and wife that escalated into religious persecution. When the couple split up, some time before, the wife had joined the Family, bringing her two children with her. The husband did not complain at first, but after a while he decided he wanted his children and saw an advantage in allying himself with an anticult movement that had been trying to stir up public hostility toward the Family. The authorities were already suspicious of any form of unconventional religion, so they were quite ready to believe wild claims about child abuse.

When the raid took place, most of the adults were already out of the house on their daily business. In the midst of her errands, Claire happened to phone another home and heard, "You've got to go! Your house is raided! It's full of police!"

Concerned about her seven-year-old son Steven, she rushed home. When she reached her neighborhood, the entire block was filled with vehicles and people. Members of the public were pawing through vast piles of Family literature that had been thrown onto the lawn. With a mixture of glee and feigned horror, one woman held up one of Father David's letters about revolutionary sex and squealed, "Look at This!"

Claire told the police at the front door that this was her home, and they let her in. The first person she spoke with turned out to be a news reporter, and she challenged him, "What are you doing in here? Wandering through our bedrooms!" Earlier, the house had been flooded with reporters, until a member of the commune had complained that this was a violation of the residents' rights, but apparently the police had allowed a few press men to remain. This turned out to be to the Family's advantage, because when the police claimed to have found cocaine in the kitchen towel drawer, it could not be used as evidence because any of the reporters might have placed it there. In fact, the Family was convinced the police had brought it with them. The officers told Claire and the others they had to sign a paper confessing that the drugs had been found in the house, or they would be arrested. She exclaimed, "I don't care if I'm going to jail! I'm not going to sign anything. We don't have drugs! We don't believe in drugs!"

The police made good on their threat, hauling Claire and a dozen other members away. The women were thrown into solitary confinement cells where they were held incommunicado. They were not allowed to contact a lawyer or anyone else, and they received no food at all for the first three days. Claire's cell was completely dark, with no light or window, and she had no blanket. Cement walls and a steel door enclosed a narrow space, hardly more than three feet by six. The women would have to scream sometimes for hours before the tough policewoman would take them to the only toilet in the cell block. The place was appallingly filthy, infested by rats and cockroaches. The water was undrinkable, and Claire became violently ill. Not permitted to go to the toilet, the best she could do was sit in the darkness and vomit into an old carton. Ordinary prisoners in a regular cell turned up their radio so she and the other women of the Family could listen to a news report of their arrest, and they heard that the state was planning to put their children up for adoption.

After a week, the women were released but placed under house arrest. The men who had been seized were confined for two full weeks before the case against them collapsed. The judge of the minors' court concluded, "I am convinced that these minors are living in a suitable environment for their physical and moral development, and this court of law is therefore not called upon to intervene." Returned to their parents, the children could begin to recover from the trauma they had suffered.

Spain, Australia, France

The following July, police and social workers raided a home in Barcelona, Spain, seizing twenty-two children and locking them in welfare institutions for nearly a year. The persecution paused for many months, then resumed all the way around the world.

Before dawn on May 15, 1992, dozens of police and agents of the state community services departments of Sydney and Melbourne, Australia, assaulted six Family homes, dragging away 142 children aged two to sixteen. Television cameramen went on some of these raids, tipped off by the authorities, and enemies of the Family fed horror stories about supposed child abuse to the media. Quickly, however, sympathetic attorneys and the Family's own efforts turned the tide of opinion, and after six days the children were released.

Family homes in France near Lyon and Aix-en-Provence were raided at dawn on June 9, 1993. In later affidavits distributed by the Family, victims recalled the wild brutality of the attack. "My first impression was that terrorists or robbers were storming the house," said a 15-year-old American named Amor, "as armed men were running everywhere. One of the plainclothesmen banged our door open and was frantically swinging his gun at us and shouting loudly!"

Forty-three-year-old Richard Leclerc, a lightly built Canadian clad only in his underwear, was the target of a military charge. "Four men dressed in bullet-proof vests, wearing helmets and carrying automatic weapons, came rushing around the corner of the house, screaming and then heading straight towards me. One of them had an axe, which he swung into the door of our caravan, which immediately flew open. They then grabbed me and dragged me from the caravan across the gravel driveway, leaving my right knee badly bleeding and bruised. I laid on the ground while three of them pinned their guns on me and the fourth handcuffed my hands behind my back." They threw his wife out of their mobile home onto the ground, cuffing her hands behind her back, not caring that her thin summer nightgown left her unprotected against the early morning cold.

Awakened by shouts and screams, Canadian Denise de Brocke Michaud hid in a closet with her baby girl and four small sons. "It sounded like some insane killers were breaking everything and killing everybody!" One child asked if they were going to be killed, so she led them in prayer. "Then some-one kicked open our unlocked bedroom door and in a couple of seconds, the closet door flung open and a man wearing a helmet and all dressed in black pointed a gun at us and shouted at me, 'Put the baby down!' At first I still did not know it was the police and I said, 'No, she's just a baby! Can I take her with me?'"

The police took thirty-eight children away from their parents, and told some they would never see them again. The ten children of Samuel and Heidi were dispersed to several foster homes and institutions: the twin babies Celeste and Angelique, two-year-old Nicholas, Marie-Claire, Christophe, Raphael, Olivier, the twelve-year-old twins Benedicte and Agnes, and Etienne who was fourteen. The parents and children did not see each other again for fifty-one days, when a judge finally ordered the children's release.

Argentina II

In Argentina, The Family had followed the French seizure closely. When the children in France were released, the Argentine group distributed thousands of leaflets announcing the judge's decision and explaining that the attack had been proven unwarranted, hoping thus to forestall a similar action in their own country. But there were many dark signs. Each home seemed to be under covert surveillance, and one of their landlords exclaimed, "Hey, you people are in big trouble!" Helicopters frequently buzzed the largest Family home and school, called the Heritage, and trespassing photographers attempted to snap pictures of the children. One day Claire was working in the Heritage, preparing for a press conference, when a chopper roared right over the roof, shaking doors and windows. She ran into the courtyard to see what was happening, and the machine was so low she could clearly see the pilot's mustache.

The Family had seen the handwriting on the wall. No matter what they did, no matter how much effort they invested in telling the mass media about their innocence and their faith, the forces of destruction continued to rage against them. Worried meetings produced a decision to move most of the non-Argentine members out of the country, using this opportunity to shift their efforts to more propitious mission fields. They held a farewell party at the school. Members got their travel documents in order, bought airline tickets, and packed their most precious belongings. The courtyard at the Media Home filled up with miscellaneous things they planned to sell. Claire believes the police learned about their plans and moved up the date of the raids to catch them before they could leave Argentina. Despite all their preparations, the raids caught them by surprise, and thus they fell victim to the most massive persecution the Family had suffered.

The police bus took Claire's son, Steven, to a huge institution that had been abandoned for a long time and was just being renovated. Encircled by a three-story-high wall, the building was dark and damp. Plaster was crumbling off the moss-covered ceiling and walls of the two warehouselike rooms in which they were thrown. During their incarceration, a construction company fixed up several other rooms nicely, but the children were never allowed to use them. For the first week, there was no electricity and no water in the pipes. When water did begin flowing, and the children drank it, they became sick. The roof leaked so badly they could not sleep when it rained.

When the children first arrived at the institution, they received little cups of soup and were then subjected to marathon medical and psychological examinations. In self-consciously friendly voices, the psychologists tried to get the children to admit they had been abused sexually. "Oh, we know you're parents have brainwashed you. But there's nothing wrong with that. All you need to do is tell us." The youngsters refused to submit to interrogation unless Family adults were present, but any parent who objected to the proceedings might be hauled off to jail.

At the beginning of the medical exam, the doctor would ask each child if he or she had ever had sex or had witnessed parents having sex. When one of Steven's friends answered "no," the doctor left the answer space blank on his questionnaire so he could write in "yes" later on. Over and over they took Steven's fingerprints; twelve times he had to press each fingertip on the ink pad and paper documents. The girls were subjected to vaginal exams, under the primitive assumption that only an intact hymen would prove their virginity, and in the chaos of the examination area all kinds of people wandered through while the girls were so intimately exposed.

As days passed, older children and some parents who were allowed to stay with their children began trying to make life livable in the institution, because they realized they might be imprisoned there for a long time. After a while the toilet paper, soap and lice shampoo ran out, and despite the filthy conditions the director refused to provide any more for a long time, so all the children contracted lice. They were not permitted to use the institution's washing machines, and the police had not let them bring more than one change of clothing, so every night Steven had to wash his shirt and underwear by hand. The few adult women permitted to stay had to clean the babies' diapers as best they could. There was no schooling, few activities were possible, the food was disgustingly greasy, and the meager staff of the institution did practically nothing for the inmates. It began to look as if the real child abusers were not the Family but the authorities.

Steven was deeply shocked to realize that his mother was in prison, and unlike the many young people from families of eight or even ten children, as an only child he had no contact with any other relatives. Representatives from the Canadian embassy visited a few times, because Claire was from Canada, and one wantonly terrified Steven by confidently predicting that his mother would spend the next thirty years in jail. Men from other embassies offered to take some of the children to nonmember relatives in their countries if they would forsake the Family, but every single one of them refused. More than a month passed, and Steven was not allowed to see his mother.

In the hours after the raid, Claire, Sunny, and many other adults were thrown into the Martinez district jail. The holding cell where they put Claire and seven other women was barely ten feet on a side, with one dirty mattress on the floor. Forty of the men were crammed into a small group of cells with no furniture, just concrete and bars. The weather was bitterly cold, and the few blankets they had brought with them were the only protection they had. They soon exhausted the tiny bit of food a few had brought with them, and because the jail gave them none they starved until friends learned where they were and began bringing gifts.

As a sign of their incompetence, the police had arrested four people who were not even members; two of them were mothers of members and the others, boarders in their homes. These strangers were amazed when the members of the Family responded in the way they always did to calamity: They sang hymns and prayed. One jail official was so enchanted by the men's singing of "Amazing Grace," that he asked them to repeat it over and over, and he opened all the hall doors so that the glorious sound would reach the women prisoners on the other side of the building.

All around the world, members of the Family prayed for the captives in Argentina, and at Father David's personal urging every home gave up its weekly movie or entertainment night in solidarity with them. Soon, members were demonstrating at Argentine embassies or at other places where their voices might be heard. Jackie and John had been away from Buenos Aires completing arrangements for their emigration from the country when the raids hit their home. Mindless of the danger to themselves they rushed back to the city and launched a campaign to free their friends. While they were in the midst of a television broadcast, the police arrested them directly from the studio. After two days, several people including the nonmembers were allowed to leave the jail, leaving five women and sixteen men.

At first it seemed mysterious why some were being kept in prison and others released, but as the prisoners compared notes they began to see a pattern. Claire was among the best-known spokespeople for the group, and a dissident had fingered her as a leader. Sunny had recently celebrated his twenty-first birthday, so he was merely guilty of being technically adult in a home chiefly composed of minors. A French member named Daniel had a computer in his room, thus possibly was responsible for the Family's documents. A German member named Juergen had defied police orders during the raid by trying to put a jacket on a child being led out into the rain. In one case a member was held merely because he had signed his name to the lease renting one of the homes. The common thread was that each of these members looked as if he or she might be a leader, or in some way had ever so slightly resisted the persecution.

On the sixth day, they were taken to the court house, and this gave them their first opportunity to make their case to the media. The police wanted to put coats over their heads, but they refused, so as they were led manacled into the building they were able to shout to the waiting news people: "Religious persecution! A gross violation of human rights! What are you doing with my children? I just want my children back!"

Inside the building, each member was interrogated with a list of questions, while a secretary wrote down the answers, often changing them. "They asked me about our sexual beliefs," Sunny recalls. "I said our sexual policies are very clear. Sex for minors is definitely prohibited. When you become of legal age, which here is twenty-one, you are a free moral agent and no one has control over you. They put on that declaration that I had said when someone turns twenty-one they're initiated into sex. They made it sound like some kind of initiation process, kind of a ceremony." As Sunny was urging the secretary to correct the document, he heard footsteps coming up behind him, and a hand reached over his head and grabbed the paper away from him. "I looked around, and there was a heavy-set man standing there with a scowl on his face. The guy looked insane; he looked like a nervous wreck. He was shaking."

"What are you doing?" the man demanded angrily.

"I'm correcting my declaration. I have a right to correct my declaration."

"You don't have any rights here!" the man screamed. "I tell you your rights! You don't tell me the rights here!"

Sunny seized the document back from him, saying, "This is my declaration, and I'm going to make it the way I want it." He returned it to the secretary. "Please keep correcting this." With the wild expression of a raving maniac, the man stormed from the room, slamming the door. Only then did Sunny learn that he was the judge himself, the man who held Sunny's fate in his hands.

John had a similar experience when he was interrogated. At one point, he reported, the judge lost his self-control and began yelling, "Do you believe in the Virgin Mary? Do you recognize the Pope?" To John, a French member of the Family, this sounded like the Holy Inquisition.

Like Sunny, Claire had to struggle for every grain of justice. "The woman who took my answers lied unashamedly at every turn. I asked for my lawyer to be present; she claimed that he had never presented himself at court at any time, and she assigned me a court-appointed lawyer. My lawyer, I found out later, was right down the hall and had asked for me several times. He had also been lied to and told that I wasn't there.

"When the woman finished typing my answers and gave the form to me to sign, I saw she had twisted several points I had made, trying to make them say the opposite of what I had intended! I had a hard time getting her to correct them, but she finally did. It was obvious that there were no means they wouldn't resort to, to accomplish their purpose."

Three days later they were again transported to the cells in the court house to learn their fate. Desperately, they prayed, Claire remembers. "We had already read in the papers that the judge had raided our home a second time and held a press conference in front of it, at which time he declared that due to the serious nature of the crimes, we would not be freed pending our trial. However, on the radio the night before, it had been announced that we were to be released and all the policemen at the station had also told us from 'inside sources' that we would be released."

This time they were transported not in cars but a truck with a canopy on the back, made especially for prisoners. For Sunny, it was an infuriating experience. "They did a lot of things to try to weaken us. For example, when we were brought to the court house, the judge's order was not to give us any food. In tiny little cells all day, twelve hours without any food at all. They gave us water, that was it. So it was worse than bread and water; it was just water. So all those things just built up and made me really angry! How someone could come into our peace-loving, Christian homes and raid them and tear them apart, tear the children away from their parents, put us in this horrible dungeon cell, and not even feed us, transport us in these horrible vehicles, not tell us what was going on. All of that together, it was just amazing to me how somebody could do that. Obviously it was the Devil right behind it himself—the classic examples all throughout the Bible of evil persecuting the good. That's the only explanation, because it was amazing how any human could do the things they did to us. We waited. Finally at the end of the day they told us the judge had ordered preventative prison. In Argentina, that means you go to jail for as long as the judge says, whether they have any evidence or not." The charges covered a wide territory of vice: multiple rape, slavery, conspiracy, discrimination, child abuse. Sunny thought it was outrageous that he was being charged with child abuse simply because he was twenty-one, while his friends a few months younger had been sent to institutions as abused children.

The police manacled Claire's hands behind her back, and as they led her out of the court house, she began to sing, "God Is Our Refuge and Strength." Soon the captives were all singing. The prisoner van waiting for them was a horrifying torture device, divided into windowless, steel cells, like coffins standing on end, each large enough for only a single person. But the police pushed two people into each cell, where they were forced to stand in the darkness, squashed against each other, gasping to breathe the weak stream of air coming through the tiny slot in the door. One man was left in the narrow aisle between the cells, and he tried to fan air into them and give comfort by reciting scripture. They sang "Amazing Grace," and they prayed. A terrible, long ride that slammed them around in the cells, during which one member fainted, brought the men to one prison, and the women to another.

Their greatest fear was that they might be separated and that alone each member would be beaten or even killed by violent inmates who believed the stories that they were cultic child abusers. At Caseros Prison, the men's prayers were answered as an entire, huge "pavilion" dormitory room was provided for the sixteen of them. Except for an hour on each clear weekday in the exercise yard, they would spend all their time there, sleeping on the metal bunk beds, cooking on the stove, using the toilet, and washing in the laundry sink. The institution was managed on military lines, as most of the prisoners came from the army or police, and the sixteen learned to march in formation with their hands clasped behind their backs, to stand at attention for inspection, and to answer smartly "Yes, Sir!"

At Ezeiza Prison, the five women were far less fortunate, placed in a cell with four ordinary prisoners who at first would not let them sing hymns or pray above a whisper.[8] Threats of violence constantly terrorized them, and during their incarceration another prisoner actually was beaten to death by inmates who were jealous that she was about to be released. Two months into their captivity, a pair of extremely dangerous women were added to their cell, an AIDS-infected lesbian couple named Deborah and Cristina who acted out their brand of sexual intercourse for all the other women to see. They brought a filthy pet toad with them, which attracted flies, and a contraband knife, which reminded everyone that Deborah had been convicted of murdering an elderly couple with a razor. Another band of inmates conspired to kill the Family members, but their complicated plan fell through. Deborah and Cristina were removed to another cell, and three weeks later they instigated a riot that nearly overwhelmed the guards. Several times, inmates attempted to attack Claire, but the nearest she came to death was an uncontrollable attack of vomiting and collapsing blood pressure aggravated by months of poor nutrition.

At both prisons, the religious captives witnessed to the other inmates. The men gave Bible classes to trustees who were allowed to enter their pavilion, telling them about the coming Endtime, and after a few weeks they received a guitar. Sunny recalls, "All sixteen of us guys would get together and we would sing sometimes, and we would have real fun times, singing all kinds of songs, rock and roll and everything. The music would ring throughout the whole prison and all the prisoners would hear us singing." The women had a much rougher time, but they ministered to the individuals who shared their cell and to the guards, many of whom responded appreciatively.

Eventually, children were able to visit their parents once or twice a week. On his twelfth birthday, Steven embraced his mother as the two of them wept softly, remembering that she had been imprisoned at his eighth birthday as well, during the 1989 persecution, and wondering whether she would ever be free again.

On December 13, three and a half months after the raids, an appeals court ordered the immediate release of the twenty-one adult captives, and over a period of days the children were also released. Their homes, all supposedly under guard by the police, had been thoroughly looted. Everything was gone, even the toilet seats. Not a single possession remained from Steven's childhood, not a toy or a personal photograph. The food in the kitchens stank with rottenness. There was no money left. Claire and the others struggled painfully to prepare a home for the children. When she and Steven joined again in freedom, he kept telling her excitedly, "Mummy, I'm so thankful I'm in the Family!"

Reflecting on her experience, Claire says, "After this Argentine experience, I can see the Endtime a lot more clearly." The persecutions seemed to confirm the Family's millenarian prophesies, but the valuable help of friendly outsiders and the simple passage of time might seem to disprove them. Most members left Argentina, as most had left France after the persecution there, moving on to more favorable mission fields in several other nations. The Family writes and speaks out about the injustice of Waco, and they have met a few of the surviving Branch Davidians, but they have not yet experienced their own deadly persecution in America. The Endtime seems so close, but the Antichrist has not yet revealed himself, and the chief concern of the older generation has become the care and education of their children.

Reflections

In 1994, about the time of Father David's death, his son Hosea thought back to the beginning of the movement, when the Children of God had expected the millennium immediately. "When we were younger and we were talking about the Endtime and how soon things would come to pass, we had a much more narrow view of what needed to be done in the world before Jesus could come back and before the Antichrist could take over. Much to our surprise, God has allowed twenty-five years to take place to enable us to preach the gospel a lot more, to reach a lot more people. And also during this time he has caused a lot more Christians to wake up to see that we are living in the last days." Returning to the United States for the first time in twenty-two years, he discovered a society that had fallen deep into violence, depravity and social disintegration. Yet the Endtime had not yet begun.

"People say, 'What about your father? He said the time was short so long ago. Doesn't this show that he's a false prophet? That he's not really reliable?'" Hosea believes in the power of Bible prophecy, but he knows that the shadow of uncertainty lies over every precise prediction. "Jesus' disciples thought he would be coming back before they died. But now we certainly don't believe any less that we are in the Endtime than we did twenty-five years ago. I never thought I would have children and they would grow up and have children of their own, but that's happened. I'm not complaining." He smiled and gazed across the wide, green fields that surround a rural Family commune in the eastern part of the United States, a warm and healthy home, filled with the laughter of children.

"God is restraining the Antichrist forces from taking over the world and establishing the one world government," he explained. "I'm very happy because I thought time was short. I gave my life to the Lord, and I went to preach the gospel with all my heart and with all my life as much as I could. The fact that he has continued to espouse that urgency of reaching the world with the gospel right now, it's important, we cannot wait." He recalled his years of mission work in Macao, unsupported by any prosperous American denomination, and he looked ahead to the opportunity of evangelizing China in the Mandarin language he was studying. "So the Endtime, the end of the world has not come for me or for you. But the end of the world has come for millions of people who have died in the past twenty-five years, and many of them without the gospel. There are millions of people who are dying every year without the gospel. It's the end of the world for them. Are we wrong because we think that time is so short?"

CHAPTER 2

Survey

With the notable exceptions of a study about the narrow topic of recruitment in the Unification Church performed by Eileen Barker, and a report prepared by E. Burke Rochford for the International Society for Krishna Consciousness, we lack systematic survey data about new religious movements.[1] Sociologist James Richardson, who has observed the Family over the years, has called it "possibly the most controversial of the early new religions."[2] Thus a systematic questionnaire study of the Family should be doubly welcome, as a pioneering application of a standard methodological tool to an area where it has seldom been applied, and for the unique description it provides of one of the most radical new religious movements.

This chapter will introduce the questionnaire survey that provided much of the data for this study, and illustrate its value by describing the life conditions of members using this unusual set of data. Among the topics covered will be the demographics of recruitment and residence in communal homes, relative insulation from secular mass media, the economic basis of Family life, activities in the homes, and charitable work by the missionaries. The chapter concludes with a consideration of the scientific value of this study of a high-tension religious movement.

The General Social Survey

During my research on the Family, I visited a total of twelve Family homes in or near the cities of Baltimore, Chicago, Los Angeles, Paris, San Francisco, Toronto, and Washington. In addition to extensive field observation, I did tape-recorded interviews with thirty-five members, averaging nearly two hours each and ranging from half an hour to six hours. But the distinctive feature of the

21

project is a questionnaire, filled out by 1,025 members around the world, largely based on the General Social Survey (GSS), a large-scale questionnaire administered to a sample of American adults that has been carried out periodically since 1972.

For more than six years I managed investment in the General Social Survey, while I was director of the Sociology Program of the National Science Foundation. I can take very little credit for supporting the GSS, because the funding decisions were the natural result of the peer review process, involving a large number of sociologists who wrote reviews of the GSS proposals, and the members of the Sociology Advisory Panel who weighed investment in the GSS against other scientific projects that had to be rejected. I was at least partly responsible for the extremely successful GSS web site that went on-line in June 1996, because I encouraged the researchers to submit a proposal to create one. When I decided to undertake the present research project, I verified with the Foundation's attorneys that doing so would not be a conflict of interest. Subsequently, I left the Sociology Program to take on other responsibilities at NSF.

The data collected over the years in the General Social Survey have been archived at the Roper Center associated with the University of Connecticut, but in fact I obtained the GSS data I used from a variety of other sources. First, the MicroCase Corporation, founded by Rodney Stark and Lynne Roberts, provided versions of the GSS files for their excellent data analysis system. My textbook, *The Sociology of Religious Movements*, and my third book with Stark, *Religion, Deviance and Social Control*, employed GSS data in the MicroCase format. Second, the printed codebook for the GSS gives the frequencies of responses to all the questions, broken down by certain groups of years.[3] Third, the web-based General Social Survey Data and Information Retrieval System from the National Opinion Research Center (NORC) and the Inter-university Consortium for Political and Social Research (ICPSR) gives frequencies across all the years in its trend analysis section. Finally, I often used the on-line analysis service of the Computer-assisted Survey Methods (CSM) Program at the University of California at Berkeley.

Guided by the codebook and also by the extensive bibliography of over 3000 reports and publications based on the GSS, I selected over 200 items for inclusion in the Family survey. They covered religious beliefs, attitudes toward society, values and norms concerning human behavior, and a variety of other issues. Most were of a simple "check the box" format, but the response categories varied so I assembled the items into more than twenty blocks that fit together logically either in terms of topic or response format. In some cases, I selected variants of the GSS items that had been used in its transnational version, the

International Social Survey Program. In a few cases it was impossible to employ exactly the same format in a paper questionnaire as in the interview-based GSS, but I did my best to make the formats comparable. A small number of other fixed-choice items were written from scratch concerning facts peculiar to the Family, always in the same form as regular GSS items.

The first section of the questionnaire, however, consisted of six open-ended items unrelated to the GSS. Three asked the respondent to describe something he or she "did yesterday," "recently did alone, all by yourself" or "recently did with another person or with a group." The other three called for descriptions of something that happened to the person "yesterday," "recently which made you happy" or "recently which made you unhappy." I quote illustrations from this material throughout the book, to flesh out the narrative organized around the quantitative tables. A second function of this section was to focus respondents' minds on the unaccustomed task of filling out a survey about their experiences and feelings. And a third function was to provide me with one more check that respondents were taking the assignment seriously.

In this pioneering study, I intentionally chose to leave out some variables that sociologists might wish had been included, feeling that they could far better be studied later on, possibly by other researchers. I asked only a few questions about the composition of the respondent's household or migration history, for example, because the Family possesses a great wealth of detailed data on these questions, notably from periodic questionnaires that all members fill out. A demographer might wish to work with the Family to achieve maximum scientific benefit from analyzing this treasure trove of information. Peter Amsterdam, a key spiritual and organizational leader, was the group's statistician for many years, and when I interviewed him for an entire day I found him to be an extremely competent person. In earlier studies, I discovered it was possible to achieve real scientific gains from quantitative data provided by the Scientology and Transcendental Meditation organizations.[4] Therefore, I am convinced the present study can be the basis for high-quality future research using data already collected by the Family itself.

The questionnaire was administered in the only way possible at the time I did the study, by employing the existing communication network of the group. I submitted a camera-ready copy of the questionnaire, and duplicates of it were sent to regional centers where publications were ordinarily printed. From there, copies of the questionnaire went to separate communal homes. It was accompanied by a one-page letter from Family leader Peter Amsterdam, dated August 1997, stressing that participation was voluntary and anonymous, but urging members to do the survey. The letter emphasized, "If you do choose to fill one out, please be completely honest in your answers." The questionnaire itself reinforced this point, saying "We should like you to feel that you are expressing your true feelings as you answer this questionnaire, so please fill it out in private, by yourself."

Once someone had completed the survey, he or she was asked to mail it directly to me, at a special mailbox I had set up and which only I had access to. As the surveys flooded in, I kept track of the colorful foreign postage stamps and the postmarks from all around the world. In addition, it was easy to see that the questionnaires had been printed at several different locations, as I had expected, because several different kinds of paper were used. Of course, there was the possibility that completion of a questionnaire could be blocked at any of these steps. Some regional centers could have been less industrious than others in sending sufficient copies to all the homes. Members who were on missionary trips, who were establishing new homes (a new one is opened about every three days), or residing in remote areas may not have received their copies. Those who are not fluent in English may not have been able to respond, and for respondents in places like Uzbekistan, mailing the questionnaire to me may have presented insurmountable difficulties. And, of course, ultimately participation was voluntary.

It is possible to estimate some aspects of the representativeness of the respondent sample. The Family itself calculates that 30 percent of members were born in the United States, and an almost identical 29 percent of our respondents were. Some non-English speaking nations are underrepresented, such as Brazil with 4 percent rather than 8 percent, Japan with 3 rather than 6, Mexico with 2 rather than 4, and Argentina with 2 rather than 3. Respondents to the survey were 60 percent female, versus 40 percent who were male.[5] It is not particularly surprising that a majority are female, because this is also true for many surveys of the general population. In 1996, 56 percent of the respondents to the General Social Survey were female.

We would prefer a true random sample of members, and I can imagine a future study that might employ the address list of the central organization to mail questionnaires to individuals. At present, the addresses of all the homes are highly privileged information, and chapter 1 explained why. The residents of each home have the right to decide how widely they want to share this information. Given the logistics of striving for a high response rate, directly mailing to the individual members would be extremely expensive, and the present pioneering study was done without the benefit of grant support. Such a study would also require a very high degree of trust and cooperation from the leadership of the religious group, something hard to obtain with groups that suffer frequent government persecution.

A book like this one, intended for a diverse audience, is not the right place for elaborate statistical analysis. Our data tables are limited to number counts of people or percentages, and we occasionally go so far as to calculate an average. Because we have fully 1,025 surveys, however, I was able to carry out complex analyses to determine whether results would change much if we controlled for variables such as gender and age that might correlate with the response rate and thus could be a source of bias. This book does not come close to exhausting the scientific potential of the data set, and a number of technical journal articles can be written examining the correlations between variables. Here we will limit ourselves to the simple facts of Family life and culture.

Demographics

We will begin our analysis by considering a representative range of questionnaire items that provide an overview of lives in the Family. Respondents to the survey were born as long ago as 1914 and as recently as 1983. The average birth year was 1966, but ironically only 2 of the 1,013 respondents who told us their birth date were actually born in that year. After 1943, 1966 was the year in which fewest respondents were born. Figure 2.1 shows how this could be true: membership in the Family is sharply divided into two generations, older people who primarily joined as adults, and a younger generation consisting of their children.

Of the 1,013 respondents who answered questions about how they came to be members of the Family, 414 or 41 percent were born into it. The mean age of those who joined the group was 20.3 years, and the median was 20. But 6 percent joined before age 16, so they undoubtedly were brought in by parents who became members. By far the largest number of members, 88 percent, came in between the ages of 16 and 27, with at least 10 arriving at each of these ages. The age at which the largest single number of people joined was 18 years, when 96 became members of the Family. Only about 2 percent joined after their twenties, and the oldest recruit was fifty.

Life at home is very different for Family members, compared with the general American public. Half of the Family respondents live in homes having fifteen or more members.[6] In the entire history of the General Social Survey through 1996, only two respondents lived in homes having fifteen or more members. More than half of all GSS respondents either live with one other person or live alone. Only 19 percent of GSS residents live in a home with a child under age six, compared with 86 percent of Family members.

Figure 2.1. Two Generations in the Family

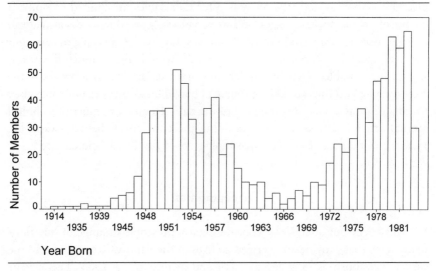

In 1986, The General Social Survey asked respondents how long they had lived in their current city, town, or community, and how long they had resided in their present home. Most Family members live outside the United States, despite the American origins of the group, but the general U.S. population provides a good benchmark of a highly mobile population against which to compare this missionary movement. These particular items were included in the International Social Survey, so future research could use other nations as benchmarks. Only 9 percent of GSS respondents had moved from a different community during the previous year, compared with 35 percent of Family members. And just 18 percent of American adults had moved into their current homes during the past year, versus 52 percent of Family members. This is a high rate of mobility indeed.

As a worldwide missionary movement, in which members constantly move from nation to nation, geography is a crucial fact of life. The 1,002 respondents who told us where they currently live reside in fully fifty-nine different countries. The largest number, 227 live in the United States. The other nations contributing at least 10 respondents are: Brazil (87 respondents), Japan (69), Thailand (60), Russia (56), Taiwan (35), Hungary (32), Canada (30), India (29), France (22), Australia (21), Mexico (18), Ukraine (17), Turkey (17), Italy (17), Chile (17), United Kingdom (16), Romania (15), Indonesia (13), Spain (11), Croatia (10), and South Africa (10). Austria, Belgium, China, Czech

Republic, Denmark, Finland, Germany, Kazakhstan, Lebanon, Lithuania, Pakistan, Paraguay, Poland, Portugal, Slovakia, Sweden, Switzerland, Uzbekistan each contributed between 5 and 9 respondents. Another nineteen nations also contributed: Albania, Argentina, Colombia, Ecuador, El Salvador, Estonia, Ghana, Greece, Ireland, Kenya, Latvia, Namibia, Nepal, Netherlands, New Zealand, Nigeria, Peru, Philippines, and Venezuela.

Respondents were born in seventy-six different nations, and this is not far below the Family's own tabulation for the complete membership that natives of ninety-three different nations belonged to the group.[7] One survey question asked, "How many countries have you lived in as a member of The Family?" Sixty-five respondents said they had only been in one country, and answers ranged all the way up to one person who claimed to have been in forty-two, a high but not impossible number. Half of the respondents had lived in six or more nations, and a quarter had been in nine or more.

This is not the place to do a complex statistical analysis of international migration flows, but a simple look will tell us much. Table 2.1 shows geographic distributions for the twenty-five nations with at least ten members in one of the columns. The first column shows the number of recruits born in each of the nations, and the second shows where these people joined the group. The third column then tabulates where members born in the Family were born, and the fourth gives the total numbers of members currently living in those nations.

Take Australia, for example. Twenty of the respondents were recruited there, and sixteen more were born there in Family homes. If none moved away, then thirty-six should still be living in Australia, but the last column of table 2.1 shows that only twenty-one respondents are currently living there. Thus, at least fifteen moved away. Probably the number is even greater, because some members may have been born or recruited elsewhere before moving to Australia. Actually, close examination of the original data show that only nine of the twenty-one currently living in Australia were born there, and just one person currently living in Australia was recruited there but born elsewhere. Thus, in fact fully twenty-six of the thirty-six born in Australia have moved away.

Despite the advantages that a more detailed, technical analysis might provide, table 2.1 gives a reasonable impression of which nations are sources of missionaries, and which are the more active mission fields. Clearly, nations like Japan, Russia or Thailand are mission fields, whereas the United States, Great Britain, and Canada are sources of missionaries.

Two nations deserve special explanation. Thirty-three people entered the Family either by recruitment or birth in Germany, but only six live there today.

Table 2.1. Geographic Distribution in 25 Nations (Respondents)

	Recruits Born In	Met Family In	Family Children Born In	Current Home of All
Australia	17	20	16	21
Brazil	16	19	27	87
Canada	39	38	15	30
France	23	25	31	22
Germany	28	19	14	6
Hungary	10	10	0	32
India	5	18	14	29
Indonesia	1	0	4	13
Italy	10	16	9	17
Japan	7	6	20	69
Mexico	5	7	16	18
Netherlands	13	24	7	1
Philippines	6	7	14	1
Poland	14	13	0	7
Romania	4	4	0	15
Russia	13	10	0	56
South Africa	3	1	0	10
Spain	21	19	17	11
Switzerland	10	11	8	9
Taiwan	2	2	1	35
Thailand	3	4	10	60
Turkey	0	2	4	17
Ukraine	3	4	0	17
United Kingdom	33	22	15	16
United States	221	202	63	227

A prime reason is the fact that Germany forbids home schooling, and as we shall find in the final chapter, most Family children are taught at home. Therefore missionaries active in Germany often live just outside its borders, and foray in on what the group calls "road trips." Fifty-six respondents entered the Family in France, but only twenty-two live there today. When I interviewed Samuel and Heidi at their home outside Paris, they explained that many members moved out of the country after the brutal seizure of children in 1993. Most of them still do not feel their kids are safe in the country today.

Prior to the death of Father David in 1994, leadership in the Family began assembling ideas and writing drafts of a formal handbook governing life within the homes. Published early in 1995 and revised subsequently, this is *The Love Charter*, a formal constitution of the rights and obligations of members of the missionary communes called Charter homes.[8] Among the chief areas covered are the proper procedures for establishing a new home and for individuals moving between homes. Adult members may open a home on their own initiative in the country where they currently live, so long as one does not already exist in the immediate area. However, pioneers may need the advice and support of existing homes, and before witnessing in a different nation they need clearance from the Family continental organization. A young woman in China wrote on the first page of her questionnaire that she was very happy, because "I received permission to open a new home."

Homes that need members will advertise through the Family's communication network, perhaps describing the kinds of skills that would be useful. Individuals, whether in response to these requests or on their own initiative, will ask a home to accept them or will advertise for homes in a particular area to invite them. In general, two thirds of the voting members of a home must agree, before a member is accepted into it. A girl living in a nine-person Taiwan home reported, "I sat in a meeting (Home Counsel) where we decided to invite some certain people to our home."

Individuals who want to transfer from one home to another also need to find the money to clear their share of debts from the first home and to pay for transportation to the second one. Because everyone involved wants to support missionary work, people who want to move frequently get help. A girl in America said, "I participated in a group skit to help a brother raise fare to Russia. He's a clown and does parties." At a twenty-one-person home, a young woman rejoiced, "The home decided to give us a monetary gift to help us on our way to Nigeria." Born in Australia, she had already lived with the Family in fifteen nations. A middle-aged British woman who had already worked in eight nations was happy to get "an invitation to go to Taiwan (first step to China!!). I also got the tickets and the visas, wow!!"

Separation from the World

Although members live within the world, often in major urban centers, in many respects they do not belong to it. They have largely created their own culture consisting of a vast corpus of literature, hundreds of songs, and the thousands of drawings that illustrate the publications. A veritable flood of internal publications links the far-flung homes to the executive body of the Family, which is called World Services and has its official address in Switzerland.

Other than the Bible and bound versions of their own publications, the worldly books I have seen in their homes tend to be reference works or classics selected for their educational value to children. The homes have television sets and often computers hooked to Internet, but few if any magazines.

The GSS has measured newspaper, radio, and television use among the American public. In 1996, 42 percent of GSS respondents said they read the newspaper every day, compared with only 17 percent of Family members. One man who never read the newspaper wrote in the margin of the questionnaire, "Too busy serving the Lord and doing activities I like such as improving my ministries." Two Americans in Russia and an Italian woman currently living in Ukraine commented that it was difficult to find newspapers in a language they could understand. The homes do get much useful information from the press about the surrounding communities, and members also are interested in world news. Only 6 percent of GSS respondents, and 8 percent of Family members never read a newspaper.

On the average day in 1996, 76 percent of GSS respondents personally watched television more than an hour, and 24 percent watched an hour or less. In contrast, fully 87 percent of Family members watch TV no more than one hour per day, and 34 percent say they never watch it. The median TV viewing for American adults was about two hours a day, versus half an hour in the Family. A Philippine woman explained she watched no television at her home in Thailand, because "I can't speak the local language and we don't have cable." Others wrote that television watching consisted primarily of a two-hour movie each week, evening news, and occasional educational programs for the children. The Family has produced its own series of children's programs, called Kiddie Viddies. A sixteen-year-old girl who watches two hours a day said, "I do aerobics 1 hour and watch Kiddie Viddie with the kids another hour. It's not really TV."

The Family has compiled a huge list of recommended commercial movies with brief descriptions and age-appropriate recommendations. For example, the film *Dead Man Walking* was considered appropriate only for members age eighteen and above: "Intense realistic drama based on the true story of a nun who gets involved in spiritually counseling a death row inmate. Well-acted, with clear message of Salvation through Jesus & loving the sinner while hating the sin. This movie contains repeated flashbacks of the rape/murder scene & a graphic description of the act by the parents of one of the victims, which may be disturbing. Everyone will probably appreciate an extra good cleansing prayer after viewing this one, & avoiding watching these scenes if they might disturb you." As this example shows, the Family does not avoid films with difficult themes, but many of the recommended movies are standard films such as *African Queen, Cinderella, Gone with the Wind, Lawrence of Arabia,* and *Star Wars.*

Some tapes of movies circulate among Family homes, but the homes I know about generally get them from video rental stores. A man at a dozen-person home in Namibia "went to give back the video tape that we rented." A woman sheepishly admitted, "Yesterday I was given ten movies to return to the video shop, which were all overdue."

The GSS has not asked about radio listening since 1983, but in that year 37 percent of Americans listened to it an hour a day or less. In the Family, 96 percent listen an hour a day or less, and 75 percent never listen. A woman in Canada wrote "fifteen minutes—news." Another in Hungary said she listened about two hours "usually while I'm driving." A girl in Indonesia reported, "I listen to Family tapes a lot, but not the radio." Sometimes when I have ridden in a car driven by a member of the group, he or she would play a cassette tape of music recorded by other members, but never the radio.

The 1993 General Social Survey examined how people prioritized each of eight fundamental values, such as "being financially secure" and "having children." Respondents were supposed to rate each one on a five-point scale from "one of the most important" to "not at all important." Table 2.2 shows how both groups weighed these life goals. Because respondents could give high ratings to any number of values, the percentages in the table do not add up to 100.

In both sets of respondents, the value receiving the most votes is "having faith in God," but twice as high a percentage consider this one of the most important goals in the Family as in the American public, 92 percent compared with 46. "Having children" scores slightly higher in the group, but the Family rates all of the others lower. The GSS respondents are far more likely to consider the materialistic goals of "being financially secure" and "having nice things" to be important. "Having a fulfilling job" rates more than twice as high outside the group, and indeed members tend not to have jobs in the conventional sense of the term.

Economics

At the beginning of the 1980s, James Richardson noted that much of the Family's money came from street witnessing, but he added, "Funds and donations of property and other support have been received from members and sympathetic outsiders. Some methods of obtaining support have been quite

Table 2.2. Fundamental Values

One of the most important values . . .	Family	1993 GSS
Being financially secure	4.3%	26.8%
Being married	8.3%	19.1%
Having children	26.2%	23.6%
Having faith in God	92.2%	46.0%
Having nice things	0.6%	4.3%
Being cultured	1.8%	3.8%
Having a fulfilling job	10.1%	21.2%
Being self-sufficient and not having to depend on others	31.1%	44.2%

The number of cases ranges from 1,015 to 1,022 for the Family, and from 1587 to 1593 for the General Social Survey.

ingenious—'house sitting' for financial institutions in England, for one example. But many of their operations such as their music businesses and special youth-oriented night clubs have not usually been money-making. These have been a drain on the coffers of the group because they were developed primarily as efforts at evangelism."9

Only 3 percent of respondents had a full-time secular job outside the Family, and another 10 percent had part-time jobs. That means that 87 percent had no work outside of missionary activity. Some respondents have held higher administrative positions in the Family at one time or another. Just 2 percent had been "Continental Overseers" holding one or another of these titles depending on which were being used at the particular point in the group's history: King and Queen's Servants, National Officers, or Central Reporting Officers. Twenty-six percent had held office at the National Area Overseer level, having titles like these: National Area Shepherd, Greater Area Shepherd, District Area Shepherd, Local Area Shepherd or Visiting Servants. The bureaucratic organization of the Family has changed several times, becoming alternately more and less hierarchical. But much of the time, the administrative jobs above the level of the individual home are very few.

To understand better the work responsibilities people have within the group, the questionnaire asked, "What ministry or ministries are you currently involved with in your home?" The fixed-choice responses were worked out in cooperation with spokespeople for the group. Table 2.3 lists the twelve responses, and individuals could check as many boxes as applied to them.

Table 2.3. Ministries in the Home

Involved in these ministries . . .	Family
Teamwork	46.8%
Outreach	69.6%
Child care	57.4%
Teacher	43.2%
Handyman	21.9%
Home care	58.5%
Consider the Poor	40.1%
Music	25.1%
Audiovisual	3.6%
Office	38.9%
Administration	23.7%
Provisioning	33.5%

Most of the terms in table 2.3 are self-explanatory. "Teamwork" means the organizational and leadership work of the home, or a committee created to carry out a particular task. The group is called a "teamwork" rather than a team, and members are "teamworkers." Outreach refers to missionary witnessing outside the home. Child care and teacher mean working with the children inside the home, although sometimes nearby homes may share their schooling. Handyman and home care are house repairs and domestic chores.

"Consider the Poor" is a service providing to poor nonmembers the food or clothing that was collected from individual donors, businesses, or in some cases from charity agencies. Many members play music, often in public as part of their missionary work, and a small number help create the group's television tapes and other audiovisual products.

The amount of office or administrative work varies from home to home, and some have special responsibilities like printing and distributing literature, which put more emphasis on these activities. "Provisioning" is a major way that members obtain food, clothing, and other material goods, through seeking donations.

There was a space on the questionnaire where respondents could write in other kinds of work. Some listed domestic jobs: "cleaning," "cooking," "dishes," "house maintenance," "kitchen," "laundry," "pantry," "seamstress," and "storage management." Others mentioned office jobs, which generally would be done in the home in a special area reserved for them: "business," "computer work," "finances," "legal matters," "mail ministry," "media spokesperson," "on-line ministry," "phone ministry," "public relations," and "secretary."

Several people worked on literature: "art," "crafts," "illustrations," "layout," "painting portraits", "photography," "publications," and "translating." A man in Indonesia did "witnessing tool production," which means producing the tracts and similar materials employed in evangelical work. The lively arts included: "clown shows," "dancing," "fund-raising with balloons," "kids' parties," "performing," "puppeteer," "show group," "studio recording," and "theatrical." In Guadalajara, Mexico, one woman said her special work was "puppets," and another said she was "promoter of our puppet show."

Miscellaneous jobs included: "animal husbandry," "driver," "fundraising," "gardening," "mechanic," "warehousing," "youth counselor," and "youth witnessing." A seventeen-year old boy said, "I am currently enrolled in a high-school correspondence course. This consumes most of my time." A woman in her late thirties wrote that her special work was "part-time college, as a student, to be an English teacher to foreign students." A sixteen-year-old boy was ready to work "in whatever needs help." A young woman who was expecting her first baby very soon said her extra job was "pregnancy."

Members generally do not have conventional jobs, yet the Family lacks the churches from which an established denomination solicits financial support. Therefore they must constantly find friendly nonmembers who respond positively to their message and are willing to help with donations of money, goods, or labor.

While witnessing on behalf of Jesus, typically on the streets or in other public places where people congregate, they often enter into friendly conversations with strangers. Often they give out tracts or little religious posters. They call this "litnessing," which means witnessing through distributing literature. They also can distribute audiotapes, compact discs, and even videotapes of music that they have composed, performed and recorded themselves in professional-quality studios. During witnessing and litnessing, the strangers may spontaneously offer donations, and members will also request donations to support their missionary work.

When a home has a particular material need, members may go on an expedition to "provision" it. On my very first day observing the Family, I watched as they provisioned a free meal from a pizza restaurant in Los Angeles. Two members entered the establishment and explained that they were part of a small group of missionaries and that a meal would help them greatly with their work. Often people decline to help, but this time the manager invited the half dozen members in for a complete meal. Provisioning is often done in person, but it can also be done over the telephone. In Toronto, one of the men explained that he had just provisioned an oil change for the vehicle he was taking on a road trip. He simply took out the yellow-page phonebook and began calling oil change services until one agreed.

When I visited a home in San Francisco, the members wanted to be good hosts, but the lunch was a little sparse because they had been without fruits and vegetables for several days. Two of the young women were optimistic that they might be able to obtain provision at a nearby supermarket they had visited, so the entire home held a brief prayer meeting at which successful provisioning was one of the topics. While I was interviewing other members, the two women went to the market. About an hour later they returned in great excitement with a box full of fruit and the promise of regular donations in the future. Often people called "friends" of the Family become long-term suppliers of particular needs. This San Francisco home regularly received free bread from an outlet of a major bakery chain that provided day-old but still edible bread to the poor at low cost. They had another arrangement with a high-fashion used clothing store to take unsalable clothing and give to the poor what they could not use themselves. A businessman provided part of their rent in a monthly cash donation.

The Edmonton, Alberta, home received a load of boxed groceries from a Safeway store each week, and a doughnut shop contributed doughnuts and muffins. The home near Paris, France, had a relationship with a health food company that provided large quantities of tasty biscuits and other food. In Toronto, Pearl told me, "We have a food terminal here. It's a huge location where trucks carrying vegetables and fruits go. It's not always the nicest place for females to go because the guys are quite rude. But the people there donate fruits and veggies to us."[10] Pearl often gives one of the warehouse operators a poster or a music tape.

The first home I visited often, in Washington D.C., had a relationship with a pizza parlor that sold by the slice. At the end of each day, there would be perfectly fine slices of pizza left over, which the pizza parlor would put in its freezer. Once each month, a van from the home would pick up enough pizza to satisfy everybody for two days. A butcher provided unpopular but wholesome cuts. For example, I twice shared a fine dinner at the home in which the meat was heart. For rent and some other necessities a home needs cash. One source for the Washington home was washing cars. The owners of a particular location permitted the young people of the home to set up an impromptu car wash, and they were quite successful at attracting drivers who made donations to have their vehicles cleaned off.

Housing is a special challenge, especially for large groups. Some of the homes I have visited were simply very large, clean, modern homes with ample space for twenty people, sleeping two or four to a spacious room. Two homes were mansionlike buildings that the owners were having difficulty selling. By agreeing to move on a moment's notice, and having no lease, the Family could get a very low rent. In two other cases, at Baltimore and San Francisco, low rent was achieved by agreeing to fix up a house. At both of these places I met Tim "Handyman" Prayerful, a member who has a fine set of tools and specializes in high-skill renovation work. The project can be minor, as when a man in Brazil "built several shelves in our garage for storage." Sometimes the work is quite extensive. From an American home with about a dozen members, a man wrote, "We spent the day preparing the bottom floor of our house for the construction of five more rooms."

The responses to the survey's open-ended questions provide many examples of donations and provisioning. A Venezuelan woman in Russia went on a trip to another town. "I was traveling on a train and by me was a lady sitting and I started a conversation and explained our work, and without asking for anything she gave me a nice donation." An American home with twenty-five members "got a large donation of bread." In Taiwan, a Canadian man was happy that "someone donated a digital camera to my work."

A group of young women from the Dominican Republic, Brazil, Hong Kong, France, and Canada were on a road trip witnessing away from their home in the United States, when they ran out of gas and became hungry. "A sweet lady donated gas that we needed to get home." "Someone donated a nice Mexican meal for the eight of us." In a different incident a Swiss father of three wrote, "My family and two friends were invited to a donated dinner at a Mexican restaurant. Even the kids had great fun eating out and staying up late." At another time, he said, "We were able to make contact again with a man who promised to donate computers. I had lost his calling card before." A woman in a fourteen-member Australian home wrote, "A provisioning contact invited myself and my whole home to his restaurant for pizza."

A teenager in Canada said that yesterday he "did provisioning pickups of milk and other dairy products at Whole Foods." One of the boys at a twenty-member home in Turkey "woke up at six o'clock in the morning to go to the market where we get fruits and veggies for free every week." But a man in the same home unhappily reported that "a promise of a tank of fuel oil fell through." A Danish father of five wrote, "My children and I went to a friend to pick up fruits and vegetables."

All kinds of things are donated. From France a woman wrote about "one of God's little miracles. We had put aside some money for a laptop, then later forsook it to help a needy widow. Yesterday a friend just gave us his laptop out of the blue!" At a small home in Romania, "The Lord supplied furniture for us." A woman in Japan was pleased that "the Lord supplied many nice baby clothes for our soon to be born baby." A Brazilian teenage girl was happy to report, "The Lord supplied some needed clothes for me." In India a man from Bangladesh, "went out witnessing to businessmen with a girl from our home. God led us to talk to some businessman and he in turn helped us with shoes." Afterward, he wrote a letter of appreciation to their benefactor.

One of the occasional but significant needs is money or tickets to travel from one nation to another. A woman in Mexico rejoiced that "a long-time supporter just gave us a large donation to visit my mom in the States." In Denmark an eighteen-year-old woman rejoiced that "we got free airline tickets to Canada." A Canadian woman was happy that her home "received a donation for our fare to go overseas." I interviewed one man who had gotten a free ride for himself and his wife in a small plane from the United States to South America, from a pilot who was delivering the aircraft there.

Sometimes a donation consists of personal help. In Thailand, a seventeen-year-old girl wrote, "I was surprised at how the Lord supplied a guide who took us to and helped us climb up some high rocks." An American man rejoiced, "I got a sponsor for a long-term visa to be able to stay in Taiwan." A man had been trying to fix the plumbing and electricity in the French home he shared with another family, having all sorts of trouble and cutting himself. But then, "The Lord made me meet a very sweet electrician who wants to help us with the electric work in the house."

Medical services are among the more specialized needs that may be met through donations and provisioning. A young man in Russia said, "I broke my tooth and I met a sweet dentist who fixed it for free." An American girl was happy when "a close friend of the Family offered to pay to get my teeth fixed with braces as a birthday gift." A British woman in India said, "I asked a local x-ray specialist if he could donate two x-rays of my arms and back for a big discount and he did." Having two children, she needed some English educational materials, but she had no way to travel to the place where they could be obtained. "A sweet Polish friend donated three round trip bus fares almost completely free. This made me feel the Lord's love very closely and personal."

Litnessing and provisioning are not always successful. In Canada, a woman "went out postering, giving out our Family posters, with my husband, a few of our children and some of the other young people in our home." One of the young people said he was not happy because "some people didn't want our posters while we were out postering." In Russia a teenage girl wrote: "I went to see a director of a flour and milk company to ask if he could help us.

He wasn't very friendly and said no! Well, the Lord probably has someone else He wants to bless." In the 1970s, perhaps in Paris, members of the Family had learned that the subway was a very good place to witness because they received many cash donations there. The police would sometimes tell them to leave, but it was worth returning again. Two respondents to the 1997 survey from a Ukrainian home said they were distributing tracts on the subway during bad weather, but police stopped them and "kicked us out of the Metro."

Home Life

The Family does not have elaborate church services or rituals. On occasion I have visited homes for Fellowship, which usually includes some singing, Bible verse reading, and possibly an informal communion with bread and wine. A young woman wrote on her questionnaire the following description of an unusually elaborate Fellowship evening: "Our home had an appreciation night, where each person had another person to appreciate by writing a poem, song or get something from the Lord for them. Everyone was very touched and some were in tears by the end. We realized that there was so many special things about each person that we often overlook or forget. Living together day after day sometimes causes familiarity and we can lose sight of the others' good qualities."

A woman in a home with more than twenty members acknowledged that they varied in their commitment: "We have one person in our home who probably won't stay full-time in the Family, who gets negative and critical about every person on our team. If he doesn't like it (us) he ought to go, but it saddened me that he didn't see the wonderful qualities of each one here. Some of these guys are saints!"

The dozen homes I have visited all blended into their neighborhoods and were not marked in any way as religious institutions. Many homes receive their mail at a post office or other locations, to preserve the privacy of their residences. For example, I saw that the mail for a San Francisco home went to an address a short distance away on a main road. A boy in El Salvador lamented, "I went walking all the way to the mail and I forgot the number of the box. So I had to come back to check the number."

Everyone contributes to the productive work of the home, and there is no artificial distinction between the employed, unemployed, or homemakers. A fifteen-year-old girl was proud that she had "cooked a liver and potato dinner for twenty-eight people." A young man who was born into the Family in

Sweden but now lived in Russia "cooked a Swedish dinner for everyone and cleaned the kitchen." But a young woman in South Africa lamented, "We had some dinner made by someone who cannot cook." A girl in a home with ten members discovered the uncertainties of a wandering life: "I made cookies, but to my surprise there was no oven. We are moving, so the pick up truck had already taken the stove. I had to ask the neighbor."

Homes sometimes get temporary aid from others. A sixteen-year-old boy was proud that he helped other members. "I went to another home that just opened up and I spent three days digging out their garden by myself." A young man in Brazil was happy because, "I received an invitation to go help on a Christmas push in Brasilia."

Every home has a certain amount of office work that must be done, and those that are very active in communications have sizable home offices. A young woman in Thailand "worked at typing, transcribing and office work." In Russia, a young man "prepared envelopes to be mailed for our mail ministry." A man in Switzerland wrote, "The other day I translated an inspiring Christmas story that (hopefully) will be part of a booklet coming out." A man in Chile "analyzed and compiled stats about visitors to our Internet site. I devised a way to transfer big computer files to another computer, tried it, and it worked." A woman in Turkey wrote that she "signed, addressed and sealed our monthly newsletter to be sent off to the States to our supporters and friends, as we live on the mission field." A woman in Turkey "wrote to almost thirty people to thank them for their help and to send them interesting food-for-thought stories," and she also worked on a new version of one the Family's videos for children, doing a "translation of *Treasure Attic #1* into Arabic."

When possible, members do their own maintenance rather than hiring repairmen. An Australian woman in Thailand wrote that yesterday she had "fixed a computer, which promptly broke down. But I fixed it for good today." A sixteen-year-old boy in Canada admitted, "I dismantled the electric dryer, so I could find out why it doesn't heat up anymore."

One man boasted, "I was able to complete converting our microbus into a motor home." Another spent a day "repairing our motor home so our family could move on to our next witnessing destination." He had to replace "the water pump and temperature sensor."

A man in Brazil wrote, "I had to get a ladder and climb on the roof of our house to see why there was a leak. Water was leaking through the tiles." As in conventional neighborhoods, there is also yard work to do. In Switzerland a man "fixed the weed-cutter, taking it apart for the first time, and cut the bank."

For a mother with many children, life can sometimes get too hectic. From the United States, a mother of thirteen wrote, "The van broke, the oven messed up, the teens were hard to handle. The Lord gave me joy to know He is drawing me closer to Him through it all." Living in a home with twenty other people, there were many to rely on. However there was "contention in the house, misunderstandings." She "sought the Lord" all alone. "I prayed desperately about my situation, and the Lord gave me wonderful answers to those prayers."

A fourteen-year-old girl was happy to report, "We got a new bunk bed in our room and me and my friend put it together ourselves." Young members are accustomed to sharing their sleeping rooms with several other people, but sometimes things become too crowded even for their tastes. A nineteen-year-old woman living in a fifteen-person home in Taiwan complained, "I was sleeping peacefully in my bed when one of my friends came and got in bed with me, saying she was sick and couldn't breathe on her top bunk. After about a half hour I had to find another place to sleep because she was pushing me off the bed and I was afraid I'd catch whatever it was she had."

When necessary, Family members make use of a full range of medical and dental services. An American woman in her early forties "went to the chiropractor." A middle-aged woman "had blood taken for a blood test at a laboratory" and was distressed to learn "I have thoracic outlet syndrome." A young woman in Mexico, "went to the dentist and got my four wisdom teeth pulled out." A fourteen-year-old boy "went to the dentist" and was happy "I only have to wear my braces at night."

Every moment that a member is outside the home presents a potential opportunity for missionary work. For example, one woman wrote, "While waiting in line at the hospital to get some tests done, I struck up a conversation with a girl, telling her of our volunteer work, gave her some gospel literature, and before saying good bye, prayed with her to receive Jesus in her heart."

Charity

An important part of Family work that this study does not directly address is the charitable work performed largely in mission fields outside the most prosperous nations. When I fished for good questionnaire items in the General Social Survey, diverse questions about person-to-person benevolent activities did not surface. In table 2.3 we saw that about 40 percent of members participated in Consider the Poor, and in my interviews members did often mention distributing food and clothing to impoverished people in their cities. Some future sociological study may have to examine how the Family's charitable activities fit in with the economy of their homes and with the activities of other charitable organizations.

In response to the first, open-ended question of the survey, a woman in Kenya said that yesterday she "did Consider the Poor at a home for street children." A girl in South Africa wrote, "I helped give food out to the homeless. Seeing the look on the people's faces when I gave them food made me happy." In Argentina, a man wrote, "We distributed donated clothes to the poor in the suburbs of town." Even in the United States, there is ample scope for Consider the Poor. In response to the question about what she had done yesterday, an American woman replied, "In the morning, a pickup truck was available for a short time. Three ten year olds and their teacher and I went down to the nearby 'slum' area distributing food to 'regulars.' All have small children."

Members of the Family are not rich in material things, so they have little of their own they can give to others. But they have developed a talent for finding donors who have a surplus of something, finding means of transportation, and finding poor people somewhere who need exactly what the donors have a surplus of. Recently, one of the Washington, D.C. homes was able to do this with educational books. In Slovakia, a girl "bagged and weighed clothes to be brought to the Ukraine, for orphanages and schools there." From Sweden, a young woman wrote, "A couple of us packed donated clothes for the relief work in Perm, Russia." A woman in Russia was pleased to say, "The customs of the country where we work gave its agreement for us to distribute a load of wheel chairs as humanitarian aid to invalid children in the local area."

Sometimes success in these efforts is not so much the result of a rational plan as of the fact that Family members are forever traveling and making contact with potential donors and recipients. A story published in the Family's *Worldwide Activity Report* (distributed to the general public) explains how this sometimes happens. Titled, "God's Mysterious Ways," this story comes from Japan. "When a company offered to donate 6,000 pairs of running shoes to our work, we accepted—even though we had no idea at the time what we would do with so many shoes!

"A short while later, Andy, a Family member who does volunteer work in Siberia, made a trip to Japan and stayed in our home. In passing, I asked if he needed a pair of running shoes, and proceeded to show him the shoes that filled two large tents in our back yard. Andy looked at all those shoes and nearly started to cry."

"He and his wife previously had arranged several shipments of humanitarian aid to institutions in their adopted city, he explained, and just before their trip to Japan they had been given a new list of most needed items. At the top of the list—shoes! Andy said that when his co-workers prayed with him for his trip to Japan, his number one prayer request was to be able to bring back shoes. And here we were, sitting on the answer to their prayers! Before long, the shoes were loaded and on their way to Siberia."[11]

Not all of the Family's charity work involved material goods, and often members provide the needy with love and entertainment. In one Eastern European country, a woman wrote, "While going to an orphanage for 100 handicapped girls, and taking a small group of them out for the afternoon to give them some personal love and attention, it broke my heart to see their living conditions and to leave a big group of them behind us because they wanted to come along too. I wished we could do more for them." In France, a young man reported, "Our band went to Slovenia and Croatia to do concerts for refugee camps."

One benefit of the Family's charity work is that it helps legitimate the group as a bona-fide religious organization in the minds of government officials. Many nations, notably throughout Europe from France through Russia, have been clamping down on new religious movements with "anticult" legislation and other repressive policies. In Romania, a woman "worked on compiling a report of our humanitarian and cultural activities in this country for the government, as they are considering legislations about religion."

The Family belongs to the broad theological tradition in American religion that believes in salvation by grace rather than by good works. That is, accepting Jesus into one's heart is far more important in gaining entry to Heaven than is doing material acts of charity. Thus, the best way to benefit the needy is to help them find their way to Jesus, and then either the Lord will provide for their material needs, or their own spiritual regeneration will allow them to take care of themselves. However, among the distinctive Family methods for bringing people to Jesus is sharing God's love with them, and material benefits are one way of showing that the Family cares for the recipients.

Science

Controversy has dogged the Family since its inception. Its apocalyptic message closed the 1960s like an exclamation mark. It was the very first victim of forcible deprogramming.[12] The FFing ministry both titillated and offended supposedly respectable citizens even as it exposed the hypocrisy of churchianity's pretence to offer God's love while despising the human body that was the Lord's creation. The mass seizure of 600 Family children caused immeasurable harm and underscored the incompetence of government to meddle in religious life. Very recently, as we shall see in chapter 4, the Family has become the most prolific channel of messages believed to come from the spirit world. Through it all, perhaps the greatest miracle is that the Family survived.

To the extent that it is exceptional, what can we learn from it? One might argue that little can be learned from a group that is so unique and does not represent any sizable population of similar groups. But I think that is very wrong, for four reasons.

First, by studying the Family we will learn how far we can take the standard social-scientific research methods. Science is a process of successive approximate of the truth, and I am sure that more rigorous studies than mine can be done in the future either with the Family or other new religious movements. But never before have we possessed quantitative data of such scope concerning a radical religious movement. If results from the survey are simultaneously reasonable and interesting, we will know that standard questionnaire methods have very wide applicability indeed. For two decades, I have been trying to convince my colleagues in the sociology of religion that they should rely more heavily on systematic quantitative methodologies, and this book is another lesson of that course.

Second, in earlier publications I have argued that new religious movements provide enlightening insights into fundamental social processes. Today I would not call the Family a "cult," because that word has become a vacuous term of abuse employed by journalists and the anticult movement. However, I still like my aphorism, "Cult is culture writ small."[13] New religious movements are like the fruit flies and bacteria studied by geneticists. By being small and fast-changing, and possessing distinctive characteristics, they give scientists clear vision into the processes that create and sustain new culture.

Third, Rodney Stark and I have argued in our award-winning books, *The Future of Religion* and *A Theory of Religion*, that secularization is a self-limiting process that does not diminish religion but opens the way for new religions to arise. When Father David died, his movement possessed something like 10,000 members, about the size of the Jesus movement at the time of the crucifixion. Both movements were distinctive departures from existing sacred traditions, even while being solidly rooted in them. We cannot guess which new religious movements will grow to become the great faiths of the third millennium. But in its resilience and creativity, the Family must be among the candidates.

Finally, this book will provide empirical clarity on the nature of the group itself. The Family has explored some of the extremes of human experience.

Despised by its enemies and mercilessly criticized by the popular press, it nonetheless retains its own self-respect. How are we to regard these people so often painted as monsters in television programs and newspaper exposés? Perhaps on close inspection we will realize that they are human beings who have created a way of life that is valid for them. In so doing, we will comprehend more fully the amazing creation that is humanity.

CHAPTER 3

Beliefs

Before it is a commune, a radical departure from conventional society, or an experiment in collective love, the Family is a religious group. Critics tend to ignore this fact, but any objective analysis of the Family must recognize its fundamentally religious nature. It was founded by a Protestant clergyman, has been guided by messages believed to come from spirits, and continues to draw much of its inspiration from the Bible today. Members consider themselves to be missionaries, and much of their time is devoted to calling people to Christ. Over the years the General Social Survey has contained many questions measuring the religious beliefs of Americans, so it makes sense to focus our comparative analysis on the beliefs of the Children of God.

For the Family, faith logically begins with belief in God, but is also rooted in the Bible. Among the areas of faith explored by this chapter are the images members of the Family have of God and Heaven, beliefs about Hell and the Devil, and the sources of possible religious doubt. Batteries of questions from the General Social Survey not only reveal the ways in which members of the Family are more religious than the average American but also highlight some of the subtleties of Family theology. However, the GSS lacks items about the End-time, so we conclude the chapter with descriptions of the Millennium drawn from the group's own unique scriptures.

Belief in God

A question in the General Social Survey offers six different opinions and asks, "Which of the following statements comes closest to expressing what you believe about God?" As table 3.1 shows, nearly 96 percent of members say, "I know God really exists and I have no doubts about it."[1] About 65 percent of

Table 3.1. Belief in God

What you believe about God . . .	*Family*	*1994 GSS*
I don't believe in God.	0.0%	2.5%
I don't know whether there is a God and I don't believe there is any way to find out.	0.0%	2.8%
I don't believe in a personal God, but I do believe in a Higher Power of some kind.	0.0%	9.9%
I find myself believing in God some of the time, but not at others.	0.8%	3.8%
While I have doubts, I feel that I do believe in God.	3.6%	16.1%
I know God really exists and I have no doubts about it.	95.6%	64.9%
TOTAL	100.0%	100.0%

This table is based on 1,021 cases for the Family, and 1,326 for the General Social Survey.

respondents to the 1994 GSS also select this option, so the Family is unusual only in its near unanimity. Just over 4 percent of members of the Family admit that their faith is not perfect, either believing in God despite harboring doubts or believing in God only some of the time. About 20 percent of the American public is in one of these doubting categories. Nearly 10 percent of Americans, but no members of the Family, say, "I don't believe in a personal God, but I do believe in a Higher Power of some kind." The remaining 5 percent of Americans are about evenly split between agnostics ("I don't know whether there is a God and I don't believe there is any way to find out.") and atheists ("I don't believe in God."). No agnostics and atheists belong to the Family.

A second GSS item about belief in God, examined in table 3.2, explores whether the respondents' beliefs have changed. About 76 percent of Family members and 80 percent of the American public say, "I believe in God now, and I always have." Interestingly, the biggest difference between the two groups is among those who believe in God now but did not used to. Nearly 23 percent of Family members and 5 percent of the GSS respondents have apparently converted from being unbelievers to believers. This fits the hypothesis suggested by many researchers on new religious movements that converts

Table 3.2. Changing Beliefs about God

Which best describes your beliefs about God?	*Family*	*1991 GSS*
I don't believe in God now, and I never have	0.0%	1.8%
I don't believe in God now, but I used to	0.2%	3.5%
I believe in God now, but I didn't used to	22.8%	4.7%
I believe in God now, and I always have	75.9%	80.4%
Can't choose	1.1%	9.5%
TOTAL	100.0%	100.0%

This table is based on 1,017 cases for the Family, and 1,335 for the General Social Survey.

come differentially from the ranks of the nonreligious.[2] However, there is an alternative explanation. The Family sets a high standard for belief, associating it with powerful positive feelings and dedication. Some members may have been only nominally religious before joining but would have said they believed in God. Now, after joining, they look back on their earlier beliefs and consider them too weak to qualify as real faith.

Miscellaneous Religious Beliefs

Table 3.3 reveals that members are not of one mind about whether everything in the Bible is word for word the literal truth. Almost 98 percent agree that the Bible is the word of God, compared with 80 percent of GSS respondents, but members are almost evenly split on the issue of biblical literalism. This shows some scope for theological disagreement within the group. However, researchers have debated whether many respondents can really make fine distinctions in answering survey questions about their feelings about the Bible.[3]

One respondent to the Family survey wrote in the questionnaire's margin, "In parts it is inspired and in parts is the actual Word of God." One considered the Bible to be the actual word of God, "except some things, i.e., us eating Jesus' body and drinking His blood, should not be taken literally, but as a spiritual illustration." Another advocated "balancing scripture with scripture under the guidance of the Holy Spirit." Others commented that the apocalyptic visions in *Daniel* and *Revelation* required "allegorical understanding," and noted that "Some of apostle Paul's advice was for his days and is outdated."

Table 3.3. Feelings about the Bible

	Family	1991 GSS
The Bible is the actual word of God and it is to be taken literally.	47.2%	32.2%
The Bible is the inspired word of God but not everything should be taken literally, word for word.	50.6%	47.9%
The Bible is an ancient book of fables, legends, history, and moral precepts recorded by man.	0.8%	14.1%
Can't choose/This does not apply to me.	1.4%	5.8%
TOTAL	100.0%	100.0%

This table is based on 1,001 cases for the Family, and 1,334 for the General Social Survey.

The writings of Father David and Maria instruct members about which passages of the Bible are literally the word of God, and which are metaphoric and require symbolic interpretation.

A standard question from the GSS asks respondents to say how religious they are, but this poses a problem for members of the Family. As we might expect, table 3.4 shows that more members consider themselves to be "very religious" or "extremely religious," but responses range across all the choices. Far more members of the Family, 11 percent compared with 2 percent, could not choose a response that expressed how religious they are.

While constructing the questionnaire, I sought advice of spokespeople for the Family, who were especially knowledgeable not only about the official beliefs and practices, but also about actual behavior among members in several nations. They explained that the word *religious* had negative connotations, implying the religiosity of conventional denominations, which members find weak and hypocritical. They refer to mainstream religious organizations as "Churchianity" and criticize their worldliness. At the same time, the Family recognizes that all denominations contain sincere believers. In responding to this standard GSS item, some members are more willing than others to suspend their uneasiness and accept the "religious" label. This example reminds us that many people may not interpret questionnaire items in the way that the authors intended, and it is essential to support survey research with other methodologies, such as the observation and open-ended interviewing employed in this study.

Table 3.4. Religiousness

Would you describe yourself as . . . ?	Family	1991 GSS
Extremely religious	13.4%	4.6%
Very religious	29.2%	21.3%
Somewhat religious	26.6%	46.5%
Neither religious nor non-religious	12.8%	16.4%
Somewhat non-religious	2.7%	3.9%
Very non-religious	2.1%	2.8%
Extremely non-religious	1.9%	2.4%
Can't choose	11.3%	2.1%
TOTAL	100.0%	100.0%

This table is based on 993 cases for the Family, and 1,334 for the General Social Survey.

In this case, many respondents wrote comments in the margin of the questionnaire, drawing a distinction between Churchianity and their own movement's faith: "I'm not a church goer or follower of traditions, but I am a full-time follower of Jesus." "I don't feel religious, like going to church. But I believe in Jesus, that he's the Sample of God's Love." "I'd describe myself as a believer and a follower of the teachings of Jesus, not that I'm religious in a way other church-going religious people are." "I don't see myself as religious because we are not a church so to speak and we don't believe in being holy but serving God from the heart and it's sometimes unconventional." "I am 'religious' in the sense I take God and His word literally, non-religious in the sense that I don't go to church and I like to have fun." "The word religious is a bit hard to deal with. I can answer I really, really love Jesus and I want to live and die for him and others if needed. I love the Word, new and old." "I don't particularly care about this term. It sounds too 'good and holy.' I'd rather call myself a believer."

Respondents rejected "ritual observance," "having a lot of traditions and pious," elaborate "ceremonies," and "an attitude of Church self-made sanctimoniousness." But they embraced "devotion to God," "believing in God and practicing what the Bible says." One who could not answer the question said, "I do love Jesus very much." Another explained, "I'm not religious, I'm just a Christian."

Table 3.5. Closeness to God and Father David

	Close to Father David, Family	Close to God	
		Family	1991 GSS
Extremely close	30.4%	42.1%	33.3%
Somewhat close	55.3%	51.6%	46.3%
Not very close	9.9%	4.3%	9.5%
Not close at all	2.4%	0.8%	4.2%
Don't know	2.1%	1.2%	4.9%
Do not believe in God		0.0%	1.9%
TOTAL	100.0%	100.0%	100.0%

This table is based on 1,004 cases (Father David) and 1,014 cases (God) for the Family, and 1,338 for the General Social Survey.

Belief in God is a cognitive, psychological quality. But traditions such as evangelical Protestantism also encourage believers to have a personal relationship with God, thus a social connection as well as intellectual conviction. The GSS has asked, "How close do you feel to God most of the time?" In table 3.5 we see that a majority of the general public feels "somewhat" or "extremely" close, but the proportions are higher in the Family. Members who do not feel very close to God undoubtedly include some who have been going through difficult periods, perhaps feeling dissatisfied with their own behavior, and getting back close to God may be a goal they are struggling toward. At the same time, Family theology makes a clear distinction between God and Jesus, and Father David once wrote, "It's almost presumptuous to talk to God; Jesus is my Mediator. I really don't know how to talk to God—He's too big for me!"[4] Thus, a higher percentage of members might have said they felt extremely close to Jesus rather than to God.

One of the open-ended survey questions asked the respondent to describe something he or she recently did alone. A girl wrote, "It's hard to describe anything I did on my own because the Lord is always with me. But he did help me make dinner the other night without the help of anyone else except me and Jesus."

The questionnaire includes a similar question about feeling close to Father David, who had been deceased for some time when the survey was administered but continued to guide the group, not only through his old writings but also through communications a number of members believe they have received spiritually from the afterlife. In a study of the International Society for Krishna Consciousness, the "Hare Krishna" movement, Larry Shinn has noted that recruits often felt a close personal relationship with Bhaktivedanta, the movement's founder, even if he was objectively remote from them in the group's social network.[5] Thus we can wonder about the bond between Family members and Father David, given that the overwhelming majority never met him.

In general, members feel very close to their departed leader, although sometimes not so close as they feel to God. One noted that Father David had helped Family members establish their relationships with God, saying, "I love him for his love of God." One respondent who felt extremely close explained, "Although I've never met him, his words are very much a part of me." Another said, "He was and is my father in the Lord!" One who was "not very close" commented, "I don't 'feel' very close to some of my immediate family either. Nevertheless I still love them."

Table 3.6 reports results from four miscellaneous belief items contained in the 1991 GSS, starting with "Do you believe in life after death?" Five responses were offered: "Yes, definitely; Yes, probably; No, probably not; No, definitely not; Can't choose." Here we will focus on the percentages who responded "yes, definitely," because this is an unequivocal measure of firm faith. Whereas about 51 percent of the general public was convinced that there is an afterlife, this was true of fully 97 percent of Family members. More members of the public believe in Heaven than in "life after death," but this is not really a paradox because later in this chapter we will see that many people conceptualize existence after death as very different from "life."

Solid belief in Heaven is thirty-eight percentage points higher in The Family than in the American public. One member gave this personal testimony: "My dearest daughter died of cancer two and a half years ago. She was four and a half years old. Now I feel Heaven closer than ever! She is 'safe in the arms of Jesus' and I'll see her again. Praise the Lord!" Less than half of Americans are convinced that Hell exists, but nearly all members of the Family believe in both Heaven and Hell.

Some comment is required concerning the last item, "Do you believe in religious miracles?" Earlier we saw that the Family associates the word 'religious' with hypocritical churchianity. One respondent who "definitely" believes, commented, "I believe in miracles but the word 'religious' doesn't have to be involved." Another said, "This word 'religious' has had a sort of bad or negative meaning to me in the past, almost synonymous with very traditional and conservative. So, please bear with me if sometimes this still 'pops up' and I

Table 3.6. Miscellaneous Beliefs

Yes, definitely . . .	*Family*	*1991 GSS*
Do you believe in life after death?	97.4%	51.1%
Do you believe in Heaven?	98.0%	59.8%
Do you believe in Hell?	95.0%	46.8%
Do you believe in religious miracles?	94.7%	42.3%

The number of cases ranges from 1,020 to 1,024 for the Family, and from 1,276 to 1,319 for the General Social Survey.

have a hard time answering you. Sorry!" A third analyzed the terms thus: "My definition of 'miracles' is: events or actions which are so far outside the realm of human comprehension and understanding as to be only attributable to the supernatural. Again this ambiguous word, 'religious'—what are you intending to credit here—God—a supernatural reality/power—or a system of prevalent, socially accepted definitions and traditional norms?"

Nonetheless, about 95 percent of those who could choose a response said they definitely believed. Concerned about the wording of the GSS item, I also included in the survey a non-GSS agree-disagree item stating, "Miracles actually happened just as the Bible says they did." Of 1,019 Family members who responded, 78.3 percent said "strongly agree," and a further 20.2 percent said "agree." Only 0.5 percent disagreed, and the remaining 1.0 percent were undecided. One who could neither agree nor disagree wrote, "The miracles did happen, but they were written as seen through the eyes of the beholder. The story might've been a little different. I don't know." Another who had trouble deciding between "strongly agree" and "agree" speculated, "What if the people of Bible times were given a 'Book of the Future' exactly as it is today. I think that most people would not believe it and would consider today's inventions as 'impossible miracles.'"

During my many hours at Family homes, I have often heard members describe good fortune as a blessing from God, practically a miracle. They see God's hand in many little things of life, from cure of a common illness, to driving safely through heavy traffic, to success in provisioning vegetables when the home had run out. Nobody needs to walk on water to prove God's mercy to these believers.

A number of years ago, Rodney Stark and I reanalyzed data that he and Charles Glock had collected back in the Northern California Church Member

Table 3.7. Percent Certain that the Devil Actually Exists

Denomination . . .	Percent	Respondents
Congregational (UCC)	6%	151
Methodist	13%	415
Episcopalian	17%	416
Disciples of Christ	18%	50
Presbyterian	31%	495
American Lutheran	49%	208
American Baptist	49%	141
Church of God	73%	44
Missouri Synod Lutherans	77%	116
Church of Christ	87%	37
Nazarene	91%	75
Southern Baptists	92%	79
Assemblies of God	96%	44
Seventh-Day Adventists	97%	35
The Family	97%	1,023

Survey, and I included one religious belief item from that earlier study to allow me to place the Family roughly on the spectrum of Protestant religious sects and denominations. The item said: "Please think about this belief and indicate how certain you are that it is true: 'The Devil actually exists.'" Of 1,023 Family members who responded, 97.1 percent checked the box for "completely true," and a further 2.8 percent replied "probably true." One lone respondent felt the statement was "probably not true," and none thought it was "definitely not true." Among the church members surveyed by Glock and Stark, only the Seventh-Day Adventists matched the 97 percent certainty of Family members, although the Assemblies of God were within the statistical margin of error at 96 percent.[6] Table 3.7 shows the tremendous range of belief across fifteen groups, and places the Family at the extreme sectarian end of the spectrum.

Images of God and Heaven

In 1983 and 1984, the GSS included twelve images of God—such as redeemer, creator, and king—asking, "When you think about God, how likely are each of these images to come to your mind? Would you say extremely likely, somewhat likely, not too likely, or not likely at all?" On average, across the twelve descriptions of the deity, members of the Family were somewhat more likely than the American public to say the images were extremely likely to come to mind, 62.4 percent compared with 50.5 percent. Of course, the general public contains many people who doubt the existence of God, and few images may come to their minds. Thus, research has found that all types of God images are more acceptable to conventionally religious respondents than to others.[7]

However, as table 3.8 shows, members of the Family are actually less likely to hold two of the images: judge and mother. One factor at work here is the vivid conception many Family members have of the Trinity, especially of Jesus as a separate manifestation of God. One Family respondent wondered if we were "thinking about Jesus? I did in my answers. God only really reminds me of father and creator. So this means Jesus, too. Sorry, but it wasn't clear. God and Jesus are quite separate in my mind, but I don't think you intended them to be in this question." Another reported, "I rarely think of God apart from Jesus." One who considered all the images very likely went through the list writing which part of the Trinity fit each description. "God" is the judge, master, creator, and father. Both God and Jesus could be described as the King. Jesus is the redeemer, lover, spouse, friend, liberator, and healer. This respondent considered the Holy Spirit to be the mother, and another wrote that the mother image referred to "The Holy Ghost part of the trinity." From the perspective of one respondent, "God is a man, and the Holy Spirit is the mother."

Sociologist Hart Nelsen and his associates have analyzed the GSS data using a technique called factor analysis, finding that imagining God as a mother goes along with imagining "Her" also as a spouse and lover.[8] Yet here we see that members of the Family react very differently to the image of mother from how they do the spouse or lover images. Also using GSS data, Andrew Greeley found that people who conceptualized God as a mother tended to be politically liberal.[9] Because Family homes are communes, one might leap to the assumption that the movement stands on the political left. However, in many respects the movement is apolitical, and members were supportive of some right-wing leaders such as Marcos of the Philippines and Pinochet of Chile for providing environments conducive to the spreading of the Gospel.[10]

The early MO Letters written by Father David judge certain nonmembers very harshly, such as Richard Nixon, whom he calls "Nitler" by analogy with Adolf Hitler. But they specifically say that God judges members of the Family with love and compassion, and later writings suggest that even Nixon has been forgiven. The 1972 MO Letter, "The Benefits of Backsliding," explains that God loves sinners. "God's idea of goodness is godliness—a sinner who knows he needs God and depends on Him for salvation—not the Devil's churchy self-

Table 3.8. Images of God

Image of God is extremely likely . . .	*Family*	*1983–84 GSS*
Judge	20.9%	46.4%
Redeemer	65.9%	59.9%
Lover	61.0%	40.8%
Master	65.2%	54.4%
Mother	16.6%	24.1%
Creator	87.9%	80.3%
Father	85.3%	61.3%
Spouse	38.4%	16.0%
Friend	84.3%	61.2%
King	86.8%	51.0%
Liberator	61.6%	42.3%
Healer	75.3%	68.5%

The number of cases ranges from 1,012 to 1,020 for the Family, and from 2,050 to 2,056 for the General Social Survey.

righteous hypocritical Pharisees who think they can save themselves by their own goodness!"[11] This message seems perfectly designed for followers with low self-esteem or who suffer feelings of guilt, shame, and personal failure. But it also links directly to the theological doctrine that salvation is to be gained by faith, rather than works. Either way, the fact that Family members tend not to conceptualize God as a judge harmonizes perfectly with their leader's teachings.

In 1983 and 1984, the GSS included ten items about the afterlife: "Of course, no one knows exactly what life after death would be like, but here are some ideas people have had. How likely do you feel each possibility is? Would you say very likely, somewhat likely, not too likely, or not likely at all?" One confident respondent crossed out the qualification that "no one know exactly," writing instead, "We know pretty well." Table 3.9 shows that afterlife conceptions in the Family differ from those of the American public in some remarkable ways.

We have already seen that 95 percent of Family members believe in both Heaven and Hell, and a few of them saw fit to write comments in the questionnaire margins reminding us that there was not one afterlife, but two. "Talking of Heaven! It depends where you're ending up after you die!" "Perhaps it depends on the person and what they want and where they go after death." "For whom? Saved? Unsaved?" However respondents apparently responded in

Table 3.9. Images of the Afterlife

Very likely life after death is . . .	Family	1983–84 GSS
A life of peace and tranquillity.	65.4%	64.9%
A life of intense action.	41.7%	11.8%
A life like the one here on earth only better.	72.0%	28.9%
A life without many things which make our present life enjoyable.	4.6%	20.9%
A pale, shadowy form of life, hardly life at all.	0.1%	5.2%
A spiritual life, involving our mind but not our body.	7.2%	46.3%
A paradise of pleasure and delights.	86.5%	35.6%
A place of loving intellectual communion.	72.7%	52.2%
Union with God.	93.1%	79.2%
Reunion with loved ones.	97.7%	71.0%

The number of cases ranges from 1,013 to 1,024 for the Family, and from 2,374 to 2,382 for the General Social Survey.

terms of the afterlife they themselves expected to experience. "In Heaven. From a point of view of a born again for born again." "For those in the Lord."

As with the images of God, just discussed, we would expect religious people to be more likely than irreligious respondents to have all of these ideas more likely to come to mind. On average across the ten items, members of the Family said "very likely" 54.1 percent of the time, compared with 41.6 percent for GSS respondents. Almost exactly equal proportions—65 percent—could imagine an afterlife of peace and tranquility. One Family respondent reserved this for "those who accept Jesus Christ as their savior." Another described it as "fulfillment and comfort in heart." A third, who considered this quite likely, nonetheless qualified the image: "Peace also, but we will still have lots of challenges and will have to step out and take the initiative and have courage. Peace and tranquility on a permanent basis will not make man stronger and help him grow to his full potential."

Whereas only 12 percent of the public thinks the afterlife may entail intense action, about 42 percent of Family members have this more vigorous image. Several expressed reservations: "I believe we'll have plenty of action. I

just don't know about the intense part." "Can this word [intense] be elimi-
nated? I like action, but can't handle stress." "Very busy, but not in the flesh so
the intenseness is gone, but active for Jesus. Thank You Lord! I guess 'intense'
bothers me because in the Spirit there's no tense to it." "Armageddon is 'very
likely' to be intense action. But generally Heaven will be tranquil though not
devoid of activity. Apparently there'll be plenty of activity, especially for the
kids." One member expected a "comfortable pace of useful work." Others anticipated variability. "As it will be everlasting, sometimes there will be peace and
tranquility and sometimes intense action. Besides, we can choose what we
want." "A mixture of both—periods of peace and tranquility combined with
periods of intense activity."

If Family members are more willing to imagine active existence in Heaven,
they are also much more likely to see it as an improved version of terrestrial
life. As one member wrote, Heaven will be like life on Earth, except "much
better for those in the Lord." Fully 72 percent of Family members believe this,
compared with only 29 percent of the American public. On the other hand,
more GSS respondents are willing to imagine "a life without many things
which make our present life enjoyable." As one member put it, the afterlife will
not be "shadowy," "except for those in the other 'camp,'" that is, those in Hell.

Almost half of the public, 46 percent, anticipate "a spiritual life, involving
our mind but not our body." Only 7 percent of Family members can imagine
the afterlife this way, and two explicitly rejected the idea: "No, we'll have spiritual bodies." "We get new bodies according to the Bible." A chapter of the
Family's book, *Glimpses of Heaven*, quotes Father David's teachings about "heavenly bodies": "We are going to have bodies like Jesus did after He was resur-
rected. Each of us is going to have a new eternal, glorified body. It will actually
be constructed as we are now, of flesh and bones—but eternal flesh and bones,
incorruptible, immortal flesh and bones. It's going to be material, natural, recog-
nizable, seeable and feelable."[12]

These new bodies will enjoy "a paradise of pleasure and delights," according to 87 percent of Family members compared with 36 percent of the American public. However, respondents added, this will be "fulfilling, with wisdom;
not mindless, hedonistic." "I would say a paradise of 'Godly pleasures and
delights.'"

The remaining three items describe images of the afterlife held by a majority of Americans, although the percentages are still higher for Family members.
The last image, "reunion with loved ones," raises the uncomfortable possibility
that some loved ones have not earned a place in Heaven. One Family respondent wistfully hoped for reunion "unless they follow a very different path from

one's, I guess," and another anticipated reunion only with those "who make it to the same place we go."

The Boundaries of Faith

In 1988 the General Social Survey included four questions about factors that might have caused the respondent to have religious doubts, and four questions about factors that might have strengthened his or her faith. These items are somewhat problematic, but as table 3.10 shows some of the results are strong enough to be quite interesting.

The GSS introduces the four doubt-producing factors by saying, "How often have these problems caused doubts about your religious faith—often, sometimes, or never?" The problem is that "born again" Christians may wonder whether they are supposed to answer in terms of doubts they may have had during their entire lives, or only since acquiring their current faith. Several respondents wrote in comments explaining their answers. Some never had doubts: "Since my salvation!" "Not since receiving Jesus!" "This is after I got saved." One had doubts often "before I knew the Lord" but never "now." Another had them sometimes "before receiving Jesus," but never "after receiving Jesus."

Certainly, adult missionaries for the Family have encountered a myriad of factors that might erode faith. A woman who joined in 1971 and has witnessed in eight countries wrote, "I've never (as far as I remember) had serious doubts about my 'religious faith' in God. I have sometimes been discouraged and felt like quitting doing anything for Him." A forty-nine-year-old Canadian man who works for Jesus in Bombay, India, said he has not felt doubts since becoming born again when he joined the Family at age twenty-three in Atlanta, Georgia.

Only 30 percent of Family members say evil in the world has caused doubts about their religious faith, compared with fully 69 percent of the American public. In contrast, personal suffering has caused more doubts in the Family than the general public. Possibly those in the Family have suffered more than outsiders, but presumably both have seen ample evidence that evil stalks the Earth. The reason evil is less likely to challenge the faith of Family members is that their faith accounts for that evil, which is embodied in Satan and has a key role in their worldview. One said the evil in the world "increases my faith," and another said it "enhances my belief." Another whose faith was never weakened by awareness of evil wrote, "It's only enhanced it and caused me to hate the Devil all the more!"

Table 3.10. Causes of Doubts and Strengthened Faith

Sometimes or often . . .	Family	1988 GSS
Caused doubts . . .		
Evil in the world	30.2%	69.4%
Personal suffering	64.0%	53.3%
Conflict of faith and science	22.7%	30.3%
Feeling that life really has no meaning	25.5%	22.0%
Strengthened faith . . .		
Death in the family	56.8%	66.5%
Birth of a child	78.4%	75.5%
Marriage	63.0%	67.9%
Intense sexual pleasure	57.3%	30.6%

The number of cases ranges from 1,007 to 1,022 for the Family, and from 1,443 to 1,463 for the General Social Survey.

The four GSS items about events that have strengthened religious faith are problematic in a similar manner to the doubt-producing factors. We cannot tell how much a person's response reflects the vitality of his or her faith, versus variations in whether each of the factors has actually impinged on the person's life. For example, two of the factors that might strengthen faith are "death in the family" and "marriage." One Family respondent reported, "never had a death in my family, never been married." A man who said "birth of a child" had often strengthened his faith reported "I have eight of my own!" Another man, whose faith had never been strengthened by the birth of a child, said, "Not yet, expecting number one shortly." Two other respondents who said these three factors had never strengthened their faith wrote, "Never happened" and "never happened to me personally."

Of the four faith-strengthening factors, one shows a remarkable difference between the Family and the general American public. In the Family, 57 percent say their faith has been strengthened by "intense sexual pleasure," compared with only 31 percent of the American public. The Family sample includes a number of teenagers who have not yet experienced sexual intercourse, so this 26 percentage point difference is an underestimate. One Family member who often feels a strengthening of faith from intense sexual pleasure said, "What a wonderful invention of the Lord. I always thank Him. Thank You Jesus!"

American Millennialism

The Family is a millennial movement that anticipates the immanent Second Coming of Christ, after a time of terrible troubles in which faith will be tested sorely. Unfortunately, we cannot easily determine how widespread this view is in the general public, because through 1997 when I wrote the questionnaire, the GSS had not carried an item concerning it. Therefore, I wrote my own question: "Do you believe that the Endtime has begun or will begin very soon?" Fully 81 percent of 1,022 Family respondents said "yes, definitely," and a further 16 percent said "yes, probably."

The GSS did however frequently contain a item I thought might be correlated with religious views about the end of the world: "Do you expect the United States to fight in another world war within the next ten years?" When this question was first asked, in 1976, 47 percent of Americans who responded said "yes." During the Cold War, this item was sensitive to short-term crises that occurred in international relations, and the same may be true for subsequent trends.[13] In 1985–1986, the proportion was essentially the same as a decade earlier, 47 percent, but as the Soviet Union was collapsing in 1988–1991 it dropped to 38 percent. The proportion of Americans expecting another world war within a decade increased to 49 percent in 1993, conceivably because now the symbolic year 2000 was within the indicated decade, but more likely in reaction to the Persian Gulf War. The figure declined to 45 percent in 1994 and 41 percent in 1996.

Many respondents to the Family survey found this item perplexing, and fully 112 of them (11 percent) were unable to answer. Many wrote in "don't know" or an equivalent phrase. However, a huge majority, 80 percent of all respondents and 89 percent of those who answered, believed that the United States would indeed soon fight in another world war.

In the GSS data, responses to this world war item do indeed vary by religious tradition. For earlier research I had combined the data from all surveys through 1993 and carefully categorized respondents' religious denominations. Just 22 percent of 140 Jewish respondents expected another world war within a decade, compared with 38 percent of 1,770 Roman Catholics. Among 1,765 liberal and moderate Protestants (Methodist, Lutheran, Presbyterian, Episcopalian, United Church of Christ, Unitarian, Reformed, Quaker), 34 percent agreed. Expectation of world war reaches 51 percent among 1,387 Baptists and 50 percent among 495 members of sects (Holiness, Pentecostal, Adventist, Church of Christ, Assemblies of God, Church of the Nazarene, Church of God, Jehovah's Witnesses). Thus among the Protestant groups that exist in some tension with secular society, about half predict a world war that could become a nuclear apocalypse.

In American religious history, by far the most significant millenarian tradition has been Adventist, and it is important to note that the Family does not derive its Endtime beliefs from that source. To see the significance of this distinction, we should briefly examine Adventism and its essential conception of the apocalypse as a specific point in time.

Legends say that a frenzy swept Europe in the year 1000, when mobs expected the wicked world to end. Christ, they hoped, would return after a thousand years to reign over a perfect kingdom. Did not the Holy Bible speak of the coming of the millennium? Indeed, Rev. 20:1–3 says, "And I saw an angel come down from heaven, having the key of the bottomless pit and a great chain in his hand. And he laid hold on the dragon, that old serpent, which is the Devil, and Satan, and bound him a thousand years. And cast him into the bottomless pit, and shut him up, and set a seal upon him, that he should deceive the nations no more, till the thousand years should be fulfilled: and after that he must be loosed a little season." A close reading reveals that the millennium is not the period that Christians must wait for the return of their savior. Instead it is the duration they shall spend in His peaceable kingdom on earth before Satan is loosed afresh in the buildup to the final battle. In fact, the legends are wrong. There is no evidence that millenarian movements existed in A.D. 1000, and they first appear in Europe more than a century later.[14]

Although groups like the Shakers came to America in the eighteenth century, the real start of millenarianism on these shores is the Millerite movement of the early 1840s. William Miller puzzled over these words from in Dan. 8:14, "Unto two thousand and three hundred days; then shall the sanctuary be cleansed." In Matthew 24, Jesus explicitly told his disciples that Daniel's prophecy was authentic, and a great holocaust lay ahead. After much thought, Miller concluded that the cleansing of the sanctuary must symbolically represent the Second Coming of Christ. Apparently the two thousand and three hundred days were a clue about when this monumental event would occur, and he suspected that the word "days" actually referred to years. Does not Ezek. 4:6 say, "I have appointed thee each day for a year?" And Numbers 14:34 echoes this interpretation, saying, "each day for a year." Further Bible reading, along with study of popular books on ancient history, convinced Miller that he was supposed to count 2,300 years after 457 B.C. Thus he concluded that the Second Coming would occur in about 1843.

The failure of anything remarkable to happen in 1843–1844 has been called the Great Disappointment, and a variety of small Adventist groups emerged from it with different explanations for the failed prophecy. Some contended the calculations were wrong and awaited Jesus again in 1854. Seventh-day Adventists decided the prophecy was correct, but the sanctuary Christ entered was in Heaven rather than on earth. They are one of two large groups in the Millerite tradition, possessing about 10,000,000 members worldwide.

The other very large group is Jehovah's Witnesses, with an estimated 6,000,000 members worldwide. Based on his own analysis of the scriptures, founder Charles Taze Russell calculated that the Second Coming had occurred invisibly in 1874, and that the millennium would become manifest forty years later, in 1914. Jer. 32:20, says that the Lord has "set signs and wonders in the land of Egypt, even unto this day," and this passage encouraged Russell to delve into the pyramidology fad that was rampant in Britain. Supposedly, the great pyramid of Cheops was built by Noah, or by some prophet divinely inspired by God, who encoded the important dates of history in this great structure. By analyzing the dimensions of the pyramid, Russell was able to deduce that Jesus would return in 1914. Instead of Jesus, it was the First World War that came. For many followers of Russell, the war seemed quite apocalyptic enough to fit the prophecy. Unlike the Seventh-day Adventists, who scrupulously avoid setting a date, Jehovah's Witnesses have done so repeatedly, the most recent disappointment being in 1975.[15]

Among the offshoots of the Seventh-day Adventists are the Davidians, founded by Bulgarian immigrant Victor Houteff who set up a millenarian commune near Waco, Texas, in 1935. His wife, Florence, took over on his death in 1955 and announced that the fateful day would be April 22, 1959. Another "Great Disappointment" ensued when the world continued as usual into April 23, and the Davidians collapsed. Benjamin Roden organized a small group he called Branch Davidians, out of the wreckage of the Waco community. The 1973 Mideast War encouraged him to believe the time of the End was fast approaching, but he died in 1979 without entering the millennium. His son George and his wife Lois competed for leadership of the Branch Davidians. Lois announced that her husband's death had accomplished the opening of the seventh seal, after which angels' trumpets would herald the destruction of the earth. In 1981, young Vernon Howell joined the group and quickly became the lieutenant and possibly the lover of elderly Lois.

In 1990 George was committed to a state mental hospital after murdering a man he thought had been sent by Howell to kill him. Vernon Howell legally changed his name to David Koresh and took charge of the tiny group, which was largely destroyed in 1993 in a siege by the Bureau of Alcohol, Tobacco, and Firearms and the Federal Bureau of Investigation.[16]

Adventism has also spawned millenarian movements in Asia. The founder of the Unification Church, Sun Myung Moon, was the child of a Korean family that converted to Presbyterianism, but while imprisoned under the Communist government of the north he was influenced by an indigenous Adventist messiah who had also been incarcerated. Rather than following Miller's example and looking for prophesies in specific passages of the Bible, Moon developed a numerological system for understanding the full sweep of past and future history. All human history consists of three stages leading toward resurrection. Two thousand years of "foundation" ran from Adam to Abraham, and from Abraham to Jesus there were two thousand years of "formation." Jesus' mission was to be the second Adam, fulfilling the role of True Father where Adam had failed. Thus there would be a second Eve, the True Mother, who would express the Holy Spirit which is female and unite with Jesus and God to form the Trinity. But Jesus, unfortunately, was crucified, so the union of mankind's True Parents was postponed for a later and more propitious time. Some believe that Moon's own wedding in 1960 was the "crossing junction between good and evil," and for several years afterward the Unification Church seemed to be setting dates for the Second Coming, or to be hinting that Moon himself was "The Lord of the Second Advent."[17]

Shoko Asahara, founder of Aum Shinrikyo, which was responsible for the nerve gas attack on the Tokyo subways that killed twelve people in 1995, has studied the apocalyptic prophecies in the Bible and was familiar with their interpretations by Jehovah's Witnesses. Schooled in Buddhism and Hinduism, Asahara was certainly not a Christian, but Adventist ideas captivated him in the years immediately before the crisis that led to his imprisonment. Devoting two books to a decipherment of Revelation, he predicted that the Battle of Armageddon would begin August 1, 1999, with a wild conflict among America, Russia, Japan, and the Middle East. For a long while, the fighting will be somewhat restrained, then absolute nuclear disaster will come October 30 through November 29, 2003, with a peak on November 25 and the total destruction of Russia and China in 2004.[18]

Thus, Miller's belief that careful analysis of the Bible can reveal the date of the Second Coming has influenced many subsequent messiahs in the Adventist tradition. For at least two of these groups, the Branch Davidians and Aum Shinrikyo, expectation of the apocalypse apparently made lethal violence more likely.

It is crucial to recognize that the Family is not part of the Adventist tradition, and its visions of the millennium have a very different quality. Recall that Father David's grandfather, John Lincoln Brandt, was a leader among the

Disciples of Christ, and his mother, Virginia Brandt Berg, was an evangelist for the Christian and Missionary Alliance. Neither of these groups is Adventist, and nothing I have seen in the history or teachings of the Family suggests Adventist influences.

The Endtime

At moments in its history, the Family suspected that events happening in the world might be some of the signs of the times that would usher in the End. But it has not made elaborate calculations. Indeed, by not trying to determine the date of the Endtime, the Family feels it is only keeping faith with the teachings of Jesus. At the temple Jesus said, "There shall not be left here one stone upon another, that shall not be thrown down" (Matt. 24:2). At the Mount of Olives they asked him how they would know when the appointed time had come. "Many shall come in my name," he replied, "saying, I am Christ; and shall deceive many. And ye shall hear of wars and rumours of wars: see that ye be not troubled: for all these things must come to pass, but the end is not yet. For nation shall rise against nation, and kingdom against kingdom: and there shall be famines and pestilences, and earthquakes, in divers places" (Matt. 24:5–7). Jesus described signs that his followers would see in the skies, but he refused to name the date. "But of that day and hour knoweth no man, no, not the angels of heaven, but my Father only" (Matt. 24:36).

Throughout 1983, a team worked over Father David's writings on the Endtime, and in January 1984 the group's publishing outfit in Zurich issued a profusely illustrated volume, *The Book of the Future*. Printed on very thin but sturdy paper, like that used in many Bibles, it held 500 pages just four by six inches. Flagging the dates with question marks to express uncertainty, the book suggested that the Antichrist might possibly establish his world government in 1985 or 1986.

Although much of the Family's literature of the 1970s and the 1980s pointed out these dates as imminent possibilities, Father David warned his disciples about taking dogmatic stances regarding dates. In 1972 he thought Jesus might return in about twenty years but wrote, "Just please don't go around telling everyone that I predicted these dates, because I didn't. The Lord did! And if they don't happen just like this, don't blame Him—but blame us for not having interpreted His predictions properly . . . if there is any error, it is due to the frailty of our human understanding, and not to the failure of God! So don't keep your fingers crossed, but thrust them Heavenward in a firm salute to the Revolution for Jesus, and keep on serving Him faithfully until those days do come, and right on through until the End, whenever and however it may come!"[19]

Practically every page of *The Book of the Future* abounds in biblical references, and the truth is that much of the prophecy does stand plain for anyone to read in the Bible. Other parts of the prophecy depend on biblical interpretations, about which reasonable people may disagree. Still others came from Father David's own spiritual revelations and from his analysis of current world events. The Endtime is the seventieth week of years announced in the ninth chapter of Daniel, in which a prince, commonly identified as the Great Beast 666 or the Antichrist, will enter on the world scene after the real Messiah has been cut off. Dan. 9:27 predicts, "And he shall confirm the covenant with many for one week: and in the midst of the week he shall cause the sacrifice and the oblation to cease, and for the overspreading of abominations he shall make it desolate, even until the consummation, and that determined shall be poured upon the desolate."

Surely the signs of the times were clear, the book proclaimed, exactly in accordance with the twelfth chapter of Daniel and with the words of Jesus given in Matthew chapter 24. Plainly there were wars and rumors of wars. Data from the World Health Organization confirmed famines and pestilences, with the possibility of a billion deaths during the decade. Rapid transportation on land, air, and sea, plus the explosion of scientific discoveries, fulfilled Daniel's prophecy that many would run to and fro and knowledge would be increased. Matt. 24:14 says, "And this gospel of the kingdom shall be preached in all the world for a witness unto all nations; and then shall the end come."[20] The far-flung missionary communes of the Family fulfilled this prophecy themselves.

They believe that the world is drenched in depravity and violence, and that people long for a savior, a superman who will take the reins of power and halt the increase of war and crime. Through flattery and deceit a supreme leader will arise, induce all nations to sign a seven-year treaty, and establish his world government in Jerusalem. This will be the most perfect system that humans could devise, and at first it will seem like heaven on earth in contrast to the wickedness that went before. Probably himself a Jew, the Antichrist will rebuild the Temple on Mount Moriah and reestablish the ancient sacrifice of animals.

After one thousand two hundred and sixty days, the Antichrist will revoke his treaty with the world, erect a graven image of himself in the Holy Temple, and demand that all the earth worship him as God. But, in truth, he will be possessed by Satan and become the Devil incarnate. This reversal may come after the Antichrist is assassinated, but rises from the dead. Anyone who refuses to worship the image of the Beast will be killed, and everyone who accepts his rule will receive the mark of the Beast.

For centuries, the nature of this mark has been a mystery. Rev. 13:16–17 says: "And he causeth all, both small and great, rich and poor, free and bond, to receive a mark in their right hand, or in their foreheads: And that no man might buy or sell, save he that had the mark, or the name of the beast, or the number of his name." Father David concluded that the image of the Beast and the mark of the Beast are facets of modern computer technology. The image is a cybernetic robot; the mark is an electronic credit card, perhaps in the form of a microscopic semiconductor chip surgically inserted under the skin. At the grocery checkout counter, each customer's chip will be scanned, and only those with the mark of Beast can buy food.

Thus begins the Great Tribulation. The Beast will send forth his armies to make war on religion and to slaughter any people who do not bear his mark. Millions will rebel and be killed. Members of the Family and other Christians, especially those who have heard the message of Father David, will flee into the wilderness. Many will go underground, sustaining their faith as secret believers even in the heart of the Beast's empire, but they must do so without accepting the mark, for all who have it will be damned. In the last days, Christians must be prepared to survive totally separate from the "System." The Family antici-pates that it and other sincere Christians will accomplish a great harvest of souls, leading all who are saved and wielding miraculous, supernatural powers. But the power of the Beast will be too great for them, and they will come face-to-face with annihilation.

At the very last moment, Father David wrote, "suddenly—*BOOM!*—like a bolt from the blue, something happens!—*Jesus comes* & snatches all of His children out of this World!—All believers, all those who refused the Mark of the Beast in either their forehead or their hand & refused to worship him, but preferred to love & live & even die for Jesus!"[21] Then comes the great Rapture and the Resurrection of all true Christians. Those who survived the reign of the Beast will be lifted up into the air and rendered immortal. Then follows the marriage supper of the Lamb, a great victory celebration in Heaven.

Back on Earth, the wrath of God engages the pride of the Antichrist. All those who accepted the mark of the Beast will now be covered with sores, a horrible form of skin cancer. The oceans, rivers, and fountains gush blood, so there is no water to drink. The heat of the sun will swell sevenfold, so the wicked are scorched in inescapable fires. Then the Earth will be plunged into complete darkness, where the wicked gnaw their tongues in pain. The remaining armies of the Antichrist gather in Israel at Megiddo. A great voice shouts from Heaven, "It is done!" and the cities of the world are swept away by thunder, lightning, and earthquakes. The last, great shaking delivers the Antichrist into God's hands for judgment. It as at this point that the Battle of Armageddon occurs between the forces of God and the forces of the Antichrist.

The millennium dawns, and Jesus inaugurates the sublime period of a thousand years when He will rule a kingdom practically as perfect on Earth as it is in Heaven. The Family believes that it and other true Christians, will rule over the unsaved who rejected the Mark of the Beast, but survived the great battles. Father David rejoiced, "Right now the ungodly & Antichrist powers of the world treat *us* as aliens, & banish us & exile us & even drive some of us from our own countries, forcing us to be refugees & fugitives from their injustice. But *then*, under the supreme reign of Christ Himself, the pitiful little bands of persecuted Christians & believers & children of God are going to *inherit* the Earth & the Kingdom of God on Earth & run & govern it by love & the power of God!"[22]

The Family believes the curse that drove Adam and Eve from the Garden of Eden will be partially lifted, and people will live in beautiful harmony. The lion will lie down with the lamb in the peaceable kingdom, and both will eat straw. There will be neither thorns nor cars in this golden age, neither venomous snakes nor polluting factories. Some survivors from the reign of the Beast may resist Christ's authority, and the children of God will have to rule them with a rod of iron. "They will all be *compelled* & *forced* to obey whether they like it or not!—Absolutely no democracy, absolutely no freedom of man, of wicked man!—No more wicked democracies with wicked majorities voting for wicked governments & wicked rulers in a wicked World—but a completely total totalitarian *dictatorship* of the *righteous* with Jesus Christ as Dictator!"[23]

Meanwhile, Satan has been bound and cast into the bottomless pit, where he lies captive for a thousand years. Despite the visible rein of Jesus, there are some who will rebel, and their hearts shall be tested. Father David was convinced that there will be many people who refuse the mark of the beast and thus survive the Battle of Armageddon, sincere Muslims, sincere Jews, and sincere peoples of other faiths. They will not be saved, but they will be granted a second chance to know the Lord through the Millennium. However, some will rebel, and this will lead to the Battle of Gog and Magog.

So God will free Satan to test them. Again the armies of evil gather. No longer disguised as the Beast, Satan reveals himself and personally leads a siege against the camp of the saints at Jerusalem. Then God sends fire down from Heaven that completely devours Satan and his legions. The heavens roll back like a scroll and depart with a great noise, and the old Earth ceases to exist. The children of God escape in rapture.

Father David saw what comes next in his visions, the last act of the drama of life. There will be a new Heaven and a new Earth. The holy city, New Jerusalem, will be a pyramid 1,500 miles along each dimension. All those who accepted Jesus as their Savior will receive miraculous new bodies, flesh and spirit combined, sensuous but eternal. Existence will be like all the good aspects of former human life, with none of the bad ones. Words cannot adequately describe it, but these point in the right direction: joy, beauty, pleasure, thrill, wonder, and orgasm.

CHAPTER 4

Practices

Faith is as much about what people do as what they think, so we must consider religious behavior as well as belief. But some of the most significant forms of religious behavior are subjective experiences of contact with the supernatural, and practices such as prayer naturally generate spiritual experiences. In the two years after Father David's passing, thousands of members of the Family began to have experiences they interpreted as messages from the spirit world. The contemporary religious movement most famous for its sexual practices transformed into the source of the greatest volume of prophecy in the world.

To begin our examination of Family religious practices, we will compare them with General Social Survey respondents in terms of two very conventional activities, prayer and Bible reading. We will then compare their dediction to salvation and spiritual experiences, before concluding with an examination of the group's orientation toward prophecy.

Prayer

In their pioneering questionnaire study of American church members, Stark and Glock noted, "Undoubtedly the primary private ritual expectation of Christian churches is prayer. In all denominations members are urged to use prayer as a personal means for worshipping God and for seeking divine aid and guidance."[1] However, Stark and Glock found that the frequency of prayer varied greatly, from a low in the "liberal" or "mainstream" denominations to a high among the sects. Thus it is advisable to begin our consideration of religious practice in the Family with a question about prayer.

Table 4.1. Frequency of Prayer

About how often do you pray?	*Family*	*1991 GSS*
Never	0.0%	7.9%
Less than once a year	0.0%	2.8%
About once or twice a year	0.0%	5.5%
Several times a year	0.1%	8.3%
About once a month	0.0%	4.9%
2–3 times a month	0.2%	5.4%
Nearly every week	0.1%	5.8%
Every week	0.4%	4.6%
Several times a week	2.0%	12.5%
Once a day	1.8%	21.8%
Several times a day	95.5%	20.5%
TOTAL	100.0%	100.0%

This table is based on 1,025 cases for the Family, and 1,325 for the General Social Survey.

Immediately after the question about whether the respondent's belief in God had changed over the years, the survey asked: "Now thinking about the present, about how often do you pray?" Table 4.1 shows that almost all members of the Family pray at least several times a week, and more than 95 percent pray several times a day. One fifth of the American public prays several times a day, and another fifth prays once a day, so prayer certainly is not uncommon outside the Family. About 16 percent of the public prays no more than once or twice a year, suggesting prayer is not a personal choice for them but arises only on rare social occasions, such as a Christmas dinner of their extended family, a wedding, or a funeral. All members of the Family pray more often than this. Thus prayer is far more common within the group than outside, even though there is nothing deviant about frequent prayer in American society.

A Canadian member named Peter told me, "We believe in the power of prayer. Whenever we move into a home, we pray over the home. We pray over everything, because we believe there is a spirit world. We believe spirits exist, and there are good ones and bad ones. There are ones that are locked into houses and condemned to stay there until they are released. Jesus himself gave examples to people about spirits and devils and demons where he would rebuke them and send them off."

On several occasions when I was visiting a Family home and happened to mention some problem in my own life, the members immediately offered to pray with me about it. We might hold hands, bow our heads a little, and perhaps close our eyes. Then one of them would ask Jesus and the Lord to help me with my particular problem, referring to it specifically. Every one of the many times I rode with the Family in one of their vehicles, they would pray briefly before starting out. I never saw a member kneel in prayer, or fold his or her hands in one of the stereotypical Christian prayer positions. Rather, they could pray in any situation, posture, and position.

Many respondents wrote something about prayer in the first, open-ended section of the questionnaire. A woman in Taiwan wrote, "I had some differences with one of my co-workers, and I knew the answer to unity was by prayer. My co-worker prayed and the Lord unified us." An American woman at a South African home said she "walked in the yard and prayed." A woman from India explained she prayed "every moment of the day before I speak or do anything."

Members often pray whenever they have to make a decision, even a humble one. A Danish mother of seven at a French home remembers, "I was running out of ideas of what to do with the young children, so I prayed and the Lord showed us to play with 'Play-Doh,' and we had lots of fun." In America, a woman wrote, "I was trying to find the newly opened main post office in an unknown part of town. I prayed and felt led to turn at a light, then asked directions and once I was in the general part of town, I spotted a mail truck which led me straight to it! Ha!"

Private prayer is more like a conversation than a monologue. As a young woman described it, she had been "praying about my life, talking to Jesus and listening to Him." A man in his fifties said his prayer is "more like a question or a 'thanks' or a conversation, not usually 'hands folded, on my knees' thing. In fact, that's seldom." A teenage girl said, "I had an intimate time with the Lord, just talking to Him and explaining things about my life and listening to what He had to say." A forty-nine-year old woman "had a wonderful intimate connection with Jesus." As *The Love Charter* states, the very first responsibility of a Charter member is to "maintain a close connection with God through personal communion with Jesus, personal and united prayer and praise."[2]

In addition to spontaneous prayer throughout the day, members of the Family often set aside special time to pray. All leaders are supposed to do so every day, and each home has a day of prayer each month. A woman living in a very large Thai home said, "Yesterday we had our monthly prayer day which included the children so it was special. I had some good prayer time." A British member living in America says he prays "'normal' prayers frequently, but deep personal prayers two to three times a month." In Los Angeles, a young woman wrote, "My husband and I had a prayer vigil together for one hour. It was prayer day. We made a list of prayer requests then prayed for it and claimed verses."

Couples often pray together. A Brazilian women living in Croatia reported, "My husband and I had a beautiful prayertime together!" Similarly, a Canadian woman in Mexico said she "had a really nice prayer time and discussion with my husband on our rest day." A man in his sixties writes, "Usually in the late afternoon I go for one hour's walk with my wife. She is pregnant with number seven. We usually pray and thank the Lord for how wonderful He is, and He speaks to us and encourages us, also gives us instructions and solutions. He's wonderful!"

One of the twenty-two members of a French home was happy that he "had a united prayer and communion with the members of our home teamwork praying for greater unity among ourselves." The fifteen members of a Polish commune "had a Home Council to talk and pray about our financial situation." A woman in China said, "We had a prayer meeting with all the voting members of the home to hear from the Lord on some important decisions."

Members often pray concerning other members and even non-members. For example, a man in Brazil "Prayed and received some prophecies for nine friends, the ones I'm ministering to." With two brothers, he "gave a Bible class in our friends' house. It was touching." But he regrets a lost opportunity, saying "A friend of mine died and I didn't pray with him to get saved." Prayer does not always come easily, as testified by a Polish woman at a small home in Russia: "I felt that I'm failing the Lord in my prayer life and it made me quite discouraged. My husband and I prayed and the Lord and him encouraged me."

An American woman in Greece "spent time with the Lord, praying for the children and the many poor people we passed on the streets." At a large home in Hungary, a young woman "got together with two others to pray and hear from the Lord for a couple of people who need encouragement and direction." A woman in Canada "prayed for healing for some people with health problems." Elsewhere, in China, a mother of seven children was delighted to report, "My baby was healed of bronchitis (after I asked local homes for prayer) from one day to the next and did not require hospitalization as the doctor had forecast."

A Sri Lankan woman living at a small home in the United States watched her son play in a football game. "The Lord answered my prayer for our team to win as they really needed the encouragement. From a score of 0–14 they went on to win at 21–20. It showed me that nothing is too mundane for God." In the United States a man "went with my wife to look for a place to go camping. The Lord answered prayer and we got a discount on a camp area for a large group." A man and woman in Britain both reported that their home had prayed for new furniture, and "the Lord gave us lots of new furniture" "quite cheap, which has been a real blessing to our home." Often members seek the Lord's protection. A nineteen-year-old American man reported that the day before filling out the questionnaire, "I prayed for the evil spirits on the bus not to harm me!"

It is said that God always answers prayers, but sometimes the answer is "No." One of the constant challenges is finding an appropriate residence for a communal home, large enough, cheap enough, and available for group occupation. In Brazil, a home with twelve members needed to move. One of the members, a forty-nine-year-old American man with four children, privately "knelt and prayed desperately for God to give us a certain house we need—fasted twenty-four hours." Soon he was disappointed to get "a negative answer about a house we were to move to." His unhappiness was balanced to some extent by relief that "somebody in my home got an OK to move" to a different home. "He's not such a hard worker and is sometimes a burden."

Disappointment often merely encourages further prayer, as illustrated by this comment by an American woman in Brazil: "It was 'in the air' that I would possibly get free tickets back to the States to visit my family as I haven't seen them in nineteen years. But the offer fell through. I'm still praying for the Lord to supply the money." Sometimes the wait for prayers to be answered is a long one. A member of a fifteen-person home in Pakistan reported, "We heard some new Family volunteers might come and join our home soon. We've been praying for six months for this."

A father of four children was very unhappy about his nineteen-year-old's decision to leave the Family, but rationalized this as part of God's inscrutable plan: "A son decided not to serve the Lord full time; but when we prayed, the Lord encouraged us to see His hands in everything that happens."

Reading the Word

In addition to prayer, the first responsibility of a Charter member is maintaining a close connection with God in "personal and united reading of His Word (both the Bible and the Letters)" and "Scripture memorization."[3] An item in the General Social Survey asks, "How often have you read the Bible in the last year?" Fixed-choice responses range from "several times a day" to "I did not read it." Because the Family considers not only the Bible but also the MO Letters and some other group publications to be God's Word, I added a similar item phrased thus: "How often have you read the Word as written down by Father

Table 4.2. Frequency of Word Reading

	Family: Reading the Word of Father David	Bible Reading	
		Family	GSS
Several times a day	43.2%	4.7%	3.3%
Once a day	38.6%	9.2%	9.2%
Several times a week	16.7%	46.6%	10.7%
Once a week	0.9%	15.5%	8.8%
Less than once a week	0.5%	23.4%	30.3%
I did not read it	0.1%	0.5%	37.8%
TOTAL	100.0%	100.0%	100.0%

The number of cases in this table ranges from 1,017 (Word of Father David) to 1,022 (Bible) for the Family, and is 1,474 for the General Social Survey.

David or Maria in the last year?" Table 4.2 shows the patterns of Word reading for both of these questions.

The table reveals that Family members are not unusually frequent readers of the Bible, compared with religiously dedicated members of the general public. About 14 percent in the Family read it every day, compared with nearly 13 percent of outsiders. However, a big difference appears at moderate levels of Bible reading, because three quarters of members read it every week, compared with only a third of the American public. Only about half a percent of members failed to read the Bible during the previous year, compared with 38 percent of GSS respondents.

One reason some members may not read the Bible very often is because they have already internalized so much of it. A fifty-year-old man who reads the Bible less than once a week explains, "The Bible changed my life. There was a time I read it more and I do need it more. I've memorized a lot of it!" Another man about the same age reads it once a week. "I know it by heart in large parts, and can quote whole chapters. It's my foundation, and sometimes I have a Bible-binge and sometimes don't open it for three weeks." Many members underline passages in their Bibles, and a man in Japan reported he had recently "transferred some notes from my old Bible to my new Bible."

For the early years of its history, the Family emphasized memorization of large numbers of single Bible verses, and members may not count this as reading. One evening I joined a home in reading Bible verses, and we all took slips of paper from a basket, each one printed with just a single verse, and we read them in a circle around and around, children and adults alike. A man in a Japanese home wrote in the margin beside the Bible-reading question, "and also verses from the Bible are often included in the writings of David and Maria." A woman in Slovakia wrote that she read the "Bible itself about once a month, Bible verses daily, and we have Bible verses or Grandpa quotes hanging up around the house." Grandpa quotes are sayings by Father David.

Table 4.2 reveals the possibly surprising fact that members read scriptures written by Father David or Maria far more often than they do the Bible itself. About 82 percent say they read "the Word as written down by Father David or Maria" every day. The first article of belief of Family members is "that David was God's Endtime Prophet and that Maria is God's chosen and anointed successor, who has inherited David's mantle as God's Prophetess."[4] Therefore, in much that they wrote, David and Maria spoke for God, transmitting his Word through the frequent Letters and other publications.

Nonetheless, Bible reading is common in the Family. A girl in Thailand wrote that the most memorable thing she had done alone recently was, "I sat in the garden and read my Bible." Many members have undoubtedly read the entire Bible, in addition to memorizing portions of it. In contrast, new Letters are constantly being published every week, so a member will want to read the new ones as they are issued, as well as reading older ones that relate to particular questions that arise. Ideally, each home will have a bound set of the early letters, printed in several Bible-like volumes on thin but sturdy paper. In addition, many of the letters have recently been issued on CD-ROM and can be read on the computers found in many homes.

Another reason members may read the Bible less often than Letters is the style in which they are written. The Family uses the King James version exclusively, rather than one of the simpler editions produced for modern readers, considering it to be authoritative as well as more beautiful. But this means that some members find it difficult to understand, especially when trying to comprehend whole chapters and books rather than selected individual verses. The MO letters are written in a highly colloquial, conversational style that could even be described as American rather than English. They are clear, often emotional, and even sometimes fun. The original MO Letters and many of the later publications carry lively illustrations like those found in comic books. The Letters speak the members' own language, yet are considered every bit as much the Word as the King James Bible with its archaic grammar and vocabulary.

Dedication to Salvation

Among the most potent survey questions I have used in earlier questionnaires is one employed by both the Gallup Poll and the GSS: "Would you say you have been "born again" or have had a "born again" experience—that is, a turning point in your life when you committed yourself to Christ?" In Gallup's survey, 34 percent of Americans said they were born again, and table 4.3 shows that the GSS got a similar response, 37 percent. In general, being "born again" is part of the Protestant evangelical tradition. When I included this item in a survey of 1,439 students at the University of Washington, 20 percent of the Catholics said they were born again, compared with 25 percent of members of liberal Protestant denominations, 34 percent of moderate Protestants, 52 percent of conservative Protestants, and fully 80 percent of members of Protestant sects.[5] In table 4.3 we see that about 91 percent of Family members report the born again experience.

In the University of Washington study, being born again was strongly associated with frequent church attendance, with definitely believing in God, with liking religious books and articles, and with liking hymns and spirituals. Born again students were far more likely than others to say: "God or some other supernatural force has a very strong influence on my life." "Suffering often comes about because people don't obey God." "Miracles actually happened just as the Bible says they did." They rejected the secular idea that "man evolved from lower animals."[6] Members of the Family have agreed with my impression that few of them experienced decisive conversion experiences, but they believe that accepting Jesus into their heart can initiate a gradual process of spiritual growth that they consider being born again.

A twenty-one-year-old man who was born in the Family wrote, "I've always had the Lord and can't recall a specific time of committing myself or a 'turning point' because I have to keep renewing my commitment." A woman of similar age also born into the Family said, "I asked Jesus into my heart at two years old but at twelve I committed myself to serving Jesus." Both of these respondents said they were born again. Some members were reborn before encountering the Family. Michael Pioneer, for example, received Jesus when he was ten. When he met the Family years later, and heard them praying to save other people, he recognized that the prayer was almost exactly the one he heard when he was saved. In interviews I asked the born again question of Marie, Pearl, and Mannie.

Marie said, "I was twenty-one years old, and I was a very lonely girl, living by myself. I was looking for deep answers, like a meaning for my life. I went to

Table 4.3. Salvation and Grace

Yes . . .	Family	1991 GSS
Would you say you have been "born again" or have had a "born again" experience—that is, a turning point in your life when you committed yourself to Christ?	90.8%	37.1%
Have you ever tried to encourage someone to believe in Jesus Christ or to accept Jesus Christ as his or her savior?	99.5%	46.5%
At your family meals at home, does anyone say grace or give thanks to God aloud before meals?	94.2%	50.2%

The number of cases in this table ranges from 1,012 to 1,023 for the Family, and from 1,459 to 1,469 for the General Social Survey.

college, but then I found out that school was not preparing me for life. I quit school, and of course I got into drugs and drinking with all kinds of questionable friends. I let go of those things when I realized they were not bringing me any answer. I was quite lonely and searching, I guess depressed." It was 1975, and she was living in a small town in Quebec, when a group of Family members came through on a road trip from their home in Montreal. At that time her English was not fluent, and she had difficulty talking with them, but "there was something about the spirit that they had. I was fascinated." The road team needed a place to stay, so she invited them to her place. "That night I prayed, and I asked Jesus into my heart. It was funny because when I prayed I thought I've always known about Jesus, because I was raised Catholic. But that made a change in my life. Because after that I was different. Little things of life, like what you do around the house, didn't mean anything any more. My soul was really hungry . . . That was a turning point in my life . . . I just wanted to go with them and serve the Lord with them."

Pearl recalled that one of her friends was a member of the Family, but she had not initially been open to his message. "I was twenty-one, and I had spent most of my life searching for real love and truth. One night I was on the point of suicide. I called out to God, I said, 'Take my life.' I was actually afraid to take my life, but I gave everything to him, the whole world. We always hold something back for ourselves, but I said, 'Take my life. I don't want to live any more. I give it to you now.' The next day my friend started witnessing to me. I don't specifically remember praying for the Holy Spirit, but I know I got saved. It was a tremendous experience, because I felt God right there. I knew God was real."

Mannie did not join the Family in the 1970s like Marie and Pearl, and becoming born again was for him more a confirmation decision than a conversion experience. "I was born in the Family. When I turned sixteen I had to decide for myself if this was really what I wanted to do. So that was when I made the choice to stay. I'm glad I did, because it's really nice to see people's lives change for the better. It was tough at first, because my parents left the full time Family, and I could have moved with them and done some other secular thing. For me it was a little bit of a struggling point, but when you get past that, you know you've made the right choice and then you feel a lot better afterwards. You constantly have to be praying for strength, guidance, asking the home to support you in prayer. That's a key factor, too."

As data for the second item in table 4.3 shows, essentially every member of the Family has tried to encourage someone to accept Jesus Christ, because that is the prime focus of the missionary work they call witnessing. In an interview, Mannie explained, "You go on what we call personal witnessing, when you go one on one and talk to people. So you go to a park and see someone that needs help or somebody that's sad or sitting there by himself, or even a group of people. And you explain it to them, you basically just give them the choice. Tell them about salvation and that Jesus died for them, and then it's up to them to accept. If they do, it feels really good to pray with them. You know you'll see them again up there [in Heaven] one day." I have done this myself with the Family in San Francisco's Golden Gate Park and the nearby Height-Ashbury section famous as the countercultural Mecca of the 1960s.

In Thailand, a Norwegian member described successful witnessing: "Last Sunday we went with the children to a nice park where we got to talk with four students about sixteen years old. They ended up receiving Jesus. Four eternal souls born into His kingdom." A girl in Thailand "talked with a young exchange student from Australia and got him saved." In South Africa, a woman "witnessed to an actress who is a single mother and led her to the Lord." A teenage girl in America "got the chance to pray with three young people to receive Jesus. It was so beautiful to see Him touch their lives." A Belgian woman entered a proverbially American environment: "I went to a truckstop and talked to the truck drivers about God's love. Ten souls got saved, and we were able to distribute some Christian inspirational tapes and posters."

A young man wrote, "It made me very happy to pray with some of the people with a severe case of AIDS, to receive Jesus into their hearts, knowing that despite their pain and suffering now, they would soon be in Heaven with

Jesus." In Russia a boy wrote, "I was at a Metro and there was a family of midgets; we were able to witness to them and cheer them up." An American woman wrote she "had a friend from out of state call and prayed with him to receive Jesus over the phone." But an American woman in Australia illustrated how success did not always come easily: "While witnessing, a young fellow about eighteen years old tried to intimidate me. He crumpled up our tract and said he lived in hell already. Later he virtually apologized, prayed to receive Jesus and was very appreciative."

Table 4.3 also reveals that almost all Family homes regularly give thanks to God aloud before meals. I have enjoyed many meals at several different Family homes, and I have never heard them recite a standard "grace" verse. Instead, they might sit reverentially, possibly holding hands, and spontaneously thank God. Individuals, in their own manner and tempo might exclaim, "Thank you Jesus!" or "Thank you Lord!" On occasion, one member might say an extemporaneous prayer for the home, but there is no standard format that all homes must follow. Indeed, mealtimes in larger homes are often chaotic feasts as people come and go at different moments, sometimes congregating by age groups. A mother with ten children commented on how hard it was to organize thanks for the Lord at mealtimes, "We try but have a lot of kids so a lot of times it doesn't work as I try to feed the toddler and then take him out."

Spiritual Experiences

In 1988 and 1989, the General Social Survey included five items about religious or spiritual experiences, asking how often the respondent might have had each one. For example, the "deja vu" item asked how often the person "thought you were somewhere you had been before, but knew it was impossible." Another item, "felt as though you were in touch with someone when they were far away from you," was labeled "ESP" by the GSS researchers. The wording of these items is not always ideal. For example, "seen events that happened at a great distance as they were happening" is supposed to be about clairvoyance when it could just as easily be talking about television. The fourth item is quite clear: "felt as though you were really in touch with someone who had died." The fifth is widely used in religion surveys, yet its metaphor may not have the same meaning for all respondents: "felt as though you were very close to a powerful, spiritual force that seemed to lift you out of yourself."

Noting that substantial fractions of the GSS respondents claim to have had each of these experiences, sociologist Andrew Greeley proclaimed, "The paranormal is normal."[7] In research done in collaboration with William Mac-Cready, Greeley found that having "mystical experiences" actually may produce a happier and healthier life.[8] Rodney Stark has noted that "many common, ordinary, even mundane mental phenomena can be experienced as contact with the supernatural," especially if strong social support is provided for this interpretation.[9] Life within the Family provides very intense social support indeed. Table 4.4 shows that Family members are significantly more likely to have these spiritual experiences, with the exception of the dubious clairvoyance item. A small number of respondents in both groups who said "I cannot answer this" were removed from the analysis.

As we saw in the previous chapter, the Family has a very active image of the afterlife, and table 4.4 indicates that two thirds of members believe they have been in touch with deceased spirits. But this does not mean seeing a ghost on a dark and stormy night. Indeed, the reports I have from Family members sound more like expressions of feelings than anything that might be described as illusions or hallucinations. Many of the most vivid spiritual experiences occurred in dreams, but the belief system of the group encourages members to feel that some dreams are at least partly real.

About a week before Michael Pioneer met the Family, he had a dream in which his long-deceased grandfather came to him and said that soon Michael "would meet some people and I was going to go with them, and that others would throw rocks at me. He was steadying a ladder, and I had to go up this ladder, and he was holding the ladder for me. So we were very much anticipating something happening when we met the Family in January 1972." Michael has continued to have contact through dreams. "I saw him recently on a park bench in the Heavenly City with Father David."

Marie told me she had been in touch with her father, shortly after he died. Some time before, she had been very concerned about whether her Catholic parents really were saved, and she helped her mother pray to accept Jesus into her heart. Marie was not as close to her father, and from the Family she wrote to her mother asking her to urge him to accept Jesus. After her father died, Marie briefly sensed his spiritual presence in her home, almost as if she could see his face high up toward the ceiling—but not quite a vision she was seeing with earthly eyes. This reassured her that he was going to Heaven.

I included an item in the questionnaire, written with the help of spokes-people for the Family, asking if respondents had received prophecy, visions, or messages from the spirit world. The Family teaches that "The spirit realm is an eternal, invisible dimension which exists concurrently with the physical world."[10] It is not far away, but right here with us, thus potentially entwined

Table 4.4. Religious or Spiritual Experiences

Have you ever . . .	Family	1998-89 GSS
Thought you were somewhere you had been before, but knew that it was impossible?	85.3%	65.9%
Felt as though you were in touch with someone when they were far away from you?	81.7%	60.9%
Seen events that happened at a great distance as they were happening?	26.5%	26.2%
Felt as though you were really in touch with someone who had died?	67.7%	38.2%
Felt as though you were very close to a powerful, spiritual force that seemed to lift you out of yourself?	68.6%	30.8%
Received prophecy, visions, or messages from the spirit world?	95.4%	

The number of cases in this table ranges from 956 to 1,004 for the Family, and from 2,423 to 2,450 for the General Social Survey.

with our lives. Unfortunately, the General Social Survey has never contained an item about the spirit world, so we cannot compare. But it seems remarkable to me that 95 percent of members report having received prophecy at least once, and 56 percent say they have such experiences often.

Marie believes that we have entered a period of prophecy, because the Lord wishes to guide his people through the storms of the Endtime. "Prophecy is a beautiful gift that the Lord gives us at this time, because He knows we need it. This world is a terrible place, and we need that close link with the Lord to be able to go on." It often happens when she prays, either alone or with her husband. "The Lord gives me something, like a picture or words. Sometimes it's just a feeling of the Lord. And it's very important." When receiving prophecy, she says, "You have to have your mind not full of your own answers. You have to clear your mind or your heart. You have to be ready for whatever the Lord will give you."

During Prayer, Michael Pioneer often has a sense—call it a vision—that Father David is looking down at him from a hill behind Michael. Soon after joining, Michael had witnessed in Sweden together with Father David's son, Aaron, who died in 1973. "Whenever we would pioneer a new place, and get down to prayer and ask the Lord, many times I would get a vision of Aaron, and he would say a few things. And one of them was that we were on a mission to Alberta." Michael helped set up a home of more than a dozen people in Edmonton, but soon after they had established relationships with donors and with needy people they could help in a shelter for transients, the anticult movement ignited a media frenzy against the Family. The group rushed its children out of harm's way, and both Michael's home and another home in Calgary had to close. But scholars Susan Palmer and Gordon Melton offered encouragement, the Family's own media experts went on the counterattack, and Michael now feels that exposing the anticult movement was the reason Aaron's spirit encouraged him on a mission to Alberta.[11]

Linda, Michael's wife, does not have his talent for rich visions and spiritual experiences. "I compare myself with my husband. We both hear from the Lord, but it's in two very different ways. He'll get a specific person who speaks a message, I'll just get either a verse or a feeling that the Lord said this. Either two by two or in our prayer meetings, I always get something. We have a prayer day every month, and we try to record things the Lord shows us or praying about a situation or for people. We always get a verse or a picture. Especially in our life, which is not very set, there are a lot of things we need direction about. I mostly get verses. That's how I hear things. I haven't ever gotten it like I felt that someone was speaking to me. I know my husband has. Maybe some people are just better channels."

Mannie explains how prophecy helps him make important decisions. "Whenever we ask the Lord for a verse or a specific reading I usually get an impression. On a day to day basis I've been taught to pray for every little thing, no matter what it is. If you start practicing with the small things, like 'Where shall I go today? Shall we witness here or there?' Then finally when the big things come, like 'Which country should I go to as a missionary,' then you'll be used to that. Like recently, I was asking the Lord whether I should go to India, Romania, or any other place. It was a pretty big struggle. But I was praying and asking the Lord and I got a specific burden [sense of a calling] for India, to reach the people there who have not heard so much about the Lord as other countries. It was an ongoing thing for about a month. I'd stop, then I'd pray and ask the Lord, because I really didn't know what to do. Usually at night or in the morning on my bed. And sometimes I'd write down the prophecy that I got, usually something small."

Born in the Family, Mannie had memorized many Bible verses, plus many quotations from Father David's voluminous writings. These then pop into his mind as prophecy. "You get an impression like a verse of something, that I'd memorized when I was a kid. Then you'd get a few more verses. And altogether after you read it, you get the basic idea of what the Lord is trying to show you. The first one I got was Mark 16:15, 'Go ye into all the world, and preach the gospel to the whole creation,' so I knew that was my basic job to go out and win the world, but I didn't know where. But then I got another quote from one of the early letters that Grandpa wrote, he said that the people of India are like diamonds that the world wants to have in its crown.[12] So at that point I felt I want some of those in my crown. So that was an encouragement for me to just go and do it."

As Mannie's cases illustrates, one way prophecy can manifest is through Bible verses. A person can be praying for prophecy when a memorized Bible verse pops into mind. Then the person can think about how to apply that verse to his or her own life, or seek advice from other members of the home. For example, an American woman in Mexico wrote on her questionnaire that she was happy because, "When I was confused about something, I got a verse from the Lord that was perfect for that situation and took away my confusion."

Because they believe God is always present, Family members can logically attribute even their own thought processes to Him. A young woman was worried by doubts, cried, and was drawing artwork. "I was feeling very low. The Lord taught me through memories and I got the victory." Another woman remarked, "I almost forgot that I had an appointment and then the Lord reminded me so I was able to make it. Thank The Lord!"

Although prophecy can come at any time, some members of the Family find that lying on a bed is conducive. In Nigeria an Austrian boy was happy because, "I was laying on my bed praying and the Lord gave me a prophecy." An American in Russia said he had "received and wrote down some prophecy and words from the Lord." Many members keep a diary or notebook for this purpose. Some use a tape recorder when they are praying for prophecy, so they can remind themselves and be better able to apply the prophecy in their lives.

Often members get prophecies in groups. An American woman in Brazil "prayed and received a prophecy." But she was especially happy about the prophecy received by another member. "Someone received a beautiful message from the Lord for me, which very greatly encouraged me and gave me invaluable specific guidance for a certain situation." In Uzbekistan, a woman wrote, "When praying with my daughter she received very clear prophecies for a situation in our home as well as directions for a road team." A Canadian mother of five, with children ranging from fifteen years down to eight months, said "My life being now busier than ever, I challenged my husband to help us find time for prophecy and the Lord came through with wonderful encouragements." For his part, her husband noted the "Lord told me to read the Book of Zechariah."

Sharing prophecies with other members strengthens each individual's faith in their reality. A teenage girl in Japan "talked with a bunch of my friends. One of them had just gotten a prophecy but was worried that it came from her own head. We all tried to encourage her and share testimony about how we've all gone through that too. I got a revelation about myself and the way I act that needs changing and wrote about it in my diary."

Prophecy

Over the years, Father David received many messages from the spirit world, by many channels, and he distributed them to his far-flung followers through hundreds of MO letters. Thus he guided the lives, loves and migrations of his flock, even though he kept a physical distance from them, living modestly in various secret locations and not intruding on the daily work of the communes. Then, a quarter century after founding the Children of God, David Brandt Berg died. The mantle of prophecy passed to his young wife, Maria, and members began to see Father David in their dreams. The Family he had created counted 9,000 full-time members, two thirds of them children, at 200 homes in forty-three countries.

Maria succeeded David as part of a triumvirate, sharing leadership with Gary and Peter Amsterdam who is Maria's husband. In June 1995, I interviewed Amsterdam at a secret location, and he explained to me the difficulty they were having filling Father David's prophetic shoes. He said that sociologists had a false impression about leadership in the Family, supposing that Father David devised strategies then concocted theological justifications to convince his followers to carry them out. "That is completely wrong. I was there for sixteen years, and I watched how things happened. Dad wouldn't have any idea on something to do. He would pray, or the Lord would give him a revelation or some sort of direction, and he'd say let's do it because the Lord said to. Then the mechanics of how to put it into place developed as it went on.

"It's something that Dad taught us at home. He tried to teach the Family at large through the letters, too, that the key is to really pray and to hear from the Lord. He was dynamic. He had years of Christian experience with his mother and his grandfather. So for us it's a loss that he is gone. And for us at the top, like Maria and myself and Gary it is awesome to think we can't just pop in the other room and ask Dad what to do." Maria is timid, and Amsterdam's own attempts to prophesy were halting at first, but they gradually were able to receive divine messages. "We pray and the Lord speaks to us in prophecy, and what He says to do, that's what we do. If anything, I would say that's how it has always been with Dad. But he was so much more articulate, that when he would get something from the Lord it would flow out like fountains. He could talk for hours and hours and hours. That's the way it was."

I asked him to describe the experience of those prayers and how the answers came. He explained, "One thing about Maria is she has always from the beginning loved the Words. She loves to hear from the Lord. She loved it when Dad spoke. She loved it when Dad got things from the Lord. Actually we had been expecting that when Dad went she would get the gift of prophecy, which she didn't have. The Lord said He was going to give it to her, that she would be a prophetess, so that was the expectation. I was looking forward to that." Talking with Amsterdam that whole day, filling tape after tape with his words and watching his face closely, I had no doubt that he was sincere. If receiving divine guidance was a cunning deception, he would not have admitted the struggle that he and Maria went through, as they lay on their bed straining to receive the Word of God.

"The Lord through prophecy said, 'I'm not going to do that right now, you won't get the gift right now. Because if I did it would be a little too easy for you. It would be like calling Me up on the phone instead of having intimate fellowship with Me, and I want you, Maria, when you pray, to really have to go deep in the mine and really dig it out so that we will have good communication. But because you have to hear things, and you can't spend all of your time doing that, you can use Peter's gift of prophecy and others.' And that's basically what has been happening.

"She keeps this list of questions that she wants to know. She has an insatiable desire to know everything. We'll pray for a certain thing each day. For example we prayed about music. We had published some Contemporary Christian Music some years ago. We had more, and she and I listened to them and weren't so thrilled, and didn't know if we should put them out. So we brought it before the Lord. She usually prays, beautiful prayers, she's very desperate. Then we lie there quiet before the Lord.

"Prophecy comes different for different people, but I usually get the first sentence. It's always a little hard to give it, it's a big responsibility. I give the first sentence and then it flows. Some are short, some long, some fast, some slow. Sometimes the prophecies are from Dad, some from the Lord."

Amsterdam explained that he usually gets a sense, just before the words begin to flow, whether they are coming from the Lord or from Father David. "But sometimes you don't know. One time there was a prophecy about tests and trials and the Apostle Paul gave it. At first I didn't know who it was, but then through the content, you could tell." I asked whether he would get a sense of the words, rather than hearing them in a particular voice. "Yes, the words just come. Like if you were a faucet, you turn it on and the water comes through. You start and then the words just come. It's not like you hear a voice and then repeat it."

The Lord told them not to distribute music by outsiders among their communes, even if it was Christian. And in another prophecy the Lord reaffirmed that they should not employ artificial birth control techniques, either satisfying each other sexually by means other than full intercourse or going all the way and accepting any children that resulted as gifts from God.[13] Over the following year, the Family developed increasingly greater capacity to receive divine guidance, and every commune was encouraged to open its souls to such messages. As we saw above, the overwhelming majority of members now receive prophecy.

Members often send the most striking prophecies to Maria or World Services for a reaction, other prophecies are received by members of World Services itself, and some from both sources appear in the Family's frequent internal publications. Tragic news came on July 16, 1995, that a van carrying Family teens had smashed on a Texas highway, killing five of the girls. By August, Maria had received the following prophecy from one of them: "Hi, Mommy Maria! My name is Joy, and I just want you to know that the girls and I are very happy! And of course you know everything Here is happiness and joy! We've already seen Grandpa [Father David] and we are so excited! We all got to sit on his lap and give him hugs and kisses, and we are very thrilled and happy to be Here! We already see what is going to happen, and that this seeming tragedy is not going to be a tragedy at all! When you write to our families, please tell them that we are doing just fine and we are happy. Tell my daddy that I love him, and tell all of our moms and dads that we love them and we are doing just fine and we are happy and that our personal problems are over now."[14]

Later I interviewed Marie, a friend of Joy, who told me, "In one of the mailings there was a message from Joy from the other side. And when I read it, it was just like her style. Everybody has a different way of expressing themselves, of course, but it was just like Joy talking. This is true, this is real!"

Any member can write while feeling inspired and justifiably feel that the words had come from the spirit world. For example, a teenage girl in America wrote triumphantly on her questionnaire that recently she had "received a spirit story, ha!" A woman in China was happy to report, "Mama [Maria] sent word that the first three chapters I sent in of a story from Jonah were terrific and asked if I could try to hear from Job!" Literature channeled from deceased persons or supernatural entities are called *spirit stories*, and the collection is called *Heaven's Library*. By the end of 1997, Peter Amsterdam reported that 381 spirit stories had been received, from novels like *The Perfect Ones* down to short stories and even dramas. About three-quarters were submitted by members in the field, and the other quarter came from personnel at World Services.[15]

The Perfect Ones, by Sir Walter Scott, is an *Ivanhoe*-like adventure tale concerning the persecution of the Cathars. In his introduction, the author explains, "I am Sir Walter Scott, and this is my first attempt to write a story through the medium of a helper on earth. This helper has argued with me that my style is a touch old-fashioned for this day and age, and so I have attempted to bring my style of writing a little more up to date, so it is more contemporary. And yet, I feel that I must also stay true to the way that I have been taught and the way I know how to write."[16]

Another spirit novel is the quest allegory, *The Return of the Seven Keys*, written posthumously by C. S. Lewis. It traces the adventures of a young man named Gabe, as he follows the guidance of whispers in unlocking mysteries until achieving heavenly translation at a battle clearly meant to represent Armageddon. Far less bellicose are the novellas by Scheherazade, "Amaris" and "The Scimitar and the Rose," published together in a single volume. Amaris is the daughter of the British ambassador to an apparently Islamic society, who was kidnapped in early childhood and raised by the king. The stories explain how prophecy leads her to discover her real relationship to her two fathers and find her destiny. "The Greatest of These" is a five-act play attributed to William Shakespeare but written nearly four centuries after his death.

Parasociology

The canon of sociological methodology does not currently approve of data collection from the spirit world. However, to members of the Family the spirit world is real, and the first rule of ethnography is to consider important anything that the people under study consider real. During my research on the Family, the leadership has delivered to me three long documents of prophecy they said they had channeled on my behalf from the spirit world. Whether or not we believe they really came from departed spirits, they contribute to an understanding of the Family.

When I interviewed Peter Amsterdam in 1995, he brought me five pages of prophecy he said he had received for me from the Lord. Particularly interesting was a passage that compared me with a crucial but obscure person in the New Testament: "Therefore be prayerful and seek the counsel of Godly people and lean upon Me, much like Gamaliel. Even though a wise man, he was wiser yet in coming unto Me and seeking the Godly counsel, seeking the truth. In like manner, I have called thee a Gamaliel, that thou mayest know the wisdom that cometh from My heart. Seek Me in the early hours. Listen to the whispers, as I would guide thee, for I have need of thee."

Gamaliel appears in Acts of the Apostles 5, and verse 34 describes him as "a doctor of the law, had in reputation among all the people." Some time after the crucifixion, the apostles were promulgating the teachings of Jesus, which the authorities had forbidden them to do. All the key disciples were seized, and interrogated by the high priest. It appeared likely that they would be executed, but Gamaliel argued against this, in Acts 35–39: "Ye men of Israel, take heed to yourselves what ye intend to do as touching these men. For before these days rose up Theudas, boasting himself to be somebody; to whom a number of men, about four hundred, joined themselves: who was slain; and all, as many as obeyed him, were scattered, and brought to nought. After this man rose up Judas of Galilee in the days of the taxing, and drew away much people after him: he also perished; and all, even as many as obeyed him, were dispersed. And now I say unto you, Refrain from these men, and let them alone: for if this counsel or this work be of men, it will come to nought: But if it be of God, ye cannot overthrow it; lest haply ye be found even to fight against God."

Thus Gamaliel described the fates of two earlier new religious movements that had perished, undoubtedly because their beliefs were false. Similarly, if Christianity were false, it also would perish, without the cruel necessity of executing its missionaries. But if Christianity were true, no power could extinguish it, and anyone who tried would merely earn the enmity of God. With this argument, Gamaliel, who was himself not a Christian but a just and righteous man, saved the lives of many disciples of Jesus. Social scientists might serve a similar mediating role today, communicating to authorities and other outsiders why the Family should be allowed to live in peace, either to thrive or perish depending on the truth of its beliefs.

In 1996, I received a further set of prophecies from the Family, just as I was completing my book, *The Sociology of Religious Movements*, which contains a chapter about their group. "Well, Bill," Father David purportedly wrote to me from beyond the grave, "you've come a long way, son. From the time you first met us until now—what a marvel it is, even to the Family, how you've come to know us, to appreciate us, our purity, our dedication, and you've come to understand us in ways rare for those who live outside of the Family."

This apparently posthumous missive from Father David hoped that social science could translate his message into terms that outsiders might appreciate. "They've heard a lot about our radical past, but what about our radical present? And how does that fit into the maturation of a movement? You know, I wrote my own kids about this many years back, to try to help them to understand that when they were young and wild and wooly, runnin' around the country-side helter-skelter sometimes, yellin' and screamin' out the message of God's prophet, they had to learn how to adjust as they had children, as they pioneered countries, to establish a work which in the beginning was revolutionary, wild, radical, impetuous I would say, impulsive, yes!—Like myself, I was a very impulsive prophet, and I acted when God told me to do things. Oh yeah, I made mistakes, that's true—many of them! But we went somewhere and we made ourselves known. And we yelled out the message as best we could, and like the Rechabites of old, we stayed dropped out of that ol' System."

The message noted that many people in the world were mired in ruts or wildly thrashing about in confusion. "The times they are a-changin', just like Dylan said, and buddy, you'd better hang onto your hat, 'cause the next few years ahead of us are going to be the wildest you've ever seen—not just in the Family, but in the world around you. These times are what the Family has been equipped for and prepared for." Then it explained that members of the Family had been transforming themselves into experienced, trained missionaries, capable of using computers or any other appropriate means for spreading the Word.

"Why is it that the Family continues to live outside of mainstream society? Why don't they register and do things like all the other churches? Explain this to the people, because you know what, Bill? It's always been like that. Why did God choose Noah to drop out of his society and build a boat to the saving of his house—and I might add to the saving of the world? Why did Jesus and His weirdy-beardy disciples live—their motley crew of fishermen, tax collectors and whores—running around the countryside preaching an eternal message that has been echoed down throughout the ages? They didn't fit in. Why did Jesus seem to preach things that seemed to contradict his own forebears and those who bore the message of the Old Testament? He was blasphemous in the eyes of the Pharisees and the scribes, and yet it was necessary for Him to be as radical as He was, in order to give birth to the Early Church."

The message attributed to Father David advised me to take my time, to do my research while listening for the voice of the Lord, and to communicate to other people the values of the Family. "That's where you come in, Bill. You can help others to appreciate things which seem odd and strange, even as you've come to appreciate this weird group, these funny people who do the funniest things and change directions on a dime."

In September 1997, when the questionnaire was on its way to the respondents, Peter and Maria send me a third document of prophecies, specifically for this section of the book I planned to write. These written prophecies said that Jesus himself spoke to me by name: "How pleased I am, Bill, with your desire to do that which is right in matters concerning your writing. I hear your prayers, I read your inner thoughts, I know the intents of your heart, and I am pleased as you turn them towards Me. I am pleased with your desire to look to Me, as you ponder in your mind and heart these matters on what to write, how to write, when to write, and on how you might be able to acknowledge Me and My voice of prophecy in your book."

After further encouragement, the message offered me my own spirit guide, a deceased author who had already begun to communicate spirit writings from beyond the grave, and one the Family knew to be my favorite from childhood, Edgar Rice Burroughs. The name of this popular American writer, the creator of Tarzan and a pioneer of interplanetary science fiction, was signed to another long message contained within the prophecy. Part of it correctly summarized Burroughs's biography, and it explained that his perspective on life had broadened considerably since entering Heaven on his death in 1950.

From beyond the grave, Burroughs apparently explained that the members of the Family were just ordinary, weak human beings, but that they were capable of great deeds in the service of God. "Each Family member knows it's not in them, but they had to be willing. Each one had to make that decision to follow. As anybody who is or ever has been greatly used of God, they had to be willing to say yes to the Lord. They had to accept His offer in their life to follow where He's leading. And you've been willing, too, Bill, so I take my hat off to you! You've been willing to stick up for the Family, and that takes a lot of guts!"

Whether these words really came from the Lord, Jesus, Father David, and Edgar Rice Burroughs, or were the imaginings of the Family, does not really matter for the purposes of this book. The prophecies received in recent years by the Family, which they sincerely believe have come from the spirit world, are among the most remarkable religious phenomena of our times.

CHAPTER 5

Alienation

Scholars and ordinary citizens alike have conjectured that new religious movements are the result of alienation from conventional society.[1] For example, a disappointed former member of the Family, Miriam Williams, has said that she and the others "received relief from alienation at the price of exploitation."[2] However, there are several problems with this theory. Clearly, only very small numbers of people join radical religions, yet in chaotic modern society the numbers who are alienated must be vast. Indeed, given the state of society today, one could argue that any aware person would have to be alienated. Lest we become trapped in a subjective argument about the quality of modern life, we should note that it is not easy to nail down the definition of the term, and social theorists have used such words as *alienation* and *anomie* in a confusing variety of ways. Nonetheless, the General Social Survey contains many items meant to measure estrangement from society, and responses of members of the Family can help us understand their relationship to the world.

One tradition in alienation research focuses on the degree to which a person feels oppressed by the society's ruling elite, rather than personally involved in public decision-making. Related to this form of alienation is the personal experience of anomia, or the societal condition of anomie, which are sometimes defined as normlessness. Other varieties or aspects of alienation are interpersonal distrust, lack of confidence in societal institutions, lack of autonomy, and powerlessness at work. In addition to considering these forms of nonreligious alienation, this chapter will survey Family opinions about the proper relationship between church and state and the group's attitudes toward the sinful world.

Measuring Alienation

In 1974, sociologist Benjamin Zablocki administered a survey to 398 members of urban communes to understand the dynamics of alienation and charisma, including some of the very items I chose from the General Social Survey.[3] One set listed five statements, and asked, "Do you tend to feel or not . . . ?" Originally derived from the Harris Poll, these items supposedly measure alienation, and table 5.1 reveals that a majority of Americans were alienated on four of these measures. Zablocki found that his commune members either responded about the same as the general public, or appeared less alienated, especially on items that concerned the conditions surrounding their own lives.

On two of these measures, members of the Family appear more alienated, because they are more likely to agree that the people running the country do not care what happens to them and that the rich are getting richer at the expense of the poor. Large majorities of the Family respondents agree with these two statements that criticize people with power and money. We should note that some have in mind the situations in very unfortunate nations. For example, an American member living in Paraguay responded in terms of Paraguay, not the United States, writing, "I live in a very corrupt country."

On two other measures, which do not concern the rich and powerful, Family members appear less alienated, apparently feeling that what they think does count and that they are not left out of things. They may, of course, mean that what they think counts within the Family, where they are never left out of things, rather than that they are happy with their status in the surrounding society. An American member living in Indonesia checked both the "yes" and "no" boxes about being left out of things, explaining, "Yes, for what's in the world. No, for what we're doing." On the final item about people with power, there is no significant difference, but both groups appear somewhat alienated.

Anomia

In the early 1970s, the researchers conducting the General Social Survey developed a nine-item measure of *anomia*, based on earlier work by Leo Srole.[4] For example, one item says, "You sometimes can't help wondering whether anything is worthwhile any more." Another asserts, "Most public officials are not really interested in the problems of the average person." Agreement with statements like these indicates the respondent is suffering from *anomia*, which is the personal feeling of normlessness, living in a world where there seem to be no

Table 5.1. Alienation Measures from the Harris Poll

Yes, feel . . .	Family	1978 GSS
The people running the country don't really care what happens to you.	76.0%	51.3%
The rich get richer and the poor get poorer.	95.3%	73.8%
What you think doesn't count very much anymore.	42.8%	55.1%
You're left out of things going on around you.	25.3%	28.3%
Most people with power try to take advantage of people like yourself.	54.3%	55.6%

The number of cases ranges from 996 to 1,014 for the Family, and from 1,517 to 1,520 for the General Social Survey.

rules or moral guides for action. According to the traditions of research in this area, anomia is a variety of alienation. However, over the years sociologists have developed doubts about what these nine items measure, and research using them has become progressively less frequent. The year 1976 was the last year in which all nine items were used, and the 1994 GSS contained only three of them. I was present when the GSS governing board debated dropping anomia from the survey altogether, and there was general agreement that the items and possibly also the concept of anomia had outlived their usefulness.

Research on religion and anomia using the GSS has been inconclusive. For example, in a study using these same nine variables, Lawrence Hong found an inconsistent relationship between religion and anomia, which was measured simply by counting how many of the nine items the respondent agreed with. People who attended church more often showed less anomia than those who attended infrequently. But other religion variables Hong investigated did not show this correlation. However, he did not consider the possibility that the nine GSS items really do not validly measure "the personal level of normlessness" that he thought it did.[5]

Using five of the nine items and the same data, Eugen Schoenfeld found little impact of religious involvement on anomia.[6] In contrast, Jack Martin and Steven Stack found a slight tendency for religious belief and church attendance to reduce anomia. Several authors have found that the anomia scale is statistically reliable but probably measures powerlessness rather than normlessness. The most important factor predicting a high score on this scale is low social class.[7] Zablocki found that his commune sample differed from the GSS in different ways on different items, so it makes sense for us to examine the items one by one rather than assume that responses to them can simply be added together to create a meaningful scale.

Table 5.2 shows what percentage of Family members agreed with each of the nine anomia statements, compared with respondents to the GSS in 1976 (the last time all nine items were included) and 1994 (the last time any were included). First note that the three items included in both the 1976 and 1994 GSS seem to indicate rising anomia in the general public over these eighteen years. Increasing majorities believe "the lot of the average person is getting worse" and "public officials are not really interested in the problems of the average person." But still higher percentages of Family members hold these pessimistic views of the status of ordinary citizens. However, we can hardly call the Family radical on the basis that almost all members agree with the overwhelming majority of Americans.

The remaining anomia item from the 1994 GSS tells a very different story. Among the American public a minority, but an increasing one, feel "It's hardly fair to bring a child into the world with the way things look for the future." Only a mere 9 percent of Family respondents agree, apparently indicating that members are far less alienated than nonmembers. But this item mixes at least two very different things: pessimism about the future and attitudes toward having children. As we shall see in the concluding chapters of this book, members of the Family have far more favorable attitudes toward reproduction than do many Americans. A father of seven children wrote in the margins of the questionnaire, "God gives the children. He takes care of His own!"

The next two items consider a person to be anomic if he or she values money highly and apparently lacks scruples about how to get it. A cynic might disagree with this interpretation, arguing that these acquisitive items express central American values. However, only minorities of GSS respondents agree with these two items, and only tiny fractions of the Family membership do. Indeed, some who agree may be answering not in terms of their own values but in terms of what they think other people value. In any case, by these two measures, Family members are far less anomic than nonmembers.

The sixth anomia item appears to measure despair or depression: "You sometimes can't help wondering whether anything is worthwhile anymore." Nearly twice as high a fraction of the American public agrees with this dismal statement as among the Family. The next item, asserting that "a person has to live pretty much for today and let tomorrow take care of itself," seems ambiguous in meaning. Is this an expression of pessimism, or of a carefree attitude? Or

Table 5.2. Anomia

Agree . . .	Family	1976 GSS	1994 GSS
In spite of what some people say, the lot (situation/condition) of the average person is getting worse, not better.	82.1%	58.6%	67.2%
Most public officials (people in public office) are not really interested in the problems of the average person.	77.0%	66.7%	73.8%
It's hardly fair to bring a child into the world with the way things look for the future.	8.9%	41.5%	44.2%
Next to health, money is the most important thing in life.	1.4%	33.4%	
To make money, there are no right and wrong ways any more, only easy and hard ways.	7.6%	26.4%	
You sometimes can't help wondering whether anything is worthwhile any more.	23.9%	39.9%	
Nowadays, a person has to live pretty much for today and let tomorrow take care of itself.	32.6%	46.6%	
These days a person doesn't really know whom he can count on.	69.5%	74.9%	
Most people don't really care what happens to the next fellow.	70.0%	58.6%	

The number of cases ranges from 1,002 to 1,016 for the Family, from 1,494 to 1,498 for the General Social Survey in 1976, and from 1,251 to 1,253 for the General Social Survey in 1994.

does it express a lazy, hedonistic attitude at variance with the work ethic? One family member who agreed with this statement explained, "We trust the Lord for tomorrow." In any case, Family members were significantly less likely to agree that nothing was worthwhile.

The remaining two items concern the extent to which people can be counted on for support and care about each other. Majorities of both groups of respondents express pessimistic views of human altruism, one being higher on one item, and the other on the other item. The overall picture sketched by these anomia statements is that the Family is not especially anomic, scoring lower on six of the nine than the American public.

Trust

Alienation from the world is partly a lack of trust in other people, and several of the items in Tables 5.1 and 5.2 concern lack of trust. In 1996, the GSS contained three questions about whether other people tended to be helpful, fair, and trustworthy. The GSS can be criticized for relying too heavily on simple question-and-answer formats that may obscure important facts. For example, the nine anomia items discussed above consider a person to be anomic to the extent that he or she agrees with the statements. However, it has been known by survey researchers for many decades that respondents differ in their tendency to agree or disagree with statements, regardless of what they say.[8] The GSS items on interpersonal trust ask respondents to choose between two alternative statements, rather than just agreeing or disagreeing with one, thus balancing against the "yeasaying" or "naysaying" bias.

One question asks, "Would you say that most of the time people try to be helpful, or that they are mostly just looking out for themselves?" As table 5.3 reveals, Family members are far more likely to say people "try to be helpful" than that they "just look out for themselves." GSS respondents tend to tilt the other way. We should note that Family homes exist on the generosity of friends and other nonmembers, and thus this missionary movement has tested the human capacity to be helpful.

Similarly, Family members are far more likely to feel people try to be fair rather than take advantage of others. Members of the Family are about evenly split about whether people can generally be trusted, but a clear majority of the American public cautions against trusting and says "you can't be too careful in dealing with people."

These three items concern "people," but which people do Family respondents have in mind? One woman wrote, "I'll answer these from 'Family' viewpoint. I'm talking about Family members here." Another wrote "in the Family" next to all the trusting responses, and "in the System" next to all the responses indicating lack of trust. A man who thought people are mostly looking out for themselves, said he was "answering with Worldly people in mind." Another man thought people try to be helpful "in the Family" but would take advantage of you "out in the world." He explained, "Everybody can be trusted in The

Table 5.3. Interpersonal Trust

	Family	1996 GSS
Would you say that most of the time people try to be helpful, or that they are mostly just looking out for themselves?		
Try to be helpful	69.8%	43.4%
Just look out for themselves	18.5%	48.9%
Depends or don't know	11.7%	7.7%
TOTAL	100.0%	100.0%
Do you think most people would try to take advantage of you if they got a chance, or would they try to be fair?		
Would take advantage of you	18.9%	42.1%
Would try to be fair	64.6%	49.9%
Depends or don't know	19.5%	8.1%
TOTAL	100.0%	100.0%
Generally speaking, would you say that most people can be trusted or that you can't be too careful in dealing with people?		
Most people can be trusted	42.4%	33.8%
Can't be too careful	41.9%	60.7%
Depends or don't know	15.6%	5.5%
TOTAL	100.0%	100.0%

The numbers of cases range from 973 to 993 for the Family, and from 1,912 to 1,921 for the General Social Survey.

Family, but you can't be too careful out in the world." Another man wrote, "People are mostly selfish by nature. They need Jesus to feel the joy of helping others."

The GSS has other items that can be interpreted as measures of trust, for example one concerning how threatening the respondent perceived government to be. In 1985 and again in 1996, the GSS asked: "The government has a lot of different pieces of information about people which computers can bring together very quickly. Is this a very serious threat to individual privacy, a fairly serious threat, not a serious threat, or not a threat at all to individual privacy?" In 1985, 30 percent of 666 respondents judged that this was "a very

Table 5.4. Lack of Confidence in Societal Institutions

Very little confidence or no confidence in . . .	*Family*	*1991 GSS*
Business and industry.	39.9%	20.9%
Government departments.	62.8%	32.9%
Churches and religious organizations.	48.6%	18.4%
Courts and the legal system.	45.6%	27.1%
Schools and the educational system.	44.3%	18.1%

The number of cases ranges from 993 to 1,013 for the Family, and from 1,312 to 1,328 for the General Social Survey.

serious threat," and by 1996 the proportion had risen slightly to 37 percent of 1304 respondents. In the Family, fully 62 percent give this response.

Confidence in Institutions

Over the years the GSS has included a battery of items naming "some institutions of the country in which you live," and asking how much confidence respondents have in "the people running these institutions." Seymour Martin Lipset and William Schneider have argued that these are valid measures of how much faith versus distrust people have in societal institution and leaders, thus they are good measures of a form of alienation.[9] I included twelve of these items in the questionnaire, but used the format from the international version of the GSS known as the International Social Survey, so only the five shown in table 5.4 are strictly comparable to the GSS.

On average, 48 percent of Family respondents say they have "very little confidence" or "no confidence" in these five institutions, compared with only 24 percent of GSS respondents. This is a ratio of two to one in alienation from societal institutions. Relative to the GSS respondents, Family members have much less confidence in "churches and religious organizations" and "schools and the educational system." Churches represent "churchianity," the godless institutions that stifle faith and are hostile to the Family to the extent that they recognize its existence at all. Schools represent secularism, and as we shall see in chapter 7, the Family provides education for its children at home.

Members of the Family do not work for business or industry, but businesspeople often contribute to provisioning the homes. Except for the frequent necessity of getting passports in order to cross national boundaries, members tend to avoid contact with government departments. For example, they frequently do not register their organization as a religious charity, considering their status to be a private matter between themselves and God. Also, many members do not consider themselves to have incomes or property that would require interaction with tax collectors, or have obtained tax-exempt status due to their charitable work. As we saw in chapter 1, the Family has suffered a number of persecution episodes at the hands of legal authorities, but the courts have always eventually released the children who were seized, thus giving some reason for confidence. A man who expressed a great deal of confidence in the courts explained, "We know exactly what to expect."

The figures in table 5.4 show that members of the Family have a relatively high level of alienation from the society in which they find themselves, but we must remember that most do not live in the United States, so part of the difference with the GSS respondents may be the nationality of the institutions being judged. Three of the respondents who did not answer these questions provided explanations. A Ukrainian woman wrote, "I just came to USA and do not know anything about people running all these different institutions." A Swiss woman in Thailand commented, "I can't choose most of these because I've only been in this country three months, so I don't know much about it." And an American woman in Poland said, "I don't know enough yet about Poland to judge." However, even though many members of the Family live in nations with incompetent, hostile, or unfamiliar governments, the fact remains that they have relatively little confidence in the people running the institutions in their immediate environment and thus are alienated.

A German member currently residing in the Czech Republic expressed a widespread feeling in the Family: "As far as society goes, or the 'System' as we call it in the Family, in general I couldn't say it's godly, and therefore I wouldn't have much confidence in the 'System.' I'd have confidence in particular individuals, but it would be a case where each individual or situation would have to be judged on its own merits."

Just 33.4 percent of Family respondents said they have little or no confidence in "the scientific community," a smaller degree of alienation than toward any of the five institutions listed in table 5.3. However, only 0.5 percent have "complete confidence," and 6.5 percent have "a great deal of confidence." The largest group, 45.2 percent, express "some confidence," and another 1.4 percent cannot make up their minds.

Scientists like to think that their disciplines are the authoritative sources for truth, and most fundamental scientific research is funded by the government. Two questions that could measure the relationship between the Family's faith and scientific ideology were adapted from the 1994 GSS, changing the response format slightly so that they could fit into the long battery of agree-disagree items measuring attitudes toward a wide range of issues. One focused on the enduring debate between evolutionary biologists and creationists about the origins of the human species. Avoiding the loaded term *evolution*, the GSS asked how true the following statement is: "Human beings developed from earlier species of animals." Of 1,341 respondents, 8.8 percent said "definitely true," and 39.5 percent said "probably true," for a total of 44.3 percent of Americans who tended to feel this evolutionist statement was true. An almost equal but slightly larger proportion, 47.3 percent, felt it was "not true."

The figures for the Family could hardly be more different. Just 1.5 percent of the 1,020 respondents who responded agreed with the pro-evolution statement, and 97.9 percent disagreed. Indeed, 93.5 percent disagreed "strongly." Although firm in their opposition to the theory of evolution by natural selection, the Family believes that some ancient animals have become extinct, and the "leviathan" mentioned in Job 41:1 and elsewhere may have been a dinosaur. The Family's movie guide approved the dinosaur movie *Jurassic Park* for ages 14 and over, saying "The movie is entertainment only & we of course don't agree with the less than subtle pro-evolution slant." I observed Family members make tyrannosaurus and brontosaurus balloon animals at the birthday party of a nonmember.

The other GSS item about the relationship between science and religion concerned the validity of horoscopes: "Astrology—the study of star signs—has some scientific truth." Of the 1,347 Americans who responded, 48.3 percent thought this pro-astrology statement was true, while 44.1 percent believed it was not. Among 1,019 members of the Family, fully 91.1 percent considered the statement to be true, and only 7.1 percent considered it to be false. I included this item in the questionnaire because I knew from my interviews that the Family had an unusually favorable opinion of astrology. Among respondents to the GSS, religious people are less likely than irreligious people to believe in astrology.[10]

The youth counterculture of the late 1960s, from which many early recruits to the Family came, embraced astrology in the famous slogan from the rock musical *Hair*, "This is the dawning of the Age of Aquarius." Astrology was dawning in American long before the 1960s, but by that decade it had established many of its concepts in popular consciousness.[11] In a 1971 MO Letter, Father David wrote, "I can prove to you from the Bible that God has ordained the stars and the planets to control and influence our lives and at least our personalities, if not actual events! I'm not much for this daily forecast business, but you can certainly determine pretty much what a person is going to be by the month they were born in, believe it or not."[12] I have not observed any particular manifestations of astrology in my visits to Family homes, and Father David cautioned against relying on ungodly astrologers rather than direct communication with the Lord. But he suggested members ought to purchase the astrological guide he himself used, and the Family continues to consider that astrology contains much truth.

The Family's strong pro-astrology and anti-evolution beliefs raise an interesting question about the extent to which the group is "deviant." Standard scientific ideology asserts that the theory of evolution is probably true, and that the claims of astrology are false. Members of the family overwhelmingly disagree, but a slight plurality of the general public also disagrees with scientific orthodoxy.

Of 1,164 respondents to the 1994 GSS who answered both questions, just 25.5 percent agreed with the modal Family belief that evolution is false while astrology is true. Indeed, almost exactly a quarter of Americans take each of the four possible positions on these two science-related issues, with the smallest proportion (23.4 percent) agreeing with scientific orthodoxy that evolution is true but astrology is false.

Church and State

Through its witnessing activities, the Family publicly proclaims its faith, but we have just seen further evidence of its suspicion of Churchianity. Therefore it is worth asking what attitudes members have about religion becoming more involved in public affairs. The questionnaire included several attitudinal items from the GSS about the role of religion in society. They do not concern life in the Family, and the group is not actively involved in such standard institutions as the public schools and government. Given the Family's suspicion of formal "religion," "Churchianity," and "the System," we might expect negative attitudes toward conventional religious involvement in the affairs of the world. On the other hand, the Family opposes secularism and might therefore hold positive attitudes.

One 1991 GSS item concerned religious censorship: "Some books or films offend people who have strong religious beliefs. Should books and films that attack religions be prohibited by law or should they be allowed?" Certainly the Family itself has often been the target of negative books, articles, and television documentaries. During the time I was engaged in active ethnography with the group, a Canadian television crew produced an hour-long documentary.[13] Because it approached the Family in an apparently open-minded and respectful manner, several members cooperated by giving interviews. But the completed documentary turned out to be an exposé that apparently exploited for commercial gain the former sexual radicalism of the group. Understandably, the members who had innocently contributed were sorely disappointed. Family members are more ready to prohibit antireligious material than are average Americans, 47.6 percent compared with 29.7 percent. Members of the general public are about three times as likely to say such material "definitely should be allowed, 27.9 percent compared with only 8.3 percent in the Family."

On the other hand, slightly more Family respondents could not choose one of the offered answers, 17.1 percent versus 11.8 percent. A young American woman expressed an ambivalence that others probably felt, saying a decision about a particular film or book properly "depends on the content, according to its own merits." Two other women were perplexed about the possible harm from such material: "If something hurts anybody it is bad and has a bad effect." "You will always be offending somebody no matter what you say!" A young woman born in India but living in France was unable to answer but felt antireligious books and films had a positive side, "as they're good sometimes as they test your faith." A man in Britain worried, "Banning may be a Pandora's box for other bans!" An American woman in Brazil had a similar concern, writing, "This is tough! If they're banned, what else would get banned? Freedom of speech?"

An older man in Belgium felt antireligious materials should not be banned, because "they help the End to progress," meaning that they may be part of the buildup to the final battle between Christ and Satan, and thus are a good sign. A Brazilian man opposed censorship, arguing, "Everybody has to choose what to see." An American woman in Australia remarked, "It's amazing how the Lord can turn persecution into praise!" She also cited Romans 8:28, an optimistic verse I frequently heard quoted in my visits to Family homes: "And we know that to them that love God all things work together for good, even to them that are called according his purpose."

A series of four items, also taken from the 1991 GSS, concern religious involvement in government. Table 5.5 shows that the Family is much more accepting of religious involvement in politics, and proportions of the two samples agreeing with four statements on this issue differ by ratios averaging two to one. Family members tend to agree that "Politicians who do not believe in God are unfit for public office" and that "It would be better for the country if more people with strong religious beliefs held public office." In contrast, members of

Table 5.5. Religion in Government

Agree or strongly agree that . . .	*Family*	*1991 GSS*
Politicians who do not believe in God are unfit for public office.	61.3%	28.9%
Religious leaders should not try to influence how people vote in elections.	35.1%	63.1%
It would be better for the country if more people with strong religious beliefs held public office.	74.1%	37.0%
Religious leaders should not try to influence government decisions.	15.4%	51.5%

The number of cases ranges from 1,010 to 1,014 for the Family, and from 1,334 to 1,337 for the General Social Survey.

the general public tend to agree that "Religious leaders should not try to influence how people vote in elections" and that "Religious leaders should not try to influence government decisions."

The proverbially longest legitimate word in the English dictionary is *antidisestablishmentarianism*, which refers to being against the separation of church and state. Apparently this word applies to many members of the Family, despite their distrust of the System. They want God to rule through godly leaders, rather than wishing to turn power over to the mainline churches.

Several respondents wrote comments next to the item about it being better for the country if more people with strong religious beliefs held public office. An American woman currently living in Romania exclaimed, "America was born and built on Christian leadership! Look at her now! God help us!!!" Like her, a Swiss man living in Italy strongly agreed, but he wrote, "I don't like religion! I hate religion! I'm not religious! I just do what the Lord told me: love God and your neighbor." Here again we see the Family's negative conception of conventional religion. Two respondents who agreed less strongly qualified the item about the office holder's religious beliefs with "if Godly" and "if it's strong beliefs in Jesus as Savior."

A Brazilian man who mildly disagreed remarked, "Churchianity no, but Christian yes." An Indian man also disagreed, saying it "depends what kind of religious faith it is. It has to be motivated by love." An Italian woman in Ukraine would not consider disbelievers really unfit for public office "unless they've rejected God and promote everything that the Bible is against." A Canadian man living in India strongly disagreed with the statement, explaining, "In India, where religious leaders have too much control, there is lots of strife. But in the West, I think it's a different case."

A Polish woman living in Russia expressed what must be the general opinion of Family members: "I'm not good with politics but I believe that people that are right, good religious people should influence the world for better, however possible." An Australian man was ready to give religion a greater influence with the state, "unless these 'religious' leaders are themselves guilty of utter intolerance, narrow-mindedness, and discrimination. In this case they should step aside and let a 'sinner' take over. He might be closer to God than they proclaim to be." He then cited the parable from Luke 18, in which a humble publican sinner receives God's mercy rather than a self-righteous Pharisee, "for every one that exalteth himself shall be humbled; but he that humbleth himself shall be exalted."

A final question about religion in public life from the 1991 GSS asked, "Do you think that churches and religious organizations in this country have too much power or too little power?" Family members expressed a wide range of opinions, but fully 31 percent could not choose among the responses offered them. If those who cannot choose are removed from the analysis, 30 percent of the Family feel that religious organizations have the right amount of power, compared with 59 percent of the American public. Family members are somewhat more likely both to feel the churches have too much and too little power, although fully 45 percent judge they have too much, compared with 23 percent of Americans.

We should consider these results in the context of real social conditions. Many Family homes are situated in nations where the church and state exist in a close alliance, and they may rightly attribute persecution they have experienced to the machinations of the churches. Among 220 respondents who live in the United States, fully 40 percent cannot choose a response to this item. Of those 132 who can choose, only 27 percent feel the churches have too much power, compared with 41 percent who feel they have too little. Outside the United States, fully 50 percent of Family members expressing a definite opinion believe that religious organizations have too much power, and just 21 percent believe they have too little.

The fact that nearly a third of Family respondents cannot choose which degree of power the religious organizations should enjoy undoubtedly reflects the quandary that conventional politics presents to them. They are torn between wanting a society that is governed by faith and rejecting the authority of the churches.

The World

Quite apart from feelings about societal leaders and institutions, members of radical religious groups may be suspicious of the material world in general, feeling that it is inherently corrupt. In 1985, the GSS contained a series of seven "world" items, two of which were also contained in the 1996 survey. These items are written in a complex format that seeks to avoid the "yeasaying" or "naysaying" bias mentioned above.

In the Family survey, this section begins with this GSS-derived preamble: "People have different images of the world and human nature. We'd like to know the kinds of images you have. Below are some sets of contrasting images. On a scale of 1–7 where would you place your image of the world and human nature between the two contrasting images?" The questionnaire has two statements about the world, separated by a "1 . . 2 . . 3 . . 4 . . 5 . . 6 . . 7" number scale. "Look at the first set of contrasting images. If you think that 'The world is basically filled with evil and sin,' you would circle the number 1. If you think 'There is much goodness in the world which hints at God's goodness' you would circle 7. If you think things are somewhere between these two you would circle one of these numbers: 2, 3, 4, 5 or 6. Where would you place your image of the world on the scale for . . . ?"

For example, in 1996 just 5.5 percent of GSS respondents marked number "1," indicating they completely thought "the world is basically filled with evil and sin" and did not feel at all that "there is much goodness in the world which hints at God's goodness." In contrast, 10.7 percent of Family respondents marked number "1" and felt the world was filled with sin and evil. At the other end of the scale, 13.8 percent of GSS respondents marked "7," indicating they completely felt that there is much goodness in the world, compared with only 3.8 percent of Family respondents. This complex response format balances the items, so that respondents who tend to be especially agreeable or disagreeable will not bias results.

Table 5.6 compares Family responses with data from the 1985 GSS, simplifying the data somewhat to increase comprehension. Among Family respondents, about 54 percent gave either a "1," "2," or "3" response to the first pair of statements, indicating they agree that "The world is basically filled with evil and sin." Roughly another 20 percent gave a "5," "6," or "7" response, indicating they agree with the other statement that "There is much goodness in the world which hints at God's goodness." The pattern of responses is almost exactly the opposite among GSS respondents, who are much more likely to feel the world is good rather than evil.

Table 5.6. Attitudes toward the World and Human Nature

Tend to agree with one or the other statement in a pair . . .	*Family*	*1985 GSS*
The world is basically filled with evil and sin.	54.2%	16.3%
There is much goodness in the world which hints at God's goodness.	19.8%	54.0%
Human nature is fundamentally perverse and corrupt.	64.2%	15.7%
Human nature is basically good.	11.8%	66.7%
The good person must avoid contamination by the corruption of the world.	24.7%	20.5%
The good person must be deeply involved in the problems and activities of the world.	41.4%	51.9%
God is almost totally removed from the sinfulness of the world.	20.1%	9.0%
God reveals himself in and through the world.	63.6%	64.1%
It is dangerous for a human to be too concerned about worldly things like art and music.	6.7%	8.5%
Through such things as art and music we learn more about God.	73.6%	69.0%
The world is a place of strife and disorder.	83.2%	33.8%
Harmony and cooperation prevail in the world.	3.1%	28.5%
Most human activity is vain and foolish.	35.4%	12.7%
Human achievement helps to reveal God in the world.	32.0%	67.0%

The number of cases ranges from 967 to 1,000 for the Family, and from 1,476 to 1,506 for the General Social Survey.

Each of the pairs of statements contains one that can be described as world-rejecting, and one that is world affirming. Family members are more likely to feel that the world is evil, sinful, corrupt, dangerous, vain, foolish, strife-ridden, and disorderly. On average across the seven items, they gave world-rejecting responses 41.2 percent of the time, and world-affirming responses only 16.6 percent of the time. GSS respondents, on the other hand, gave world-rejecting responses 35.0 percent of the time, and world-affirming responses 57.3 percent of the time.

Satisfaction and Happiness

Related to alienation from the world is the amount of satisfaction a person has in the community he or she lives in, and other aspects of his or her quality of life are relevant as well. Confidence in institutions and social trust are related to several aspects of personal satisfaction.[14] A heavily used set of items in the GSS asks respondents how much satisfaction they get from areas of life such as "the city or place you live in," "your family life," and "your health and physical condition."[15] Seven response choices ranged from "a very great deal" down to "none." Among the most powerful predictors of satisfaction is social class, measured by such things as income and education.[16] The lower social classes are not only deprived of material things, but they also have good reason to feel powerless and thus, alienated.

Among Family respondents, 24.7 percent said they were satisfied "a great deal" or "a very great deal" with the city or place they live in, compared with 46.5 percent of GSS respondents. Of course, we would not expect missionaries traveling throughout the world to be entirely comfortable with their momentary surroundings. They are also less satisfied with "nonworking activities" such as "hobbies," 34.4 percent compared with 56.9 percent. But members of the Family neither work at regular jobs nor have much in the way of personal hobbies, so it is hard to see how comparable this aspect of life might be across the two samples of respondents.

There is essentially no difference at all between the two samples in the percentage who have a great deal of satisfaction in their friendships, 68.6 percent in the Family and 69.2 percent in the American public. Both figures round off to 69 percent. One factor that works against satisfaction in friendships is high geographic mobility. Consider the situation of a seventeen-year-old girl, born in Spain but currently living in Switzerland, who has been with the Family in five other nations. She wrote that she was unhappy because "A lot of my friends left to other countries." The most memorable thing she recently did alone was "wrote some of my friends." A recent cause of happiness was that a "home in Thailand replied to my request to join them," so she is preparing to leave for that mission field. Family members appear somewhat less content with "family life," 64.9 percent being highly satisfied compared with 75.3 percent in the American public.

The literature on communal utopias stresses that the prime value of these social experiments is brotherhood, or essentially friendship.[17] Thus enthusiasts for communes might hope that more Family members than average Americans would be highly satisfied with their friendships and family life. Unlike the

Shakers of the nineteenth century, however, the Family is a missionary movement that actively promulgates its message throughout the world. Despite the fact that *The Love Charter* is a blueprint for life that members hope will maximize harmony and emotional closeness, the chief aim is winning souls for Jesus. Thus we can read different meanings into this 69 percent figure. Either the Family fails in achieving a more friendly life, or it succeeds in maintaining a friendly life despite the depredations of missionary life.

Religious involvement tends to enhance health among respondents to the GSS, but Family members show a very slight tendency to be less satisfied with their health, 49.9 percent compared with 56.2 percent.[18] Concerned that health varies throughout the life span, and the two samples do not have identical age distributions, I tried a somewhat complex age-adjusted analysis using a different measure. In many years, the GSS has asked, "Would you say your own health, in general, is excellent, good, fair, or poor?" Of 9,372 Americans who selected one of these choices from 1988 through 1996, and who also gave their years of birth, 31 percent said they were in excellent health, and only 5 percent were in poor health. Among 1017 members of the Family, 30 percent said they were in excellent health, and 2 percent in poor health. After doing the age-adjusted analysis, I found that there was a relative tendency of Family members to say their health was good, rather than excellent, but the differences were slight.

In 1991, the GSS asked, "If you were to consider your life in general these days, how happy or unhappy would you say you are, on the whole?" Of 1,355 Americans responding, 37 percent said "very happy," essentially the same as the 39 percent of 1,009 Family members who expressed great happiness. At the other end of the scale, less than 1 percent of each group said they were "not at all happy." In chapter 3 we saw that members of the Family feel somewhat closer to God than nonmembers, and chapter 4 showed that most of them experience communication with the divine. Research by Melvin Pollner, using GSS data from earlier years, found that interaction with spiritual or divine beings enhances happiness and satisfaction with life.[19] Using data from 1988, Christopher Ellison found that strong religious faith increases satisfaction and happiness.[20] We do not see much evidence of those effects here.

In 1996, the GSS asked: "In general, do you find life exciting, pretty routine, or dull?" Of 1,918 Americans, 50 percent said life was exciting, compared with 69 percent of 988 members of the Family. Perhaps Family life excels in the exciting challenges it offers missionaries, rather than ordinary happiness and satisfaction with the corrupt world.

Table 5.7. Determinants of Fate

Very important for how somebody's life turns out . . .	Family	1993 GSS
Such things are decided by God.	33.1%	23.3%
Some people are born with better genes than others.	2.7%	9.4%
Society gives some people a head start and holds others back.	10.5%	13.4%
Some people use their will power and work harder than others.	56.2%	57.1%
It's just a matter of chance.	1.6%	3.4%

The number of cases ranges from 999 to 1,010 for the Family, and from 1,594 to 1,596 for the General Social Survey.

Autonomy

After working his way through his data on urban communes, Benjamin Zablocki concluded that alienation should be reconceptualized in terms of a person's ability to make choices.[21] Thus we should consider the beliefs and experiences of Family members concerning the degree to which they have control over their own lives rather than being the victims of external forces.

In 1993, the GSS listed five possible "reasons why a person's life turns out well or poorly," asking respondents how important each one is "for how somebody's life turns out." As table 5.7 reveals, Americans tend to believe that people create their own fate. Fully 57 percent say that a "very important" reason for inequality is that "some people use their will power and work harder than others." In contrast, only 3 percent consider chance to be very important.

The Family holds very much the same view, with 56 percent saying will power is very important, and less than 2 percent saying chance is important. The fraction saying God is very important is significantly higher in the Family, 33 percent versus 23 percent, and the Family rates biology ("genes") and sociology ("society") lower than the American public does. But on the surface, something is strange here. The way the items were scored, nothing prevented a person from saying all five factors were very important; these were five separate questions, rather than a single item that required respondent to rank the choices. Indeed, the sum of the percentages is 104 for the Family, and 107 for the GSS respondents. Thus, nothing prevented all of the Family respondents from saying God is very important, and we might have expected them to do so.

However, the question does not merely refer to God's influence. Rather, it says, "Such things are decided by God." That statement simply does not match the way Family members and many other Christians think about human life. They are not Calvinists who believe God pre-ordains human fate. Rather, they believe that the all-powerful Lord gives people the freedom to choose.

Five members of the Family wrote revealing comments in the margin of the questionnaire beside this item: "A lot depends on our own decisions within God's will or out of it." "But we have a choice also, to do right or wrong." "Yes, our lives can be decided by God if we yield and let him lead." "A person who is yielded and obedient to God can overcome any obstacle." "God has a plan, but we need to make our personal choice and this is what determines the outcome."

Three others stressed human free will under God's law: "It mainly depends on your choice, if you choose to do right or wrong." "It's a matter of personal choice and God's plan for your life." "You can make the best out of each situation you're in. We all have gifts and talents and if used wisely can be a blessing for ourselves and for the help of others." One of those who considered will power to be most important qualified this judgment by saying, "along with their faith in God and His help."

Another Family member recognized that society had influence, but argued, "True, but it shouldn't affect our personal happiness, because that comes from our connection with God." Another explained, "We can think of 'chance' as an opportunity created by God, or at least circumstances set up, and the person confronted by it has his choices to make." Thus, within the Family, all of the other factors are compatible with God's gift of free will.

The 1991 GSS included seven agree-disagree items about the factors that govern human fate, three of which concern God. As table 5.8 shows, Family members are no more likely than GSS respondents to say, "The course of our lives is decided by God." However they are nearly twice as likely to say, "There is a God who concerns Himself with every human being personally," and more than twice as likely to say, "To me, life is meaningful only because God exists." This supports our analysis. God is fundamental to the Family's conception of life, but He is a Lord, not a dictator. He gives humans free will, and he cares about the choices each individual makes.

Very few respondents in either group believe people have no control over their lives or that life is meaningless. About a fifth of Americans, but much smaller fractions of Family membership, agree that only the person himself decides the course of fate or gives meaning to life. Several respondents wrote comments: "Even someone who doesn't 'believe' can find meaning in life if they do what God intends them to do." "Meaning in life comes from what we

Table 5.8. The Meaning of Life

Strongly agree . . .	*Family*	*1991 GSS*
The course of our lives is decided by God.	19.0%	17.6%
There is a God who concerns Himself with every human being personally.	88.7%	44.7%
To me, life is meaningful only because God exists.	60.0%	23.0%
There is little that people can do to change the course of their lives.	1.6%	4.3%
In my opinion, life does not serve any purpose.	0.5%	1.1%
Life is only meaningful if you provide the meaning yourself.	4.5%	21.7%
We each make our own fate.	7.2%	20.6%

The number of cases ranges from 999 to 1,010 for the Family, and from 1,282 to 1,309 for the General Social Survey.

put into it and what we do with it, how much we love and give. God is an important part of each person's life without which life and love are impossible." "God gave us the right of choice." "We have choices that determine if we have His blessings or not." "God gives us opportunities and we decide which ones to choose." "We have the choice. It is a gift of God."

Work Alienation

An important arena of autonomy or alienation is the world of work.[22] The 1991 GSS included several items measuring the respondent's degree of control in this realm. One offered four choices and told the respondent to check the box "indicating the one which best describes your job (the work you generally do)." Nearly a tenth of 895 employed Americans, 9.6 percent, reported, "Someone else decides both what I do and how I do it." This response represents a high level of work alienation, and only 2.5 percent of Family members selected it. Nearly a quarter of GSS respondents, 23.9 percent, said, "Someone else decides what I do, but I decide how I do it." This shows some autonomy, but gives power to a boss, and just 12.9 percent of Family respondents gave this answer. The most common response for both groups was, "I have some freedom in deciding what I do and how I do it." Among GSS respondents, 36.6 percent said this, compared with fully 61.8 percent of Family members. Finally, 29.8 percent of GSS respondents and 22.9 percent of the Family selected, "I am basically my own boss."

It is worth noting two things about these differences. First, members of the Family generally decide their work plans together, so nobody is either the boss or the employee. Thus the majority do indeed have considerable freedom, and are not alienated from their labor, even though they share decision making with the other members of their collective. Second, unlike the case in American society, there is no distinction between employed and unemployed members in the Family. Everybody is a missionary, sharing in the productive work of the home.

A man currently doing missionary work in Ireland explains, "My wife and I pray and counsel together." A woman in Venezuela said she was basically her own boss, "but strive to meet the need at hand which thus determines what I need to do and how to do it." A man in Indonesia said he had "lots of freedom but do council with others."

The 1991 GSS also asked how true each of three work-related statements was.[23] Only 19.3 percent of Family members said it was very true "I can work independently," compared with 45.9 percent of GSS respondents. Sociologists should not leap to the conclusion that being independent is a good thing, or that admitting one's interdependence with other people is a sign of alienation. Indeed, one could argue exactly the opposite. A woman in Venezuela said, "I'm a teacher and work with kids and other teachers." A father of ten commented, "With responsibility of a family obviously my decisions affect them greatly, so it is a sobering responsibility and requires a lot of prayer in making decisions. But no one is telling me what I should or shouldn't do. Just the Charter rules." From Japan, a woman wrote, "I like working with others and value the input, though I'm independent too." A Canadian woman said it was only "somewhat true" that she could work independently, admitting, "I need help." A Russian woman did not work independently at all: "In other words, I can but I don't want to. I'm bound to make mistakes."

About equal percentages, 38.2 in the Family and 33.4 percent of GSS respondents, said, "I have a lot to say over what happens on my job." More than half of Family respondents, 52.1 percent, felt the following was very true: "My job allows me to take part in making decisions that affect my work." Rather fewer, 35.6 percent, feel this degree of autonomy in the American public. Thus, while they may not be comfortable working independently, Family members feel that have a considerable degree of control over decisions that affect their work.

A Social World

Social science has often emphasized the relationship between the individual and "society," but the most crucial relationships are undoubtedly between individuals. In his influential books, *The Division of Labor in Society* and *Suicide*, the French sociologist Emile Durkheim wrote about anomie, the root concept of anomia and the distinctively sociological form of alienation. The extensive analysis in *Suicide* actually presents two forms of alienation: anomie and egoism. Both are forms of societal disintegration. They are characteristics of the entire society, rather than of the individual or of the small circle of relationships that surrounds the individual.

Anomie is a disruption of norms and values in the society, a cultural breakdown that degrades moral integration. Egoism is a disorganization of relationships, a breakdown of interpersonal bonds that erodes social integration. Durkheim's prime example of egoism is the disorder he sees in Protestant communities, compared with the supposedly more stable Catholic ones, and he does not connect religion with anomie. However, he could logically have argued that religion is a prime antidote to anomie, because it imbues life with meaning and promulgates coherent norms and values.

Durkheim's chief evidence for the existence of anomie comes not from survey data, or from anything else that directly examines the real lives of ordinary human beings, but from correlations between the suicide rate and economic trends. Durkheim notes that suicide rates are high during time of economic decline. This could simply reflect the despair experienced by a few susceptible individuals under times of increased stress, but Durkheim was not interested in the despair of individuals. He argued that anomie was a characteristic of the entire society, during times when standards were in flux, as they are during rapid economic change. He capped this argument with the observation that suicide rates rise not only in times of economic depression, but also in times of suddenly rising prosperity. Unfortunately for Durkheim, by the early 1950s it was quite clear that this observation was incorrect, and suicide rates do not zoom in boom times.[24]

For some strange reason, sociologists did not abandon the concept of anomie when empirical evidence showed that it was faulty. Perhaps they found the concept so useful in their competition with more individualistic sciences such as psychology that they were reluctant to lose it. Durkheim's fundamental argument in *Suicide* is that human behavior cannot be understood without reliance on distinctively sociological concepts that describe the society as a whole. Yet if our aim is the pursuit of truth rather than forging a rhetoric to aggrandize an academic profession such as sociology, we may be more ready to abandon concepts when they are proven false.[25]

My own sociological mentor, George Homans, argued that there is only one social science, and that its fundamental principles concern individual human beings in interaction with others.[26] The fundamental human group is the hunter and gatherer band, comparable in size to a communal home within the Family. For most of human existence, people lived in tiny groups of perhaps forty individuals, surviving by gathering food from nature, without benefit of agriculture or heavy industry, and frequently wandering. Such is life in the Family. All the heavy machinery of civilization, with its nations, corporations, and churches, is a later accretion built precariously on the foundation of small groups.

Thus the key problem is not how individuals may become alienated from society, but how large societies can exist beyond the individuals and small groups that constitute social reality. All human history can be viewed as a supremely difficult attempt to construct ever larger social orders. But from the standpoint of the individual, what really matters is the fellowship of a very small number of other individuals. The government levies taxes, and it defends the individual against military conquest by other governments. To that extent, the state is a protection racket, and individuals should have no fondness for it. From the ancient Greek and Roman republics to modern democratic nations, however, the state has depended largely on willing allegiance of a significant fraction of the population, on people who identify with the state and are ready to sacrifice for it. Within this system, members of the Family are free riders, untroubled by their lack of allegiance to the state so long as the state upholds principles of freedom of religion and refrains from persecuting them.

The data examined in this chapter support this conceptual framework. By some measures, the Family is more alienated than the general public, but by other measures it is less alienated. This reflects the fact that the general concept of alienation, like that of anomie, is seriously flawed. The Family has constructed its own social world, within which people may be more or less satisfied, have more or less control over their own lives. That microsociological realm is connected to the larger, somewhat chaotic system that surrounds it, but connected only loosely and only at certain points in the individual's experience of life. The great number of GSS items we have employed sketch a complex picture of social life within the Family and how it articulates with outside structures.

It is wrong to say that either the Family or the American public is alienated, because the concept of alienation is too crude to do justice to social reality. However, it cannot be denied that the conditions experienced by individuals do aggregate in some rough fashion to create a global social environment that may be relatively integrated versus disorganized. Although appearances may deceive, the late twentieth century seems to be a time of unusual religious creativity around the world, and it is reasonable to wonder why this might be true.

It may not be either alienation or anomie that generates new religions, but secularization. This process need not be the death of religion in general, but a sickness of particular religious organizations or of the hitherto dominant religious tradition. Sociologist Daniel Bell has suggested that the present era may be like the dawn of Christianity, but run in reverse.[27] Two thousand years ago, one religion arose triumphant out of a morass of competing cults. Now, besieged by science on one side and bureaucracy on the other, organized Christianity may be crumbling, creating gaps in which new religious movements arise. When they do, as in the case of Teens for Christ that grew into the Family, they arise as small groups of individuals whose social life consists primarily of their intimate relations with each other.

Successful new religions tend to share some of the most powerful culture of the dominant tradition of the society, as well as innovating in specific areas of belief and practice. Thus, the Family is not a counterculture but a culture. It is not merely an alienated reaction against the System, but a unique way of life. We see this in the complexity of the data concerning alienation in this chapter, and in the positive features of Family culture described in other chapters. Opponents and journalists tend to see this religious movement in terms of its deviance from conventional standards, but it deserves to be appreciated in its own right. It is a valid way of life for the people who have chosen to join it or remain within it, and significant features of this microculture may contribute to the development of new ways of life for some fractions of the general population in coming decades.

CHAPTER 6

Sexuality

The Family is famous for its unconventional orientation toward sex, yet we have seen that its religious beliefs are in many ways quite traditional. Religious communal movements tend to regulate sexual relations among members, which means greater unanimity but not necessarily greater conservatism.[1] This chapter will quantitatively document the group's sexual attitudes, illustrate how they function in actual lives with data from interviews, and place them in a theological context.

We begin by considering the background against which sexual relations are played out: the group's moral philosophy and the values it seeks in close friendships. We then examine the group's attitudes toward eroticism, sexuality, and marriage. The Family's practice of sexual sharing needs to be understood socially in terms of romantic instability and theologically in terms of the Law of Love.

Moral Philosophy

Over the years, the General Social Survey has included various items exploring the respondent's opinions about the philosophical roots of morality. Our questionnaire took four such items from the 1988 GSS, and three from 1991, measuring theistic versus relativistic orientations. Table 6.1 reveals that both groups of respondents are only lukewarm toward the idea that people "who violate God's laws must be punished," with slightly more Family members agreeing with this statement.

Several Family members wrote comments about this item: "Punished by God, not by us." "I strongly agree, but I also know that God is very loving and merciful." "Sometimes He forgives us, depends how much we love Him and if

117

Table 6.1. Moral Philosophies

Strongly agree . . .	*Family*	*GSS*
		1988:
Those who violate God's rules must be punished.	29.9%	22.0%
Right and wrong are not usually a simple matter of black and white; there are many shades of gray.	50.3%	40.0%
Morality is a personal matter and society should not force everyone to follow one standard.	23.7%	31.8%
Immoral actions by one person can corrupt society in general.	40.7%	18.1%
		1991:
Right and wrong should be based on God's laws.	65.8%	27.2%
Right and wrong should be decided by society.	0.4%	8.8%
Right and wrong should be a matter of personal conscience.	5.0%	14.0%

The number of cases ranges from 1,004 to 1,019 for the Family, and from 1,282 to 1,473 for the General Social Survey.

it was intentional!" "If they refuse to change or repent." "Or forgiven if sorry." "You can repent and be forgiven." "Depends on each situation. Do you mean harshly? God is not usually harsh." "If taught first and if they're Christian and committed themselves to a Christian standard in their life." "Sometimes our waywardness is punishment in itself." "Depends on their motive. God deals out punishment." "I leave that to God." One respondent cited Psalm 103, which says, "He hath not dealt with us after our sins, Nor rewarded us after our iniquities. For as the heaven is high above the earth, So great is his mercy toward them that fear him."

Interestingly, members of the Family are more likely than GSS respondents to feel "there are many shades of gray" in matters of morality, yet they are slightly less likely to feel that "morality is a personal matter." Three members expanded on the simple check-the-box responses: "I believe in the law of love. Do unto others as you would do to yourselves!" "When it affects others it's no longer just personal. But society can't necessarily decide everyone's morals, only God can." "But society has to at least give information that will help people to develop healthy morals, and not leave people ignorant." Family members are more than twice as likely to say that "immoral actions by one person can corrupt society in general."

These attitudes show a subtle mixture of liberal and conservative tendencies, and one possible source of this ambivalence is the two levels on which moral judgments of Family members take place. Within the group, there is great need for some level of conformity, in order for the group to survive. Yet the group requires a high degree of tolerance by the outside world, from whose standards it deviates.

The three 1991 items concern theories about the basis on which morality rests: God, society, or the individual. A majority of Family members strongly agree that morality rests on "God's laws." Few in both groups assert that morality is a social construction or personal preference, yet the fractions are smaller within the Family. There are alternate ways of interpreting these results. The findings are compatible with the observation that the Family is neither amoral nor immoral. Rather, it possesses a distinctive code of behavior, which members believe God endorses, even though it diverges in some respects from society's norms. Thinking back to the images of God described in Chapter 3, we should recall that members were less likely than outsiders to see God as a judge. While they do not accept moral relativism, they hope that the Lord will forgive occasional transgressions in those who sincerely love Him.

Friendship

Sexuality is a form of intimacy, so it is worth asking what Family members value in a close relationship. The 1993 GSS asked respondents to judge the importance of seven "qualities one might look for in a personal friend." The right-hand pair of columns in table 6.2 shows that for the first six items there is no real difference between the Family and the American public. From being cultured to being honest, the percentages range widely, yet the two groups stay together. Only on the last item, the importance of intelligence in a friend, is there a significant difference, with the Family valuing this quality far less.

It is not that the Family values stupidity, but purity of heart counts far more highly than cleverness.[2] Self-professed intelligence is a form of arrogance, and may be at the root of secularism. A so-called intelligent person tends to

Table 6.2. Qualities of a Friend

Very or extremely important in a friend . . .	*Family Men*	*Family Women*	*Family*	*1993 GSS*
Creative	29.5%	23.5%	26.0%	23.2%
Cultured	20.1%	20.2%	20.0%	20.6%
Dynamic	22.8%	21.1%	21.7%	19.1%
Fun-loving	63.9%	71.7%	68.5%	66.8%
Honest	94.3%	97.4%	96.2%	97.8%
Responsible	80.0%	85.4%	83.3%	88.9%
Intelligent	22.3%	21.5%	22.0%	48.7%
Spiritual	58.5%	64.2%		
Dedicated	78.3%	83.7%		
Romantic	29.3%	30.3%		
Strong	8.5%	17.8%		
Emotional	11.2%	12.5%		
Rich	2.3%	2.0%		
Conventional	2.7%	3.5%		
Sensual	25.9%	26.9%		

The number of cases ranges from 1,019 to 1,023 for the Family, from 399 to 404 for the men and 599 to 609 for the women, and from 1,591 to 1,595 for the General Social Survey.

analyze too much, pulling things apart mentally to see how they work, and thereby killing them. In that direction lies doubt, agnosticism, atheism.

The Family explains its low opinion of intellectuality in the "Carnal Reasoning" chapter of its compendium of biblical verses, *Word Topics*. This term means, "being guided by or trusting in our own human understanding, reasoning, logic, or experience, rather than by the Lord through prayer and His Word. . . . If we lean to our own understanding, we're doomed to disappointment and final failure."[3] Dozens of biblical citations are marshaled to prove these principles, for example, Proverbs 3:7: "Be not wise in thine own eyes: fear the Lord, and depart from evil." Isaiah 5:21: "Woe unto them that are wise in their own eyes, and prudent in their own sight!" Prov. 26:12: "Seest thou a man wise in his own conceit? There is more hope of a fool than of him." I Corinthians 3:18: "Let no man deceive himself. If any man among you seemeth to be wise in this world, let him become a fool, that he may be wise."

Because sexuality is a relationship between genders, table 6.2 compares responses from male and female Family members separately. One of the greatest deficiencies of the General Social Survey is that it is so costly that items must be kept to a minimum. To get a fuller picture of friendship values in the Family, I added eight more items, from spiritual to sensual. On average, women rated the fifteen items slightly higher, 38.8 percent of the women calling them very or extremely important, versus 36.6 percent for the men.

Just four sex differences achieve solid statistical significance. Men are more likely to want a friend to be creative, whereas women want one to be honest, dedicated, and strong. Marginal statistical significance is achieved by the slightly greater tendency of women to want a friend to be both fun-loving and responsible.[4] It is hard to see the gender difference of opinion about honesty in the table, because an overwhelming majority of both sexes consider this to be "very" or "extremely" important. However, 75.5 percent of the women said honesty was "extremely important," compared with 65.6 percent of the men.

Given the erotic stereotype of the Family, it is interesting to see that men and women do not differ in how important they feel it is for a friend to be romantic or sensual. We do not see in these numbers evidence that lusty men are overpowering meek women; rather we see sexual equality. It is a pity that these two items were not included in the General Social Survey, because it would be interesting to test the commonsensical hypothesis that one gender values these qualities more highly than the other in the general population. In any case, the Family does not have a sexual double standard.

Eroticism

When asked to describe things they had done or experienced recently, several members showed no inhibition against mentioning sex. A Frenchman in America said, "I gave a class on sexuality in the Bible to answer the questions somebody had on our beliefs." A woman was pleased to report, "I woke up in the middle of the night with my sweet, half-asleep husband on top of me! It was a nice surprise." Another woman said, "I had a sweet time of making love with my husband." A father of nine was happy he "had a super time loving up my wife"; a father of eleven said, "My wife was happy after our lovemaking and commented about it"; and a father of twelve was happy to report, "My wife and I had a sweet time making love together." An American in Ukraine said he "had an enjoyable time having sex." When asked to describe something they had done alone, some members admitted this was difficult because there was always someone with them. One man, whose wife happened to be away on a trip, was not ashamed to say that the most memorable thing he had recently done alone was "masturbated."

Traditional Christianity discouraged sexual indulgence and sought to spiritualize love. Christians were taught to believe that the passionate words exchanged between lovers in *The Song of Solomon* were really metaphors for faith in God. But in 1969 Father David published a MO Letter, "Scriptural, Revolutionary Love-Making," that explained they were poetic descriptions of sexual intercourse: "Let him kiss me with the kisses of his mouth: for thy love is better than wine." "Thy lips are like a thread of scarlet . . . Thy two breasts are like two young roes that are twins, which feed among the lilies." "My beloved put in his hand by the hole of the door, and my bowels were moved for him. I rose to open up for my beloved; and my hands dropped with myrrh, and my fingers with sweet smelling myrrh, upon the handles of the lock." In radical millenarian communities, especially as they mature over the early years of their existence, sexuality and family love pose great challenges. "For love is strong as death; jealousy is cruel as the grave: the coals thereof are coals of fire, which hath a most vehement flame."[5]

Historically, religious communal utopias have often experimented with radical systems of sexual relations.[6] People who are ready to give up this world are often lonely, disappointed souls. Either they lack love, or love imposes a tremendous burden because they are too poor to afford a home for their children, too sick to rejoice with their lover, or too often rejected by those they love. Even just the thought of terrestrial love may bring tears to their eyes. But any religious movement that endures for more than a few weeks draws to itself many people who seek love and are entirely capable of experiencing it.

By proclaiming that the wicked world will soon be destroyed, millenarians express disdain toward nonmembers, and the world responds with anger. When members of a group have hostile relations with outsiders, their relations with fellow members tend to intensify, often becoming passionately loving.[7]

Love between members of radical religious movements threatens group solidarity, however. A pair of lovers is a rudimentary conspiracy. In the intimacy of their embrace they can share feelings of dissatisfaction about the movement, and their commitment to each other becomes greater than the commitment each feels to the leadership. It is often easier for an entire family to defect than for an individual, if only because a family takes most of its love relationships with it when it leaves the movement, whereas an individual would have to forsake all loved ones. Thus, the leaders of these movements have developed various strategies to prevent the emergence of exclusive love relationships and to harness love to the goals of the group.[8]

There are three unusual ways that millenarian communities can handle sexuality and family affection. First, they can suppress carnal love, forbidding sexual intercourse and separating parents from their children. This was the strategy followed by the Shakers for most of their history, and it leads surely to slow extinction.[9]

Second, they can focus most of the love on charismatic leaders. Examples are Jim Jones of the People's Temple and David Koresh of the Branch Davidians.[10] As these two examples suggest, focusing too much of a group's love on a single individual can lead to exceedingly pathological results.

Third, a community can adopt forms of group marriage that give members erotic experiences with many other individuals, and it can adopt communal child-rearing. Among millenarian groups, one documented example is the Process, which said that sexuality was the glue that held them together, and each senior Processean could have multiple sex partners.[11] The best-known "free-love" commune was Oneida, which was utopian but not millenarian, where individuals were encouraged to transfer their erotic love constantly from one partner to another.[12]

Unlike Oneida, the Family encourages permanent marriage and does not attempt to pull adult lovers apart. However, it not only practices sexual sharing within the communal homes but experimented for a decade with a sexual ministry that provided orgasms as well as Bible reading to more than two hundred thousand outsiders.

The Family has published a series of first-person stories by men whose souls were saved in this way. In one, Stephen explained, "After a stern Catholic upbringing, my drug years led me into a world of promiscuity and indiscriminate sex, which I found equally unfulfilling. In the Protestant churches I felt uneasy with the often unspoken but clearly evident opinion that sex was somehow inherently 'dirty' and 'nasty.'" A woman in the Family healed his wounded soul through a spiritual form of sexual therapy. "I guess what so impressed me was the absolutely clean, pure attitude Carol had towards our lovemaking. Nudity and sex were suddenly completely natural, as I saw things through her eyes. We prayed together, talked, and lay in each other's arms for hours in real heart-to-heart communication."[13]

As we have seen, the Family arose in the late 1960s as an amalgam of the late-sixties youth counterculture and the traditional Holiness movement. Both of these sources emphasized powerful, personal emotions that could energize intense love. Members of the Family are convinced that sexual intercourse, unless of a type explicitly forbidden in the Bible, is not sinful.[14] From biblical passages such as Matt. 22:36–40, Galatians 5:14, Gal. 5:22–23, and Titus 1:15, Father David deduced the Law of Love, that any harmless act performed in God's love and with the consent of those involved, is good.[15] We shall now see how this doctrine is reflected in members' attitudes today.

Sexual Attitudes

The counterculture of the late 1960s disagreed with traditional Protestantism about the propriety of sex outside of marriage, and the Family has achieved an interesting combination of the two perspectives, condoning extramarital sex if it channels God's love. The 1994 GSS included four questions about nonmartial sex. Two concerned premarital sexual intercourse: "Do you think it is wrong or not wrong if a man and a woman have sexual relations before marriage?" "What if they are in their early teens, say under sixteen years old? In that case is it . . . always wrong, almost always wrong, wrong only sometimes, or not wrong at all." Several studies show that conventional religion is a significant factor encouraging disapproval of premarital sex.[16]

Table 6.3 shows that more than a quarter of Americans reject premarital sex among adults, compared with less than one percent of respondents to our Family survey. A man with ten children who thought premarital sex might be wrong sometimes explained, "If some third party is hurt emotionally, then it's not done in love."

Disapproval rises to more than two third of the general public if the individuals involved are under sixteen, and nearly a fifth of Family members also consider early sex to be always wrong. The man just quoted could not decide, saying it "depends how far it goes. Kids experiment. It's not allowed in the Family according to the Charter, but who knows? In an ideal society governed by love it might be considered perfectly normal. Millennium?"

A mother of twelve who thinks sex between young teenagers is always wrong said, "They can kiss and feel but not make love." A forty-year old mother with one child said it was almost always wrong, "unless it's only kissing and caressing." The father of one child felt it was wrong only sometimes, saying, "It would be good to have parental oversight and [be] kept in balance and not go 'all the way' unless contemplating marriage." A father of four could not answer the question, but explained, "It depends how far they go! Generally speaking, not all the way sex should be permissible."

The third item in table 6.3 concerns extramarital sex, traditionally considered the crime of adultery. One of the Ten Commandments proclaims,

Table 6.3. Attitudes toward Nonmarital Sex

Always wrong if . . .	Family	1994 GSS
A man and a woman have sexual relations before marriage?	0.3%	26.5%
What if they are in their early teens, say under 16 years old?	18.7%	68.3%
What about a married person having sexual relations with someone other than his or her husband or wife?	1.2%	78.4%
And what about sexual relations between two adults of the same sex?	55.0%	62.9%

The number of cases in ranges from 1,003 to 1,019 for the Family, and from 1,358 to 1,361 for the General Social Survey.

"Thou shalt not covet thy neighbor's wife" (Exodus 20:17). Yet the forms of marriage described in the Bible, and the limits of acceptable sexual behavior, are in many respects different from those that most Americans understand to be scriptural today. For example, the third and eleventh chapters of 2 Samuel make clear that the biblical David had several wives and also consorted with other men's wives, notably Bathsheba.

Fully 78 percent of Americans consider "a married person having sexual relations with someone other than his or her husband or wife" to be always wrong. Previous research based on the General Social Survey reveals that disapproval is significantly greater among religious conservatives.[17] But among members of the Family, only about 1 percent reject extramartial sex under all conditions. Two respondents who considered it wrong only sometimes explained this means "when not according to God's law of love" or "without consent." Another said, "If it hurts no one and is done according to the Law of Love, then it's fine." A man with six children said extramarital sex was not wrong at all "if it's done in love with the consent of the other party."

It is important to realize that religion influences attitudes only when the attitude in question is salient to the particular religious tradition and its teachings. For example, data from the GSS demonstrate that religiousness discourages alcohol drinking among Protestants but not among Catholics, because the two traditions have historically differed over this issue, and American Catholicism was not involved in the anti-alcohol Temperance Movement.[18] Other

GSS-based research shows that the power of religion to discourage sexual permissiveness varies across denominations.[19]

The final item in table 6.3 concerns "sexual relations between two adults of the same sex." About 63 percent of Americans feel that homosexual relations are always wrong, and religious conservatives respond even more negatively, considering homoerotic behavior to be sinful rather than a legitimate personal choice.[20] Again we see that members of the Family are less likely to feel that unconventional sexual activity is wrong, but the difference is narrower, just under 8 percentage points.

However, this is a case where responses to a simple fixed-choice-survey item definitely do not tell the entire story. Several family members wrote in the margins of the questionnaire to explain that homosexual relations between men are always wrong, but not always wrong between women. As one man explained, "Sodomy is always wrong. Lesbianism is unnatural but occasional woman-woman sexual relations is not forbidden by scripture if done in love."

Marriage

If nonmarital sex is often appropriate within the Family, we can ask how members feel about the institution of marriage. Table 6.4 collects a number of agree-disagree items about marriage, divorce, and sexuality from three years of the GSS: 1988, 1994, and 1996. This table combines "agree" and "strongly agree" responses. Few respondents in either group consider personal freedom more important than the companionship of marriage. We see that members are less likely than the American public to agree that "married people are generally happier than unmarried people," 30 percent compared with 45. Of course, the primary social unity that members live in is not the nuclear family but the Family home, and the primary social relationship is not marriage but membership in the group.

Hardly any members of the Family agree that "the main advantage of marriage is that it gives financial security," just 1 percent compared with about 17 percent of the public. Financial security is not a high value for the Family, because members believe "the Lord will provide," few hold regular jobs, and their homes require relatively little money to sustain. Indeed, the meaning of "security" is problematic for a group that looks forward in positive anticipation to the end of the world.

Three of the dozen homes I visited consisted of a married couple, their children, and other members who looked to the couple for leadership. In each

Table 6.4. Marriage-Related Attitudes

Agree . . .	Family	GSS
		1996:
Personal freedom is more important than the companionship of marriage.	7.7%	14.6%
		1994:
Married people are generally happier than unmarried people.	30.2%	45.2%
The main advantage of marriage is that it gives financial security.	1.2%	16.9%
It is better to have a bad marriage than no marriage at all.	2.4%	3.1%
Divorce is usually the best solution when a couple can't seem to work out their marriage problems.	39.8%	47.3%
It is alright for a couple to live together without intending to get married.	80.5%	41.3%
It's a good idea for a couple who intend to get married to live together first.	92.6%	33.1%
A pregnant woman should be able to obtain a legal abortion for any reason whatsoever, if she chooses not to have the baby.	3.8%	44.4%
		1988:
Homosexual couples should have the right to marry one another.	3.1%	11.7%
Couples don't take marriage seriously enough when divorce is easily available.	72.4%	64.4%

The number of cases ranges from 1,015 to 1,020 for the Family, and from 1,366 to 1,458 for the General Social Survey.

case the couple appeared to be confident, effective missionaries with a long history of successfully dealing with practical challenges. Since the time the survey was administered, the number of homes has increased, and the average size has decreased, so there are undoubtedly many homes like these three. However, members need not depend on a spouse for support, and I have observed a number of women with children living in a home without a husband, apparently as secure as any of the couples. This is not to say that marriage provides no security, but merely to note the profoundly rich social environment that surrounds couples in the Family.

Few respondents agree with the idea that "it is better to have a bad marriage than no marriage at all," and the difference between the groups is neither significant nor worth discussing. Two items about divorce give far more meaningful distributions of responses. Slightly more members of the general public than of the Family agree "divorce is usually the best solution when a couple can't seem to work out their marriage problems." In the margin of his questionnaire, a man with seven children wrote, "temporary separation first." A mother of eight children wondered about divorce: "What else is left if they can't work things out in a loving manner?" But a woman with six children opposed divorce, urging instead "love, humility, prayer." A mother of five wrote, "Each situation is different. I could have given up years ago on my marriage when it was rocky, but love, prayer and humility solved our problems."

Slightly more Family members than GSS respondents believe "couples don't take marriage seriously enough when divorce is easily available." Perhaps the most important thing to note about this item is that answers from both groups cover the full range of available responses. Thus, there is no "party line" about divorce in the Family. The differences on divorce items are statistically significant but really small, between 7 and 8 percentage points, showing slightly higher opposition to divorce in the Family.

Religious conservatives tend to oppose divorce, and despite the Family's unusual attitudes toward extramarital sex, it is possible that this factor weakly discourages divorce. However, there is a social factor that may be stronger, the great opportunities for separation rather than divorce. It is relatively easy for married couples to separate in the Family, simply by living for a time in different homes. Indeed, couples who are absolutely committed to each other often find that their work takes them to different places for a period of weeks or even months. No stigma is attached to being apart, and a couple need not even articulate to themselves any dissatisfaction with their relationship before temporarily separating. I should not imply that separation is trivial, because there can be many practical barriers, and couples undoubtedly vary in the degree to which their situations facilitate or inhibit it. Members of the Family do occasionally get divorced, for example, when one member wishes to marry someone else. But the availability of many options for informal separation, plus norms encouraging intimacy outside of marriage, may reduce the necessity for divorce.

In table 6.3 we saw that the Family was far less likely than the general public to condemn premarital sex, and table 6.4 contains two items that phrase the issue more positively. Almost twice as many members of the Family (about 81 percent compared with 40 percent) agree that "it is alright for a couple to live together without intending to get married." And almost three times as many (93 percent versus 33 percent) say "it's a good idea for a couple who intend to get married to live together first." Of course the implications of these two statements are quite different for The Family and the outside world. Members often live together in the same commune during courtship, at least initially without having sexual relations. A sexual relationship within a commune, even one that endures, need not imply marriage.

Table 6.3 revealed apparently slightly less condemnation of homosexuality within the Family than outside, but we explained that this resulted from the particular wording of the question ("always wrong") and the fact that the Family does not officially condemn erotic experiences between females. Table 6.4 includes an item about homosexual marriages, and here we see more clearly the group's opposition, only about 3 percent saying "homosexual couples should have the right to marry one another." Under 12 percent of the general public approves of same-sex marriages, but this figure is far enough from zero to reveal differences across gross religious categories.

As members of the Family interpret it, the Bible prohibits male homosexuality. The GSS item about the Bible offers three choices: (1) "The Bible is the actual word of God and is to be taken literally." (2) "The Bible is the inspired word of God but not everything in it should be taken literally, word for word." (3) "The Bible is an ancient book of fables, legends, history, and moral precepts recorded by man." Among GSS respondents who have a literal interpretation of the Bible, only 5.6 percent believe "homosexual couples should have the right to marry one another," compared with 12.8 percent of those who merely consider it to be inspired, and 25.1 percent of those who say the Bible is a book of fables. As we saw in chapter 3, members of the Family are not entirely of one mind about the literal truth of everything in the Bible, but here we see their attitude toward gay marriages is like that of biblical literalists.

Among the most serious social controversies relating to marriage and sexuality is the question of abortion. Numerous studies have shown that traditionally religious people are more likely than others to reject abortion.[21] Over the years the GSS has contained several questions about abortion, asking whether it was appropriate under various circumstances. In table 6.4 we see that less than 4 percent of Family members believe "A pregnant woman should be able to obtain a legal abortion for any reason whatsoever, if she chooses not to have the baby." This contrasts with 44 percent of the American public.

Several Family respondents explained their opposition to abortion: "It's killing—I was a nurse!" "The Lord gave her the child." "Adoption rather than abortion!" "She should know that by having abortion she's actually killing someone." A fifteen year old girl commented, "I believe in abortions only if a woman was forced against her will or for medical reasons. If there was nothing stopping her from using a contraceptive, then she should know that's what happens."

Several studies have examined the way that ideologies about different aspects of sexuality fit together in a way that reinforces the conventional influences of religion. Some people may oppose abortion on "right to life" grounds, whereas others oppose sexual promiscuity and believe that easy abortion would encourage it. In many people's minds, abortion is stereotyped as a response to unwanted pregnancy resulting from premarital sexual activity, but a more fundamental response should be avoiding premarital sex. People who favor large families could be expected to feel that having the baby is a better alternative than abortion. Conventionally religious people thus are quite consistent to oppose premarital sex and abortion, and to favor large family size.[22] Thus it will be interesting to see in the final chapter of this book how the Family feels about the connection between sex and childbearing. However, we must first examine more closely the Family's sexual beliefs and behaviors.

Sharing

Few of the people I have interviewed with the Family participated in the flirty-fishing sexual ministry, and the group abandoned the practice several years ago. However, this remarkable form of ministry is a distinctive part of Family history, revealing the limits of love-giving, and thus deserves discussion.

David Millikan, an Australian minister and author, interviewed two members about their FFing experiences in Hong Kong. Ammi told him that she and other young women witnessed for Christ at The Mandarin Hotel and The Captain's Bar, and she eventually had sex without about fifty men she met in this way, always trying to pray with them and share the Word, as well as meeting their physical and emotional needs. "There were so many lonely travelers." Joan said, "We did our best to love them and let the love of Jesus come through us to them."[23]

Miriam Williams has published an autobiographical account of her own experience FFing in the Family, and despite her publisher's insistence on promoting it as a lurid exposé, she acknowledges her own willing acceptance of the practice: "I had decided to belong to a social experiment called the Family, and this was just another variable; no one was twisting my arm. And. how would we ever start a new society if everyone balked at each new experiment? Sure, it seemed strange and deviant, but that is what living over the edge is about."[24] In 1987, the Family discontinued FFing, partly for health reasons and possibly also because the practice gave their enemies an excuse to persecute them.

Interviews I did with two women who practiced FFing provide some idea what the experience was like and also sketch the sexual sharing within the Family that continues to this day. Mindful of the persecutions the Family has experienced in many nations, I will call them X and Y.

When Father David announced the new ministry of love, X belonged to a Family commune in a nation ruled by a military dictatorship, so they had to proceed discretely. She was twenty-two years old when she started FFing with Hafez who was seventy-five. "He had lost his wife and gotten very bitter. He had three daughters, and after the wife died when he divided up the estate, the sons-in-law tried to swindle him out of the left-over money that would be for his upkeep." Hafez "was going through a very difficult time." Grief over the loss of his wife contributed to a long period of illness, and when he came out of the hospital he met the Family. "We spoke to him about the Lord. He had never really believed in God, so for him it was a special time." For most of his life, Hafez had been very wealthy, with a chain of supermarkets and servants, but now he had lost almost everything. "He was the first person that I got close to on an FFing level and had a sexual relationship with. I used to visit him two times a week. He was a very lonely man. I was pretty worried about him, too, because he lived on his own and was elderly."

FFing was meant not merely to satisfy the man's worldly emotional needs, but to help him develop a relationship with the Lord through reading the Bible and participating in religious fellowship. "Hafez was always very, very thankful for all the love and attention, not just from me but from the whole Family. We had Church of Love meetings every week, where several of these men we were witnessing to would come. He thanked my husband for being willing to share me with him. We always had new people that we were witnessing to, not necessarily through FFing, and he would get up and give a testimony to everybody about how Father David and the Family's love had changed his life. He would say how he was always such a proud man and had everything, but God had to show him how all that was worth nothing."

X vividly recalled the hesitation she felt "the first time that we got to the point where I felt that I needed to have a sexual encounter with him, to show

him the Lord's love. He was missing an arm and an eye he had lost in his childhood, and he had a false arm on I didn't notice even. When the time came and
he had taken it off, it was a little bit scary! I was quite shocked, when it happened, but I didn't want him to see that. I excused myself and went to the bathroom. I just prayed. I got in the bathroom, kneeled down on the floor and was
just praying. 'God, you've got to help me get over my feelings about this!' As I
prayed I had a vision of him in heaven. He was like a younger man, and I saw
that he was whole. In God's eyes he was a whole person. It was just a little physical thing. So, after that those feelings disappeared. That whole experience with
him taught me a lot, as a young person, about love for others, unselfish, caring
love. There is a whole lot more to FFing than just sex, there was the love behind
it and giving to others."

Some of the men who received the Lord's love provided material help to
the Family, but sometimes they also received aid from the Family. When Musa,
one of the other elderly men, underwent heart surgery and needed many trans-
fusions, members of X's Family home provided the lifesaving blood. Leo was a
totally bald Egyptian Jew who ran a travel agency, a sweet man who frequently
took members out to dinner or brought food to the home.

"Hafez would take me shopping every two weeks, maybe to the supermarket and tell me, 'Take whatever you want for the home.' So we would go
through the supermarket, and that was how we kept our home stocked, because
he was so sweet." After a while Hafez contributed part of the rent, as did some
of the other men, and he would help if there were a need for doctors. "He felt
he was too old to do much for the Lord anymore, but he knew we were, so it
was his way of supporting the Lord's work." As the channel for God's love, X
transformed the man's life. "He believed that God loved him. He continued
on in that way until he passed away, firm in God's love."

Not all the men involved in FFing were as loving souls as Hafez, Musa,
or Leo. One day X was witnessing on the street with Ruth, whose feet began
bleeding, so X stopped a car to ask for help getting home. The driver turned out
to be a retired general who was vice president of an influential military club.
"He wanted to see me again after that, so we went together a few times to see
him. His office was about the size of this whole bottom floor of our house and
had huge paintings. He would call the butler in, who would bring anything
you wanted to eat or drink. Eventually we ended up having more of a relationship which lasted for about a year. I actually ended it, because I was talking to him about the Lord, and trying to get him to receive the Lord. He was
quite a hard character, and he wasn't really accepting the Lord." The General
never contributed materially to the Family, but it was his spiritual selfishness

that convinced X she should stop FFing with him and invest her witnessing efforts elsewhere.

I will call the other woman I interviewed about FFing Y. She experienced flirty-fishing during a period when she and her husband were supporting themselves with odd jobs, living in her mom's California house as her step-father was dying of melanoma. Her husband was a former drug dealer whom Y had married in the Family, and for a time they had been "shepherd" leaders in Mexico. But he misspent "the Lord's money" hiring prostitutes for himself, and they entered a rough period, constantly leaving and reentering the group. "I always forgave him, and I really loved him," she recalls. "We were very close, almost like best friends. Both Capricorns, the same sign, almost too much alike." Discouraged, they returned to her mother in the United States, receiving Father David's literature but otherwise uninvolved with the Family.

Y says that Father David was a great teacher about sex. "When you're growing up you hear from your peers about sex, but there was so much we didn't know, like how to satisfy each other. There was a tape. I think it was called 'Revolutionary Love Making.'" When Y married within the Family, she and her husband were given a copy of this talk by Father David. Her husband had been married before, but admitted to Y that he had never helped his first wife achieve sexual climax. Y recalls, "The things we learned listening to that tape made all the difference in the world." Father David "was always so open and honest, telling us how to make sure each other is happy, and that sex is not something that is hidden or dirty." Then they began having fellowship with members who lived not far away, and they learned about the new FFing ministry.

"The FFing that we did ourselves was just with friends we met. Like we managed an apartment, so we knew some couples. There was a couple that lived next door to us. I would go share with the husband, and he would go share with the wife. They were real fat! It would really be such an encouragement to them to know that somebody could love them. It was very difficult for us. We didn't enjoy it, but sharing love with them made a really big change in their lives."

Y and her husband began cleaning homes for a living, and one of their customers had a huge dairy that milked a thousand cows a day. "That was how we met one of the workers, who had a little house, where he lived alone, and I shared with him a few times. He got saved, and we witnessed to him. My husband would give him Bible classes, and I guess it was overwhelming to him that my husband would share me with him, too, to show him God's love." Despite eight years of marriage, and an active sex life when she had been a "hippie" before joining the Family, Y had never become pregnant. But now she discovered that she was going to have this dairy worker's baby. "I was just so excited! It was such an exciting thing for me!"

After her step-father's death, Y and her husband rejoined the Family and returned to Mexico. She and her husband separated; he married a Mexican member and moved to Guatemala, taking Y's young son with him temporarily. Much of her time was occupied by office work, and she became one of the Family's most trusted secretaries. Now single, she would occasionally have sex with one or another male member. "I would tell a brother, if he was single, and I knew that he hadn't had a date for a while, I would offer to be with him. Probably even weekly." This was the Family custom called *sharing*. "It was out of an outgoing concern, making sure that the men had their needs met. And it was fun, too, you know. I enjoyed it. It was fun being with different people. It was a very fun fellowship time. The sex part's not very long, but usually it's a time when you really pour out your hearts to each other, just have fun having somebody to talk to and be close to, hold in each other's arms. It's the time when you really get to know somebody in a special way."

Thus she became pregnant for her second time, this time giving birth to a girl. The father "was a brother that I wasn't in love with or anything. I became a single mommy. Had my baby." Five years later, the same thing happened with another man. "With him I would have regular weekly dates. We had fun together. But it wasn't anything that we wanted to make serious. We were just close, very close friends and all." So when her third child and second son was born, there was no thought of marrying his father.

She says, "My children all know who their fathers are. I've never hidden anything from them. We're very open and honest about it. My girl writes her father. He likes to consider her his daughter. My youngest son's daddy is in Europe, and he has gotten to see him a few times, when he has come over here. He just saw him recently, and he bought him a bicycle." Although their fathers are still members of the Family, they live far away. "I've asked them sometimes, 'Are you sad you don't have a daddy here?' And they always say, 'No, mom, we like it just the way it is.'"

Instability

The data from our questionnaire do not allow us to determine whether the divorce rate of Family members differs from that of the American public or ordinary citizens of the nations where many members live. I decided that a simple

GSS question about whether respondents were married, separated, divorced, or widowed would not capture the potential complexity of their marital histories, and a lengthy battery of items might discourage respondents from completing the survey. Given the intimate living conditions within the communal homes, and the great geographic mobility of members, one might expect a significant degree of instability in sexual relationships. The doctrines of Fundamentalist Protestantism would seem to strengthen marital bonds, but research based on the GSS indicates that rates of marital dissolution are unusually high among Fundamentalists.[25]

A few responses to the open-ended questions that began the survey concerned romantic tensions or divorce. A mother of six was unhappy because "Two of my teen girls fell in love with the same boy and quarreled about it." A young woman with one child lamented, "I had to choose between being with the father of my baby or staying in the Family." Another young woman brooded, "My friend left the Family and her boyfriend left her alone with their baby." A middle-aged father of five children was unhappy because, "I received some e-mail from my wife pressing me to send in papers consenting to terminate our marriage." A young mother of two children wrote, "Called an embassy to check on my divorce papers. Wrote a warm letter to my former mate explaining about progress of our divorce."

Often members are able to achieve friendly relations with their ex-spouses. A father of three children who lives with his current wife was pleased: "I was able to begin communicating with my daughters. They've been living with my ex-wife." A mother of ten children was made unhappy by "Learning that my former husband's condition is considered terminal. Helped my children call and speak with their father who is dying of cancer." A woman in America "Ate a nice meal with my ex-husband visiting from Russia."

The potential complexity of romantic relationships was illustrated by three of the comments written by a mother of four: "Had a very pleasant conversation with my ex-husband and his wife." She was unhappy recently because "My fiancé broke our one-year engagement." But she had also had a good time when she "Saw my close friend and lover for a special day."

I have observed much tenderness between husbands and wives, in my visits to Family homes, and some was expressed in the questionnaire. A mother of ten children was happy when "My husband came home with some white roses for me." A woman without children was made very happy by "receiving a bouquet of red roses and a beautiful birthday card from my husband." Young people, just beginning to think about dating, experience all the romantic excitement of traditional American teenagers. For example, a seventeen-year-old girl in Russia was happy to report she recently "got my first real kiss."

Certainly many of the marriages in the Family are as solid as any in the outside world, and I interviewed several couples who had been with each other for many years. Yet for some of the men, personal relationships are unstable within the overarching stability of their relationship to the Family. When I interviewed a man I will call Z, he had moved many times and lived in many nations. He had loved many women, engendering children he would not raise and helping to raise children he had not sired. Despite this fluidity, the Family provided an underlying meaning that he could draw on whenever his life needed to be reconstructed, which it frequently did. Every once in a while, as he saw it, the Lord would send him a message, reminding him that his life was in divine hands. Even an adventurer must ultimately surrender to God.

At one point, he had separated from a woman with whom he had fathered three children, and he was falling too deeply in love with a single woman who had three children of her own. They would have a sexual-sharing date one evening each week. "She was really in love with me, but she was afraid of getting hurt, because she had been hurt so many other times by other Brothers." She and the leadership of the commune they lived in urged Z to cool off his passions and get his "eyes on the Lord." But he would not listen, and was terribly jealous whenever she would be with another Brother, so the Lord sent him a message he could not ignore.

"I was working on my car, in the back of the property one day. I had it up on some car ramps, and I had turned the tape player on. I was back there by myself. I was under the car, on a dolly, trying to put the exhaust pipe back together up by the engine. I was thinking about her. That's all I could think about—when I would see her next—murmuring against the Lord in my heart, saying 'Why can't we be together? Why can't we have two or three dates a week, instead of just one?' Next thing I know, the car comes down on top of me, and crushes me! The car came down slowly off of the ramps, and the frame rested on my chest, and crushed me! I couldn't move, and I freaked out and started twisting to pull myself out, but I couldn't get out from under it. I could breathe by a miracle, but I ripped all the ligaments in my chest, trying to get out from underneath this car." After struggling fruitlessly for two or three minutes, he heard the voice of the Lord telling him to pray. "I stopped, and I relaxed for a minute. Then I just started praying, 'Jesus, please help me through this!'" Then he began yelling for help, but with the tape player blaring, no one could hear him.

Eventually, one of the commune leaders went to close a window, and heard him faintly. Considering this incident to be a message from God, and a miracle of both bodily and spiritual salvation, Z recovered from his injuries. Like some others in the Family, his life would appear to an outsider as a series of blunders, as his love affairs form and dissolve, nations expel or admit him seemingly at random, and he stumbles impulsively through life. But to Z, himself, life has meaning. In retrospect and in prayer, he is constantly discerning what God meant by the experiences given him. "God opens one door and shuts another."

The Law of Love

When a Pharisee lawyer tempted Jesus by asking him to state the most fundamental commandments, according to Matt. 22:34–40, Jesus replied: "Thou shalt love the Lord thy God with all thy heart, and with all thy soul, and with all thy mind. This is the great and first commandment. And a second like unto it is this, Thou shalt love thy neighbor as thyself. On these two commandments hangeth the whole law, and the prophets." This is the Law of Love.

The Love Charter urges all members to "live by the principles of the Law of Love: To love and care for, and interact lovingly and harmoniously with all members of the Home in which they reside and with Family members at large."[26] This Golden Rule should govern all aspects of members' lives, and it is not merely the principle of sharing sexual love. By living the Law of Love, members believe they become free of all other biblical laws. Thus, there is no longer a specific prohibition against adultery. However, if sexual relations between a married person and someone other than the spouse would hurt the spouse, then it violates the Law of Love and is wrong.[27]

A book-length treatise on the Law of Love, published as eleven issues of the Family's internal publication *Good News*, gives the fundamental justification for sexual sharing: "Helping those in need is part of love, and when one is in need of sexual love, supplying that need is fulfilling the Lord's commandment to love. We believe in sacrificial love for the sake of our brothers and sisters, and part of that love is sharing sexually, opening our arms of love to each other. If for no other reason, we should share out of obedience to the Lord, and His Word, and a desire to please the Lord. 'Inasmuch as ye have done it unto one of the least of these My brethren, ye have done it unto Me' (Matt. 25:40)."[28]

There may be several reasons why the Family ended the FFing ministry. Increased awareness of the danger of sexually transmitted diseases, such as AIDS, is undoubtedly one. Perhaps for hygienic reasons the first edition of *The Love*

Charter permitted sexual sharing only within the home, but as the number of homes grew and their typical size decreased, this was amended to permit sharing across homes. Another reason for the end of FFing may be the fact that opponents of the Family were able to exploit it in their persecution campaigns. A third reason may be that FFing exhausted energies that might better be contained within the group, to build and sustain relationships among members. Finally, few people who are not already spiritually mature may be capable of really benefiting.

The novel purportedly written from beyond the grave by C. S. Lewis, *The Return of the Seven Keys*, teaches that sexual sharing is not for everyone. During his quest, the hero Gabe befriends a people known as the Drifters, and they teach him the arts of war so that he can triumph over the powers of darkness. When the Drifters invite Gabe into their fellowship, he discovers they have a remarkable form of "extended family" involving multiple wives and sexual sharing. Their leader, Rahim, even sends one of his daughters, Helena, to share sexually with Gabe. Rahim explains, "The freedom of love, if used wisely, is one of the most beautiful gifts that has been imparted to us from the other world."[29] But he recognizes that few people are ready for it:

"Freedom is a wonderful thing—you can use it to bring love, life and happiness into the lives of many. But many people do not know how to channel such freedom. Freedom is powerful. If it is misused it can turn upon you, and bring sadness and grief. The freedom of love is one of the most blessed gifts we have ever received. But many people do not know how to use this gift wisely, and so they prefer not to use it at all. It is not essential. In fact, unless one is able to use such a gift wisely, it is often best that it is not played with at all."[30]

For its own membership, the Family has published a sexual instruction manual, that begins with the necessity for a positive, loving attitude, stresses open communication between erotic partners, and discusses how best to arouse the other person.[31] The book offers many suggestions, rather than prescribing one particular approach. Many pages concern the arousing things people might say to each other, and foreplay with mouths and hands, as well as positions for completing the sexual act. The fundamental principle is that intercourse is communication, and that the two parties should sense each other's feelings and seek to give the best possible sensations.

Many of the Family's customs have the effect of encouraging fertility. All sexually active members are expected to avoid the use of artificial birth control techniques such as condoms, pills, IUDs and the like. Married couples are also supposed to avoid any form of birth control whatsoever. In a prophecy, the Lord said, "Unto you who are married I say, trust Me, for I am He that creates life. I am He that chooses to give unto you your children, and thus trust Me."[32] Single couples are allowed to satisfy each other in ways that would not result in pregnancy, and a married person sharing with a single person is considered single with respect to these rules. But if singles wish to trust the Lord, they may complete intercourse, and *The Love Charter* explains the responsibilities they will have if pregnancy results.

CHAPTER 7

Children

Years ago, the Children of God became parents, and now the Grandchildren of God are in the process of doing so, as well. Few religious movements survive, let alone grow, unless they produce children in significant numbers and retain most of them when they reach adulthood. Children are the fulfillment of the Law of Love that so strikingly sets the Family apart from other Christian religious movements of our era, and for many outsiders the way the Family treats its children is the ultimate test of its spiritual worthiness.

Fertility

Over the years, the GSS has asked, "What do you think is the ideal number of children for a family to have?" Table 7.1 compares the Family's responses to those from the 1996 GSS. The most common number of children considered ideal by the American public is just two, while it is four in the Family. However, the majority of Family members refuse to pick a number, selecting instead, "as many as you want." One out of nine selected "don't know." Thus, most members of the Family are really not prepared to accept the notion that a couple should plan the number of children to have. A mother of six who selected "as many as you want" wrote in "as many as possible." A father of four wrote, "as many as God wants." A mother of two wrote, "as many as God gives."

Another item taken from the 1996 GSS asked: "How many children have you ever had? Please count all that were born alive at any time (including any you had from a previous marriage)." The final columns of table 7.1 compare the answers from respondents who were age thirty or older. A fifth of American adults older than their twenties have never had a child, compared with less than 6 percent of Family members. About half of these Family respondents

141

Table 7.1. Ideal and Actual Number of Children

Number of children . . .	Ideal Number of Children		Age 30+, Actual Number of children...	
	Family	*1996 GSS*	*Family*	*1996 GSS*
0	0.1%	1.2%	5.7%	20.0%
1	0.2%	2.8%	8.5%	14.8%
2	2.4%	54.7%	7.9%	30.4%
3	6.0%	20.9%	9.5%	17.3%
4	10.5%	8.3%	9.9%	9.3%
5	4.2%	1.1%	7.5%	4.0%
6	2.4%	0.6%	10.7%	2.1%
7 or more	3.2%	0.4%	40.3%	2.2%
As many as you want	59.5%	6.1%		
Don't know	11.5%	4.0%		
TOTAL	100.0%	100.0%	100.0%	100.0%

This table is based on 999 cases (ideal) and 507 cases (actual) for the Family, and 1,960 cases (ideal) and 2,298 cases (actual) for the General Social Survey.

have six or more children, whereas a majority among GSS respondents have two or fewer. Thirty percent of Family members have eight or more children, compared with only 1 percent of Americans aged thirty or above.

This is a monumental difference in fertility, to the advantage of the Family. It has become fashionable among secular intellectuals to extol the virtues of childlessness or small families, yet this attitude is suicidal. More than 65 percent of the GSS respondents have had two or fewer children. One might think that two is a sufficient number of children per couple to sustain the size of a population, but a slightly higher number is required because some children will die before reaching adulthood. The 2,298 GSS respondents age thirty and over have had an average of 2.1, which is just at the replacement level. Although some will continue to have children after completing the survey, the average is only this high because it includes many members of older generations in which the birth rates were higher than they are today. On average, the Family respondents have 5.4 children, and many of them are still producing babies.

Whether or not the Battle of Armageddon comes tomorrow, the end of a world is at hand. It is a small world, but vital, and it is called the *family*. Within families, most people are born, develop into adults, make love, have children, and eventually die. Without a healthy family, personalities become warped, love is violently unstable, and the number of children dwindles far below the rate that can sustain the population. The educated classes in postindustrial societies smugly prattle about population explosion and the need to limit fertility. But their own numbers are collapsing, not exploding. Throughout Europe the birth rate has fallen below the replacement level, and the same would be true in the United States were it not for high-fertility religious minorities and immigrants. A decade ago, my colleague Nathan Keyfitz, among the world's greatest demographers, announced that he could see no way that Western societies could restore their plummeting birth rates, and the world would be inherited by high-fertility religions like Islam.[1]

Demographers used to think they understood the dynamics of populations that were evolving from agricultural into industrial societies. *Demographic transition theory* postulated three historical stages. First, in traditional societies the death rate is very high from disease and malnutrition, so the birth rate must also be high if the society is to survive. Second, medical advances and economic progress reduce the death rate, but the culture keeps the birth rate high for some years, and there is a population explosion. Third, the culture modernizes and the birth rate comes down to balance the low death rate.[2] Before the transition, high rates of birth and death balance off to produce a stable population, and after the transition low rates likewise balance. Unfortunately, many scientific studies on population trends seem to refute this optimistic theory. Historical demographers looked at what had actually happened in Western Europe over the past several centuries, and survey demographers studied contemporary populations around the world. A very different picture emerges.

Traditional societies have high birth rates not because they need them to survive but simply because people lack reliable means to control births. Sexual urges drive men and women to copulate, and the result is lots of babies. Many infants die, and adults often die before completing their reproductive years, but human erotic passions are strong enough to keep the species alive. Then, with the development of civilization, people discover a host of means for limiting children. The classical world of Greece and Rome developed a few somewhat effective contraception techniques, experimented with abortion methods, indulged in conception-free sexual practices, and at times legalized the killing of newborns. The population stabilized and even seems to have declined among the dominant groups. Partly in consequence, the Roman Empire fell. The Western Civilization that succeeded the Romans was based in Christianity, which opposed all these methods for limiting population.[3]

At the beginning of the twentieth century, new contraceptive techniques were developed. Adopted first by elites in the most secularized industrial nations, they quickly spread throughout Europe and many other areas of the world, causing a rapid drop in the birth rate.[4] The old theory of demographic transition assumed that some social mechanisms connected the birth rate and the death rate, so that the system would tend to stay in balance and the future of the human species was secure. But now we realize that such mechanisms probably do not exist, and little can stop the birth rate in modern societies from dropping below the survival level. The rate jumps up and down somewhat over the decades, in response to wars and economic conditions, but the American trends have been downward for a century. At the same time, the divorce rate has been rising rapidly. Now half of all American marriages end in divorce. Many of the families that endure are quite traditional and provide well for the emotional well-being of their members.[5] But for the society as a whole a grinding demographic disaster is in progress, and the disintegration of the family aggravates every other kind of social problem.

The Family resists this trend, and one reason for examining its revolutionary lifestyle is the possibility that we can learn lessons about how to prevent the populations of postindustrial societies from collapsing. Perhaps it would be necessary to forsake the constant competition for status in the highly stratified, secular world, and embrace a more egalitarian, communal ethic. Parents may instinctively realize that children from small families tend to get more education and achieve higher social-class status than children from large families.[6] Especially intriguing is the Family's almost unique combination of traditional Christian religious opposition to birth control and sexual practices that limit fertility, while promoting positive attitudes toward giving and receiving sexual love.

It is important to note that this emphasis on fertility does not mean that second-generation members of the Family begin sexual activity especially early in life or start having babies at an early age. In a survey study that compared responses from 100 second-generation members of the Family with a large non-Family sample of the same age, Nancy Vogt found a slight tendency for Family teenagers to begin sexual activity somewhat later than nonmembers.[7] Thus, by the standards of the world, Family members achieve a reasonable level of maturity before preparing to become parents themselves.

Parenthood

One of the main purposes of the General Social Survey is to chart the changing condition of the American family, so there are many questions on this topic. Table 7.2 reports responses to ten agree-disagree items from the 1988

Table 7.2. Attitudes toward Parenthood

Agree . . .	*Family*	*1988 GSS*
A single mother can bring up her child as well as a married couple.	21.5%	37.3%
A single father can bring up his child as well as a married couple.	18.7%	31.8%
The main purpose of marriage these days is to have children.	7.7%	11.7%
People who want children ought to get married.	64.4%	72.9%
Children are more trouble than they are worth.	2.1%	4.1%
Watching children grow up is life's greatest joy.	79.3%	86.3%
Having children interferes too much with the freedom of parents.	4.9%	11.1%
A marriage without children is not fully complete.	60.5%	44.6%
It is better not to have children because they are such a heavy financial burden.	1.6%	4.1%
People who have never had children lead empty lives.	18.0%	26.2%

The number of cases ranges from 1,014 to 1,021 for the Family, and from 1,388 to 1,398 for the General Social Survey.

GSS—combining "agree" and "strongly agree"—beginning with a pair about single parents. Fewer Family members agree that a single mother or single father can bring up a child as well as a married couple. A mother of five children wrote in the margin of her survey, "Children need a father figure, even if it's not their natural father, someone who loves and cares for them." A sixteen-year-old girl commented, "Kids have a strong, God-built need for both a father and a mother." A father of ten wrote, "A child needs a father figure. The mother who can provide that role well is rare. But better a single mom than a bad dad." He also felt that a child needs a mother figure. A mother of nine said a single woman could not raise a child as well as a couple, "unless she has help of a father as in our Family," and she believed that the Family gave a single father the "help of a mother figure or mothers." Thus, while Family respondents feel that the nurturance of both a father and a mother is important, they think their communal homes can often provide this when one of a child's natural parents is absent.

Few respondents in either group felt the purpose of marriage was to have children or that children are more trouble than they are worth. With respect to children being trouble, a mother of six children reacted: "What a sad thought. They're so precious. Children are old men's riches!" A father of six agreed, saying "It's not good for man to be alone (I've tried that). But, be fruitful and multiply." A majority in both groups felt people who want children should get married and that watching kids grow up is life greatest joy, but the proportions were slightly smaller in the Family. One respondent explained, "Jesus is life's greatest joy." Although Jesus should be central to the life of a Family member, a father of seven noted, "Children are God's gifts to those whom He chooses."

Most respondents in both groups reject the notion that having children interferes with parents' freedom, and a father of eight wonders, "What are parents supposed to be 'free' for?" Family members are more likely to agree that "a marriage without children is not fully complete." Both groups reject the idea that children are too heavy a financial burden. Family members are less likely to agree that childless people lead empty lives. A father of four explained, "But in the Family, even though an individual didn't have a child, he or she is surrounded by those beautiful little kids!" A father of two agreed, saying "Not in our Family, as we all share the blessings and joys of the children." A father of ten pointed out, "Some have other roles to play in life than parents." A young man who had not yet fathered a child asserted, "The main thing is to care for someone."

Two divorce items from the 1994 GSS were also included in the survey. Just 15.0 percent of Americans agreed that "When there are children in the family, parents should stay together even if they don't get along." In contrast, fully 46.0 percent of Family members agreed that parents should stay together.[8] The comparison was quite different without kids. Among GSS respondents, 7.6 percent felt that "Even when there are no children, a married couple should stay together even if they don't get along," compared with only 3.0 percent of Family members.[9] Beside the first of these items, a Canadian father of two wrote, "Pray for love." Beside the second, he wrote, "Got to have peace."

Clearly, members of the Family are not very different from the American public in their attitudes toward parenthood. They are somewhat more concerned about providing a complete family environment for children to grow up in, but this need not require marriage because of their communal life style. Although children are very important to them, Jesus is also important, and they believe that childless adults can find fulfillment in their spiritually oriented life.

Childhood

Living in communal homes, children are often grouped by age, and the Family has developed a series of code words to name them: Babies and Toddlers are less than four years old. Other children are YCs (Young Children aged 4–6), MCs (Middle children, 7–8), OCs (Older Children, 9–10). JETTs (age 12–13) are Junior EndTime Teens. Then come JRs (Junior teens, 14–15), SRs (Senior teens, 16–17) and YA (Young Adults, 18–20). People born into the Family who are older than 20 are called SGAs (Second Generation Adults), and those who joined the Family are called FGAs (First Generation Adults).

Several respondents wrote about the excitement of preparing for a child to be born. A mother of nine children rejoiced, "I'm pregnant, and when I went to my midwife for a checkup I got to hear the heartbeat of my baby." A younger woman with only one child "went to the hospital for a pregnancy checkup and heard the baby's heart and movements." A mother in her late thirties was happy because, "I am pregnant with our sixth child, after not having been pregnant for seven years." A mother with one child "went to a baby shower for two pregnant mommies in the Family." A mother of ten was happy that "some Family members from different homes got together for a baby shower, and we had prayer for the baby." A woman with eight children of her own "sewed some baby items for a young mommy due to have her first child in one week."

The father of six children listed some of the recent events in his home: "I climbed a mountain with my five-year-old son and watched a beautiful sunset together. My wife and I took our two boys witnessing and to lunch. My wife got pregnant! Thank you Jesus!"

A pregnant woman who already had one child was distressed at "having to go through all the papers required for marriage," but pleased she had "found a hospital where I would have my baby." A forty-five-year-old mother of seven was happy to see her youngest son and daughter go off to the mission field in distant countries, but this left her without children to raise. "I had a date—got off on the wrong foot—no communication, etc. Bummer. Lord Help Us! All's well that end's well—I'm pregnant!! Hallelujah!"

When giving birth, women may have the help either of a Family member trained as a midwife, or of secular medical facilities. A twenty-year-old woman who had not yet borne children herself said, "I will be taking a midwifer course, which has been my heart's desire." A mother of four wrote, "I found a good doctor who speaks English and is willing to deliver my baby on my terms, which is a super miracle in Romania." A forty-four-year-old woman was pleased when "the doctor said my daughter-in-law can have a natural delivery in spite of a minor heart problem." Another mother of the same age was pleased she "was able to be there when my first grandchild was born."

A Canadian mother of eight said, "I played a game with my baby on the baby swing outside, gently pushing the swing and giving her little kisses when she came my way." Another Canadian mother who is expecting her eighth child wrote, "My youngest son, three and a half, is excited about the new baby coming. He kisses my tummy several times a day and tells me how he is going to share his toys with the baby."

In Brazil, a father of six children "cooked and served breakfast for the kids" and "went with all our home (7 kids, 3 adults) to a presentation of the Philharmonic." One of his happiest recent experiences was "seeing my son so happy on his fourth birthday." A father of four "Had a real good time telling and acting out some Bible stories the other day to our younger children." A young mother of two reported "an indescribable feeling of joy in seeing my daughter at her fifth birthday party and realizing how much she's grown and matured!" In Japan, a father of five "spent quality time with my kids. I drove my family and some friends to a big shopping center and everyone shopped and we ate out. My five year old boy sat on my lap and I told him an animal story for thirty minutes. It was fun for both of us."

I have observed three Family birthday parties for small children, and the party for a four year old third generation member was typical. A half dozen small children sat around the birthday table, wearing party hats and having a delightful time digging into ice cream and cake, while an equal number of adults stood singing "Happy Birthday" and encouraging the youngsters' merriment. If there was someone in the home who knew how to make balloon animals, then a whole menagerie would spring to life. A mother of seven in Indonesia wrote, "We took a few of the MCs (ages 5–8) out for an ice cream because it was one girl's birthday. They wore hats and had balloons and had fun."

In Australia, the mother of eleven children took some of them to a movie, and found time to attend an aerobics class alone, just as mothers in secular society might do. The day before filling out the questionnaire, she had enjoyed a rare group meeting where she "talked and fellowshipped with other Family members for the first time in months." She was also able to take "a day off with newest baby to rest, read, and shop at the second-hand shop." All was not idyllic, however, because "recent surveillance of our home brought back traumatic experiences of my children being taken in previous raids." When I interviewed a couple whose children had been seized for several weeks in France, even six years later they said their children were somewhat anxious and even a little discouraged when planning an activity that involved the institutions of the outside world.

A young Russian mother was happy about her first child's progress, but unhappy she cannot devote herself to him. "My baby is learning how to grasp and hold toys. I was too tired and didn't have enough milk to breast feed my baby." A young woman at a home with about twenty members "took kids to the doctor."

Life for young people in the Family, as elsewhere, has its adventures and misadventures. A teenage girl reported, "Our horse stepped on my brother's foot, and it swelled up big." A mother lamented, "My son fell off his bike and had to have stitches." A mother of one living in a large home was displeased by "some of our children breaking things, unaware of God's always watching eye." A father of seven was unhappy about "the teens in my home saying and doing things which show that I haven't been able to help them feel fulfilled and excited in their lives." The day before filling out the questionnaire, he "talked to one of our teens about some problems he's been having and realized that part of his problem is that I haven't been taking enough 'personal time' with him."

A Russian home with about a dozen members experienced a terrifying accident. As one of the women wrote, "We had to evacuate our apartment due to a fire, but all was well in the end." A man was more specific, saying "One of the little children lit a match and dropped it on a bed." A nineteen-year-old girl explained her role in the disaster: "My sister's crib caught on fire with her in it. Don't know what started it, but I was held responsible for it. It was hell seeing her trapped inside screaming. Thank God she wasn't too seriously injured."

Elsewhere, a father of six was happy "having all my kids pile onto the bed with me for a big hug." From Taiwan, a forty-eight year old father of five wrote, "I played tennis with my son and a British brother and his son. It was fun and good exercise." A French mother of six wrote, "It was our 'family day.' So I went in a public park to play with my youngest children while the big ones went ice skating."

A father of nine children illustrated how it was possible to give them a fun experience while doing missionary work: "I took my youngest son to the pet shop. We passed out gospel tracts to the owner and all his workers." A young woman who was not yet a mother "took several children on an outing to the mall, passed out tracts on the way."

Parents watch their young adult children embark on their mission careers with mixed feelings. A father of nine was happy "to see my eldest daughter eighteen years old moving on to another mission field and her personal commitment to serve Jesus!"

However, parents generally are not happy to see any of their children leave the Family, and news from them is a constant source of concern. A mother of eleven worried, "My second oldest son who joined the Navy told me he was going to try to become a Navy Seal." A father of four said, "One of my sons left the Family and later got into some trouble with the law. It's been difficult."

Schooling

The Family has enthusiastically embraced the home schooling movement, both to protect their children from the secularism of public schools and to fit education into the rigors of missionary life. We asked parents, "If you have children who are of school age, what kind of schooling do they get?" Of the 485 parents who had school age children, fully 81 percent said their children exclusively received home schooling. Only 10 percent attended only public or other non-Family schools, whereas 7 percent received both kinds of schooling. Another 2 percent replied "other," and one of the eleven parents who gave this answer explained, "home schooling with an official correspondence course." One parent in Taiwan, and another who was in mainland China, considered their children to be receiving complete home schooling, but they were also getting outside instruction in the Chinese language.

Another way of looking at the education children received was to focus on the 418 who were either born into the Family or joined it earlier than age 6, and who reported how many years of home schooling versus outside school they had received. As table 7.3 shows, on average, they reported 10.2 years of home schooling but only 1.1 year of outside schooling.

A father of five in a home with two dozen members did home schooling the day before filling out the questionnaire. "I taught math—changing base 10 numbers to binary (base 2)—to our thirteen year olds." A mother of eight "taught fractions and decimals to my son and his friend." In Hungary, a young woman "made a height and weight chart with the children." A young father of three was very pleased "when my three year old son did his daily reading of about 50 words in only 10 minutes without needing much persuasion." A mother of four boasted, "My two oldest girls (11 and 9 years old) got good grades on their home schooling tests."

Table 7.3. Schooling of Second-Generation Family Members

Years of schooling . . .	Home School in the Family	Schooling Outside the Family
0	0.7%	62.7%
1–5 years	12.2%	33.3%
6–10 years	41.6%	4.1%
More than 10 years	45.5%	0.0%
TOTAL	100.0%	100.0%

This table is based on 418 respondents who were either born into the Family or joined it earlier than age 6.

Not only do adults teach, but so do the older children. Two girls in a Thailand home, one sixteen and the other fifteen, collaborated in teaching the little children in their thirty-person home: "I choreographed a song with a friend and taught it to the 4–5 year olds in my home." "I taught some 3–4 year olds choreography to some songs that they would perform in the local language." Elsewhere, a fourteen-year-old girl "cared for a two-year-old toddler. I read him a story and helped him practice his writing."

The curriculum aims not only to train the children in writing, reading, and arithmetic, but also to instill spiritual values. From Brazil, an American wrote, "I began teaching children full-time. I helped build a better world by teaching pre-schoolers good manners, the Word, how to read and how to take care of themselves." A mother of three in a small home wrote, "I taught a missions and geography and social studies class to a local home schooler's group. Of 25 students, 8 of them said they wanted to be missionaries." A father of four "Had a real good time telling and acting out some Bible stories the other day to our younger children." A young mother was pleased when, "My little girl learned to praise the Lord."

The Family uses some existing Christian home-schooling material for younger children, and has established its own home-schooling program for the high school and junior-college levels, called Christian Vocational College. The catalog explains, "It has been developed for students preparing for full-time Christian service careers, enabling them to gain quality vocational training and practical job experience along with their academic studies. Besides a basic high school diploma program, the CVC lays the foundation for careers in pastoring, teaching, counseling, missionary and evangelistic work, publishing, performing, and much more, as well as providing training in a wide range of other vocational job skills."[10] Thus, the aim is to prepare youngsters for effective lives as Family missionaries, rather than to become workers in the System. The Family realizes that some of the children will not choose to serve the Lord, and parents are encouraged to help such young people get prepared either to work in secular society or to attend college. The CVC educational materials include much Family religious literature, some other Christian home schooling material, and a wide range of secular instructional material concerning practical subjects.

CVC helps students obtain high school equivalency certificates from the U.S. states and Canadian provinces, as well as issuing its own certificates and diplomas. A seventeen year old girl in Brazil was pleased with her progress, writing on her questionnaire, "I got my certificate which shows that I finished history in high school." An eighteen year old said she was happy because, "I received my first CVC certificate for studies completed in Christian History and Heritage." A twenty-year-old woman in China wrote proudly, "I received my GED diploma."

Children living in non-English-speaking nations often use a mixture of educational materials, so they will get some experience with the local language. A French couple showed me the bookstore where they buy French-language teaching materials they use in their own children's home schooling. When they were through with the books, they could sell them back to the store to reduce the cost of the next set.

Although members of the Family have little contact with public schools, they do have opinions about the appropriate role for religion in state-supported education. In 1991, the GSS asked, "In your opinion, should there be daily prayers in all public schools?" Of 1,338 Americans who replied, 35 percent said "yes, definitely." This is less than half of the 77 percent of Family respondents who hold this view. While about 33 percent of the American public oppose prayer in public schools, only 2 percent of Family members agree with this negative attitude. A German woman wrote that prayer in the schools "would be a witness and help people know they can call out or speak to God even if they have another faith."

This is not to say that Family members are free of all misgivings about establishing religious influence in the public schools. An Indian woman in Romania could not answer "yes" or "no" but wrote, "Those who would lead such prayers themselves should have a vibrant link with God, not just a 'religious show.' Otherwise it might do more harm than good, and end up turning youngsters off to God." A Hungarian woman in Croatia wrote, "Mandatory prayers won't help people to find Jesus and faith!" And an American man in Chile asserted, "You can't force people to pray or love Jesus, it's voluntary from the heart." Others wrote that the proper answer would depend on the culture of the country in question, that perhaps students should be allowed to vote with the majority ruling, or that prayer should be allowed but not imposed on any unwilling students.

Socialization

One way of conceptualizing different approaches to child raising is to look at the values the culture seeks to inculcate into children, what sociologists call *socialization*. A linked set of items in the GSS presents the respondent with five different values a child might learn: "to obey, to be well-liked or popular, to think for himself or herself, to work hard, and to help others when they need help." It then asks, "If you had to choose, which thing on this list would you pick as the most important for a child to learn to prepare him or her for life?" The respondent is instructed to mark the highest priority value with a number "1," then rank the other four from "2" down to "5." Table 7.4 reveals that members of the Family respond very differently from the American public.

The Family gives highest priority to obedience, followed by helping others. Certainly these are the values most appropriate for a Bible-inspired communal movement. In contrast, members of chaotic, anomic, competitive American society give highest priority to thinking for oneself, with lesser priorities on obedience, helping others, and working hard.

A father of eleven children explained why he had ranked "to obey" first: "because you can't make right decisions unless you can learn to follow what is right, or to obey." In contrast, a mother of seven had ranked "to think for himself or herself" first, but qualified this by writing, "and therefore choose to obey." A father of six did not rank the values, but wrote in, "Most of all to pray and hear from God what to do!" Beside "to work hard," a mother of six quoted Ecclesiastes 9:10, "Whatsoever thy hand findeth to do, do it with thy might."

The five items describing values a child might learn were not original with the General Social Survey, but were written by Gerhard Lenski for the 1958 survey of Detroit residents analyzed in his classic study, *The Religious Factor*.[11] One finding was that Protestants stressed individual autonomy (think for himself or herself) more than Catholics did. Conversely, Catholics stressed conformity (obey) more than Protestants did. This is consistent with the classic descriptions of Protestant-Catholic differences of Emile Durkheim and Max Weber early in the twentieth century.[12] Today, Protestant-Catholic differences in the United States are slight, but across denominations higher levels of church attendance

Table 7.4. Most Important Value for Children

Most important for a child to learn . . .	Family	GSS
To obey	44.9%	18.0%
To be well-liked or popular	0.6%	0.7%
To think for himself or herself	14.8%	51.3%
To work hard	3.1%	17.3%
To help others when they need help	36.6%	12.7%
TOTAL	100.0%	100.0%

This table is based on 995 cases for the Family, and 1,895 for the General Social Survey. These are the respondents who ranked all five items properly.

are associated with greater desires for conformity in children.[13] But traditionally, Catholicism gave a greater emphasis to community, whereas Protestantism stressed the individual.[14] It is impossible to say which of these is better. Rather, they represent different value systems for living life that arise under somewhat different social conditions and have distinctive sets of advantages and disadvantages.

In 1980, the GSS included a different item about the proper balance between parental authority and children's autonomy: "Here are two statements. Will you tell us which one you agree with more? First: 'The younger generation should be taught by their elders to do what is right.' Second: 'The younger generation should be taught to think for themselves even though they may do something their elders disapprove of.'" Respondents were given just these two choices, and in the face-to-face situation of the GSS interviews, less than 1 percent of the 1,461 respondents were unwilling to select one and said "don't know." A majority, 55 percent, selected "think for themselves," compared with 45 percent who selected "taught by elders."

Of the 881 Family respondents who selected one of these two choices, only 44 percent selected "think for themselves," compared with 56 percent who chose "taught by elders." Here, again, we see a preference for obedience rather than individual autonomy. However, fully 1,004 Family members actually answered this item, 6 percent saying "don't know" and a further 13 percent checking both of the choices and often writing in that they saw no contradiction between them. Among these 1,004, only 36 percent selected "think for themselves" alone, compared with 45 percent selecting "taught by elders." In a group that believes it knows the truth, following authority and thinking for oneself will give the same answers, and thus are not mutually exclusive choices.

Some of those who chose one of the options provided comments. A childless man remarked that the answer "depends on the elders. If they are godly then 'yes.'" A mother of seven said, "First taught right from wrong as children, later to hopefully choose wisely for themselves." A father of three agreed, saying "Of course, children should also be taught to make their own decisions age appropriate." A father of seven agreed as well, "When they are small they should be taught by elders, but as they grow up they should learn to think themselves." A childless woman said, "I think a man is wiser if he learns from the mistakes of others. Being open-minded to counsel and learn from others is important!" A young woman felt children should be led by elders, "but they should also be taught to think for themselves somewhat but be aware of the consequences."

Those who could not select a single answer also chimed in. A mother of three said, "Kids need guidance as well as freedom." A seventeen-year-old girl commented, "I think a little bit of both because when we're young I think that it's right for the parents to train the child in the right way, but once we reach a certain age I think that we should be able to make our own decisions—and in some cases, maybe learn the hard way." A mother of two agreed: "Have to have both. Teach them the foundation and to think for themselves and then let them choose." A father of four explained, "They should be taught to do what is right so they will be able to think for themselves."

Others linked the question to their faith. A father of one child wrote, "The younger generation needs moral teachings of life's guiding Principles and they also need to learn how to think for themselves and most of all learn how to 'Hear from God' just as Samuel the Prophet had to learn how to 'Hear from God.'" A mother of three quoted Prov. 22:6, "Train up a child in the way he should go, and even when he is old he will not depart from it."

In 1990, the GSS contained a related item that asked respondents whether they agreed or disagreed with this statement: "A child should never be allowed to talk back to his parents, or else he will lose respect for them." Of those who answered, 57 percent agreed, compared with 55 percent in the Family, essentially no difference. However, Family respondents were more likely to be ambivalent about this item and check the boxes for "neither agree nor disagree" or "can't choose." Taking those indifferent people out of the GSS sample increases the percent who agreed only one point, to 58 percent. But removing them from the Family sample increased the percent who agreed by fully 19 percentage points to 74 percent. Thus, again we see evidence that the Family favors obedience in children.

This value is tempered by respect for the child. A mother of five children agreed with the statement but commented, "But a kid should be free to express his 'side.'" A mother of seven wrote, "The idea would be that they know how to present their opposition without 'talking back'—but have not found the way to achieve the ideal yet—ha!" In Taiwan a mother of ten wrote, "Sassiness should not be allowed, but voicing disagreement is OK." In Ireland a father of ten echoed her sentiment, "A child should be allowed to explain but sassiness should not be tolerated." And a mother of twelve reacted to the questionnaire statement by saying, "That is true, but they also need to present their point of view."

Discipline

A large majority of members, 79.6 percent, agree that "it is sometimes necessary to discipline a child with a good, hard spanking." However, before we conclude that the Family is an extremely harsh disciplinarian, we should note that a majority of the American public, 71.7 percent, feels the same way.[15] Given that older people tend to do the spanking, and younger people tend to be spanked, I thought it was worth considering the responses of the older and younger generations separately. There is no significant difference between those who were born in the Family (80 percent) or recruited (79 percent). The percentage approving of "a good, hard spanking" is only slightly lower (78 percent) for 216 respondents who were born in the 1980s and thus were aged fifteen to nineteen and might be expected to defend the interests of children.

Christopher Ellison and Darren Sherkat have used GSS data from 1988 to identify three related reasons why conservative Protestants are more likely than others to agree with this item about spanking. First, those who believe in the literal truth of the Bible are apt to follow the practices for dealing with children described in its pages. Prov. 13:24 says, "He that spareth his rod hateth his son." An explanation is offered in 22:15: "Foolishness is bound up in the heart of a child; but the rod of correction shall drive it far from him." And Prov. 23:13–14 leaves no doubt: "Withhold not correction from the child: for if thou beat him with the rod, he shall not die. Thou shalt beat him with the rod, and shall deliver his soul from Sheol." In chapter 3 we saw that Family members are more likely than GSS respondents to consider the Bible to be the literal truth.

Second, according to Ellison and Sherkat, conservative Protestants consider human beings to be sinners. To measure this sin-oriented conception of people, they used a single GSS seven-step scale on which people marked where they stood between "human nature is basically good" and "human nature is fundamentally perverse and corrupt." As we saw in chapter 5, members of the Family are more likely than the average American to consider humans "fundamentally perverse and corrupt."

Third, conservative Protestants hold that sin requires punishment. Ellison and Sherkat used this GSS item to measure this attitude: "Those who violate God's rules must be punished." In chapter 6 we saw that about 30 percent of members of the Family agreed strongly with this statement, compared with 22 percent of GSS respondents. Thus, in being slightly more likely than the average American to agree that spanking is sometimes necessary, members of the Family are merely agreeing with the large conservative Protestant segment of the population, rather than displaying a distinctive disciplinary style.

Several of the Family respondents wrote comments beside the spanking item. A mother of thirteen children thought spanking should be used only "when all else fails." A fifteen-year-old girl said, "I agree that there are situations where a good, hard spanking is what the child needs, but it can be abused. A spanking should be a last resort." A father of seven thought spanking should be used "seldom. When they do something that hurts others and when they do something evil or when they lie or steal. But you have to judge each child and case by itself." A mother of nine exclaimed, "Not too hard please! And followed with love and prayer!" A mother of twelve felt that any spanking should be done "in a moderate way and causing no harm." A father of three explained, "We need to see discipline as training, and so act lovingly, respectfully and patiently."

The New Generation

Converts to religious sects tend to be deprived in terms of wealth and status, compared with people who do not join. People born into a sect often gain wealth and status compared with recruits, and defectors from sects who join mainstream denominations typically enjoy higher social-class standing than either native sectarians or sect recruits.[16] One possible outcome is that the religious movement reduces its tension with the surrounding sociocultural environment, to suit the needs of the second generation for a rapprochement with society.[17] But some religious movements are sufficiently isolated from conventional social life and societal institutions, or sufficiently entrenched in their beliefs, that they retain their sectarian fervor. This appears to be the case for the Family, and thus we can wonder what will become of the second generation.

When Father David died in 1994, many children of his original recruits were reaching adulthood, and a few had begun to have babies of their own.

Thus the Family faced two of the classic challenges of new religions simultaneously: how to survive the loss of the founder and how to retain many of the second generation of members when they became autonomous adults. The tremendous effort to create a distinctive educational system for the children, culminating in creation of the Christian Vocational College, undoubtedly strengthened the bond holding the young people within the group. Similarly Herculean efforts to produce music and literature attractive to the young people, and to include them ever more centrally in the decision processes of the homes, undoubtedly helped as well. But a significant number of young adults left the Family, stimulating fears that many more would defect.

One teenage girl who completed the questionnaire said she prayed only about two or three times a month, explaining, "I only pray when I'm real scared, but my parents pray all the time." She has doubts about the existence of God, and she has not read the Bible for more than a year. She feels it is better for a child to think for herself, than to obey her elders. Born and raised in the Family, she has never attended school outside it, but has traveled with it in a dozen nations. Now she has started doing very secular things, like reading romance novels, playing computer games at a bowling alley, and visiting her boyfriend's apartment. She is happy because, "My boyfriend told me he loved me." But she is unhappy because, "My mom's thinking about getting back together with my step dad." All these factors suggest that she may defect.

However, anthropologist Charlotte Hardman has compared young people in the Family with those raised in the Findhorn and Transcendental Meditation movements: "The children in the Family form a sharp contrast to these New Age children. They share a strong morality and sense of mission with their parents, and they aspire to follow in their parents' footsteps."[18]

Partly in reaction to concerns about increasing losses of young people, in 1998 Maria published a proclamation: "Trash Your Trinkets and Head for the Hills!"[19] Including extensive prophecies from Jesus and Father David, it warned that members could become too attached to material goods and worldly attitudes, especially in the United States. It urges them to shake off spiritual lethargy, demonstrate their obedience to God, and leave their comfortable home for the rigors of the mission field. Over the years, the leadership of the Family has staged periodic revivals, called revolutions, and they have often been effective. I have observed many young adults and members in their late teens enthusiastically prepare to be missionaries, then voyage to Russia or some other adventurous mission field. Time will tell, and our questionnaire cannot give us a valid measure of the defection rate in the past let alone the future. But it does allow us to compare the first and second generations on some measures that may be relevant to persistence or defection.

We could describe the first generation as members who joined at age fifteen or older, and the second generation as those who were born in the group or brought in by parents before age six. Here we ignore those eleven respondents who joined between the ages of five and fifteen, because their experience (including schooling) may have been very different from either of the two "generations." Thus defined, generation is first and foremost a result of the manner by which the person became a member of the group: recruitment or birth. But it clearly is very much related to age and birth cohort. The mean year of birth for the first generation is 1956, and for second generation it is 1979. The difference between these averages, 23 years, is a good approximation of a biological generation.

Although one could profitably compare the two generations' responses to all the items in the questionnaire, here we will focus on just one set of fifteen measures of values that ought to be relevant to the likelihood of defecting. Table 2.2 compared how members of the Family and GSS respondents rated eight things that different people value. In composing the questionnaire, I added seven more values I thought might be salient for Family members, and the full list is shown in table 7.5. The first eight allow us to see whether the second generation of Family members has moved closer to the American public, or otherwise differs from the first generation in ways that might predict future defection from the group.

The two groups of Family members do not differ significantly in their average ratings across the fifteen values. On average, 34.6 percent of the first generation consider a value to be among the most important, compared with 33.7 percent of the second generation. The second generation has moved closer to nonmembers on five of the first eight values: being financially secure, having faith in God, having nice things, being cultured, and being self-sufficient and not having to depend on others. A couple of these differences are insignificant, however. Having children may be a lower value for many of the younger Family respondents—compared with both older Family members and the American public—because they simply have not yet entered the phrase of life when childbearing will be a salient question for them. On the other hand, the second generation rates having a fulfilling job higher than do either first generation Family members or GSS respondents. If they can channel their job ambitions into the calling of missionary work, and retain the erotic norms of the older generation, then children will come along without the need for intentionally trying to produce them.

Table 7.5. Fundamental Values Revisited

One of the most important values . . .	Family 1st Generation	Family 2nd Generation	1993 GSS
Being financially secure	0.9%	9.1%	26.8%
Being married	8.3%	7.9%	19.1%
Having children	34.4%	14.9%	23.6%
Having faith in God	96.5%	86.5%	46.0%
Having nice things	0.4%	0.9%	4.3%
Being cultured	0.9%	3.0%	3.8%
Having a fulfilling job	26.5%	37.8%	21.2%
Being self-sufficient and not having to depend on others	1.8%	10.7%	44.2%
Living together with many friends	9.2%	11.4%	
Spiritual change	31.6%	22.8%	
Humility	44.7%	44.1%	
New challenges	30.8%	44.8%	
Love for others	84.7%	76.6%	
Eternal life	90.1%	81.4%	
Working with others for a common goal	58.6%	48.7%	

The number of cases ranges from 563 to 568 for first-generation Family members, from 426 to 431 for second-generation Family members, and from 1,587 to 1,593 for the General Social Survey.

The seven values that supplement the GSS list show complex patterns of similarity and difference between the first and second generations. Some hint of readiness to defect may be seen in the second generation's greater interest in new challenges, and lesser interest in either love for others or working with others for a common goal. However, they show at least as much interest in living together with many friends, which relates to communal living. Three of the fifteen values are religious in nature (having faith in God, spiritual change, and eternal life), and in each case the second generation has less commitment. I have examined differences on many other items in the questionnaire, and as with these fifteen values they tend to show a complex pattern with some hints of slightly weakened commitment, but not a stark picture of a generation ready to defect.

One factor that could cause concern is the sex ratio. In the first generation, 56 percent are female, the same as the percentage in the 1996 General Social Survey. But 66 percent of second-generation respondents are female. Because roughly equal numbers of boys and girls are born, we would expect the sex ratio to be nearly equal among children, which suggests either that young men were reluctant to fill out the survey, or that they are leaving the group in significant numbers.

In earlier research, I examined age and sex specific defection rates for three radical communal religious movements of the nineteenth century: Oneida, Zoar, and the Shakers. Starting in 1850, the United States census collected data on individual persons, rather than just households as it had done before, and microfilm records of the original manuscript census schedules are available to scholars and the general public at the National Archives and a dozen local centers around the country. It is easy to find the religious communes in these records, although a great amount of hard effort is required to match the names across censuses and calculate rates of defection.

Oneida was in many respects comparable to the Family, although much smaller in total membership. Founded by a Yale-trained minister named John Humphrey Noyes in 1848, Oneida practiced a form of group marriage, in which members experienced erotic relations with many members of the opposite sex.[20] Zoar was an Anabaptist German immigrant group that practiced economic communism but had conventional families.[21] The Shakers were a celibate millenarian communal movement with 3,842 members at twenty-one locations in 1850.[22] All three movements established their communal settlements in rural areas away from the opportunities and enticements to defect provided by urban areas.

In analyzing the old census data, I carefully linked records by name across the decades, tabulating the numbers from one census who did or did not appear again at the next census. When someone vanished, I cannot tell whether he or she died or defected, but we would expect age-adjusted mortality rates to be quite similar between the sexes. In the childbearing years women's rates might have been higher than men's, except among the celibate Shakers, although young men might more often have been killed in agricultural accidents in an era when medicine had little power to cure blood loss and infection. But it seems reasonable to assume that sex differences in the data primarily represented different propensities to leave.

In 1850, Oneida had 44 males under age 20, and 25 percent of them were gone by 1860. Among the 39 females in this cohort, 13 percent vanished from the records by 1860. At Zoar, a community of similar size, the 1850–1860 defection rates were 22 percent for males and 27 percent for females. Given the small numbers, we cannot make too much of these sex differences, but for the considerably larger Shaker communities we see both much higher and much more different rates of defection. Of the 669 females under age 20 among the Shakers in 1860, fully 59 percent had vanished by 1860. For the 618 males, the defection rate was a very substantial 76 percent over this same decade.[23]

The fact that Massachusetts held a state census in 1855, 1865, and 1875 allowed me to calculate 5-year defection rates for the five Shaker communes in that state. For males under age 20, the rate steadily increased from 68 percent in 1850–1855 to 86 percent in 1865–1870. The female rate remained roughly constant at about 54 percent. My estimate of the 20-year defection rate for males under age 20 from 1880 to 1900 at all Shaker communities is 99 percent, and 93 percent for females.

The peak in Shaker membership may have been some time in the 1840s, and from 1850 to 1860 the total membership declined from 3,842 to 3,489. By 1880 the population had dropped to 1,849. In 1900 there were just 855 members, and today one might say there are none, unless we should count a tiny group in Maine that may or may not be legitimate members of the historical Shaker movement.

Because of the higher male defection rates, the percent of members under age 20 who were female rose from 51.1 percent in 1840 to 77.3 percent in 1900. By 1936, 88 percent of all members were female. It is entirely possible that the loss of male members accelerated because it was caught in a vicious circle. As males departed, they left behind an environment that may have been less hospitable to males, as well as serving as role models encouraging other males to depart. As their numbers dwindled, Shaker communities resorted to hiring farm laborers from outside to tend the fields, thereby eroding the economic autonomy of their communities. Because Shakers were celibate, they could sustain their numbers only through recruitment, and the decline in membership corresponded with a loss of the fervor necessary to attract new recruits. Thus differential defection and the changing demographics of the group were a spiral toward oblivion.[24]

The Family differs from the Shakers in two crucial respects. First, they produce an ample supply of children. The group's statistical office has counted a total of 13,093 births, an average of 422 a year. The peak fertility came in 1983, when 746 babies were born. In recent years, there has been a declining trend, from 349 births in 1997, to 293 in 1998, and 272 in 1999.[25] However, these numbers are rather volatile over time, and we would have to see a longer data series and correct for the changing age distribution of members to come to any firm conclusions about future prospects.

Second, like Oneida and Zoar, the Family offers members legitimated sexual gratification plus the opportunity to play autonomous adult roles as a missionary. One factor that retarded defection from nineteenth-century religious communes was their rural location and consequent isolation from the surrounding society. Family homes tend to be urban or suburban, but it is not clear that many young adult members are able to develop the extensive relationships with nonmembers that would make it easy for them to defect.

The Shaker communities survived economically, despite the fact that they were agricultural and all the farmwork was done by men, because they owned a tremendous acreage of valuable land. The women of the Family are quite capable of supporting themselves through provisioning needed food, clothing and other goods, and by soliciting financial donations. However, the fact that they have many children means they face greater child care challenges than did the Shakers. Thus one could worry that excessive defection of young males—or defection of both males and females who had no children—could at some point trigger a crisis with economic as well as social dimensions.

The Family does currently recruit some new members from the surrounding society, but not a large number. Figure 7.1 graphs the number of questionnaire respondents who joined in each year, for the 597 who were not born in the group and who provided their birth dates and age at recruitment. The first two joined in 1967, and the peak year was 1971 when fully 88 of these respondents joined. The great wave of gathering that created the Family ended with the 22 recruited in 1979, and just 11 respondents joined in 1980. Since then the number has ranged rather narrowly between 4 and 13 per year. Over the period 1980–1996, an average of 8.5 respondents joined each year.

Of course, many people undoubtedly joined over the three decades of this time series but subsequently defected or died. We would need a much more complete set of data to analyze the rates of movement into and out of the group with any precision. However, for a group of 597 members, 8.5 recruits a year is not sufficient to drive rapid growth. If people typically join when they are 20 years old, and live to 70, then each person spends 50 years as a member. Assume for a moment that nobody dies or defects during these 50 years. Once the age distribution evens out, one-fiftieth of the membership would die each year, or about 12 people. A recruitment rate of 8.5 per year is therefore not sufficient in itself to sustain the population of the group. Were the Family celibate like the Shakers, they would be doomed to vanish over the next century. However, their unusually high fertility rate, combined with this

Figure 7.1. Recruits to the Family

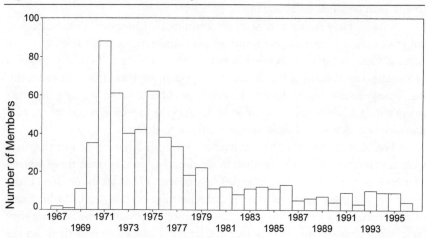

Year Joined

modest rate of recruitment, can produce substantial growth, so long as most children born into the group remain members.

The Future of the Family

We will conclude this chapter by considering the shape of things to come, not to prophesy but to understand better the nature of the Family and its sociological implications. The late 1960s, when the Family was born, was a time when many people looked toward the future with utopian eyes. Scholars wrote books about the year 2000.[26] The Apollo program sent a dozen humans to the Moon, with a promise that they would soon go on to Mars.[27] The young counterculture of hippies and left-wing radicals dreamed of remaking America.[28] And the Children of God burst out of the System to enter the Endtime.

Perhaps, any minute now, their millenarian hopes will be fulfilled. The Great Beast 666 will seize world power and require people to have computer chips implanted, so they can buy and sell. Members of the Family will know what to do. They will save thousands of innocent Christians from the mark of the beast, and lie low until Jesus comes for them. Then, triumphing in a great battle, Christ will usher in the millennium. If that is about to happen, then there is no need to worry about whether the Family will gradually lose membership, or grow slowly, because there is not time for such trends to matter. If the End does not come soon, or if our aim is to gain sociological wisdom from contemplating the Family, then we need to consider the long term future.

Some scholars had advised the Family to begin reducing its tension with the surrounding sociocultural environment, to make peace with the System, and settle down on the modern religious landscape. This strategy presents challenges. At present, the Family has missionaries who could evolve into clergy, but it lacks laity. A few outsider friends help each home, and many homes hold fellowship meetings with halfway members called Fellow Members.[29] Yet many changes would have to be successfully negotiated to transform these relatively few outside supporters into sufficiently numerous laity to support all the missionaries as their clergy.

In all the public fascination with FFing, observers of the Family have often lost sight of the fact that the period of FFing was the time of greatest social involvement with outsiders, after the formative years of the group. Without some kind of bond-building with nonmembers, the group cannot recruit effectively. Relatively few people joined the Family during the early 1980s when FFing was most common, compared with the early 1970s, and the end of FFing meant a loss of contact with external social networks that might be exploited to recruit either missionaries or laity. The recent period, in which the Family receives such a flood of prophecy from the spirit world, is as remarkable as FFing, but it does not yet involve outsiders as closely FFing did.

However, the Family has recently been increasing the importance of prophecy in its outreach. Most of the tracts currently distributed, as well as the newest posters, entirely concern prophecy. Family members are encouraged to pray and get prophecies for their closer friends and contacts. Perhaps in emphasizing prophecy, the Family again risks derision from the press and public officials. Yet done carefully and prayerfully, this could be the means by which the Family expanded its spiritual boundaries to encompass a new wave of recruits.

One can imagine a time in the near future, when each well-established missionary home led one or more homes or networks of nonmissionary members living in the same geographic area. These outer members would hold ordinary jobs in society, and have various living situations, but would fellowship regularly with the missionary home and participate in aspects of the Family's spiritual life. They would contribute material resources that would allow the missionary home to concentrate on its main mission. They would also spend their vacations from secular work going on evangelizing road trips under the guidance of full-time missionaries.

The Love Charter would specify the rules and regulations concerning relations between these inner and outer memberships. Perhaps there would be a
small category of outer members whose contributions and spiritual development
were of a sufficient level that it was appropriate for them to share spiritually and
sexually with inner members. But there might also be distinct circles of outer
members who shared exclusively with each other. Young adults growing up in
either category might be expected to devote themselves for at least two years to
missionary work, to determine if they had a calling to be full-time missionaries.
Young couples could fall in love, prayerfully discover whether they were destined
for the inner or outer membership, then take their places in the larger community of the Family.

Whether this is the way things will work out or not, the Family can make
its greatest contribution to the religious life of the future not by compromising
with the System, but by finding a new pattern of life beside the System and
most effective to influence and recruit people who still live within it. When the
Family ceased FFing, it did not abandon its beliefs about the sanctity of sharing
physical love.

There are dangers in the present shower of prophecies, as well. A person
who becomes a powerful channel for prophecy is the potential leader of a hereti-
cal schism, and thus unrestricted prophecy can threaten the integrity of the
social network, even as it strengthens many bonds within that network. Perhaps
the Family can find a way to help outer members develop their own communities of sharing and prophecy while building ever stronger commitments to Jesus.

The Love Charter establishes rules for deciding whether to implement the
guidance received through prophecies, and Maria determines which prophecies can appear in World Services publications.[30] Thus, homes that adhere to
the Charter are constrained from following prophecies that might take them
out of the governance structure of the Family.

In 1999, Maria received prophecy indicating that members must dedicate
themselves more clearly to the values of the Family, and Charter Members—
those who live in communal homes and are covered by all the regulations of
the Charter—were asked to sign a contract to this effect. In an internal publication titled "The Shakeup 2000," she wrote, "The CM [Charter Member]
Family is very much in need of a cleansing. We cannot continue on as we are. I
know you've sensed that there has been a gradual decline of purity, dedication
and spirituality in the Family, and we're not what we used to be. You've probably witnessed example after example of compromise, lack of dedication, and
refusal to live or even read the Word in many cases. . . . There are quite a few of
our YAs [Young Adults, age 18–20] and SGAs [Second-Generation Adults]

who don't seem to want to be in the Family, but who don't take the step to leave."[31]

Maria expressed concern specifically about "the movies being watched, the Internet sites being surfed, the computer games being played, the System music that's being listened to, the System books and novels being read, the ungodly religious and New Age doctrines that are being pondered, and all the ungodly attitudes being developed by those who want to see how far they can push their own agendas in the name of 'freedom.'"[32]

In addition to much prophecy from Jesus, Maria also received prophecy from her deceased husband. From five years beyond the grave, Father David reportedly wrote, "They say that no revolution or even reformation has lasted past the first generation, the pioneers, the ones who fought and bled and died for it. I can see why people have come to that conclusion, because usually the ones who have the truth and freedom handed to them without their having to fight for it don't appreciate it. Many on Earth and Here in Heaven have been watching the Family, to see if this will be proven true once again.

"Will those of you of the second generation, who didn't have to live in the hell of the System, who didn't have to forsake a whole life and all your loved ones and friends, who didn't have to make the initial decision to leave everything to take up your cross and follow Jesus, will you have the depth of conviction, the true heart of the Revolution to such a degree that you will carry it on?"[33] The full answer cannot be written in these pages; the life of the Family continues, but this book is reaching its conclusion.

By October 12, 1999, all adult members were asked to sign a Charter Membership contract, agreeing to obey the Charter's rules. Senior teens (age 16–17), who were voting members of their homes but not yet adults, were asked to sign a Provisional Charter Membership contract. Those who did not sign became Fellow Members and must do without much of the communication and communion restricted to Charter Members, or leave the Family altogether.

From the time of Father David's death in 1994 through 1998, the Charter membership of the Family had grown from 8,646 to 10,167, but by the end of 1999 it had droppped slightly to 9,918. The number of Fellow Members had followed the opposite trend, dropping from 3,957 in 1994 to 2,776 in 1998, then rising to 3,022 at the end of 1999.[34]

A move had been in progress to increase the fraction of the voluminous literature that is available to Fellow Members, and to include them in more frequent Fellowship meetings. Thus, Shakeup 2000 may go some distance toward creating a viable laity to which Charter Members could minister as clergy. In addition, the year 2000 saw new efforts to increase witnessing, recruit disciples, and build a stronger movement.[35]

Imposing discipline on the second generation during a time of spiritual revival carries risks. Most notably, an increased requirement for commitment may stimulate defection of young adults who are enticed by the attractions of secular society. On the other hand, revival has a tendency to generate small schisms as high-solidarity local groups start acting on the prophecies of one or more charismatic members.

At the same time, the Family must resist the corrosive effects of the surrounding secular society. Many young people may leave temporarily, only to discover to their misery that life in the System lacks the intimate emotional closeness and sense of profound purpose they enjoyed in the Family. As in the early 1990s, anticult activists may impel government officials to launch devastating persecutions. Yet, if the Family remains true to its principles, willing to adapt and to experiment but not to compromise, it will survive. In so doing, it will fulfill the words of Luke 20:36: "Neither can they die any more; for they are equal unto the angels; and are the children of God, being the children of the resurrection."

Conclusion

The Family is a novel religious movement in considerable tension with the surrounding sociocultural environment, yet its members are very similar to nonmembers in many respects. Of course they differ from outsiders in some of their religious beliefs and practices, and in those aspects of their lifestyle that are grounded in their distinctive religion. Yet perhaps the biggest surprise from our analysis comparing members with respondents to the General Social Survey is how similar they are on so many variables.

Some readers may also be surprised to see how much members of The Family differ from each other in their responses to most questions. Clearly, this is a group with considerable diversity of opinion, very much like that found in the encompassing society. We found no sign of the "brainwashing" or "mind control" that the mass media or extreme secularists might have expected.

If these results seem puzzling, then it is worth noting that the Family is a community as well as a faith. Members must work together and rely on each other to accomplish the practical tasks of life, as well as to carry out their difficult missionary activity. Success requires competence, cooperation, and realism. To cooperate successfully, members must be trustworthy, and the greatest benefits of cooperation come when a diversity of people contribute their complementary skills and perspectives to achievement of the group goals. Three decades of survival are a very substantial measure of success for such a high-tension religious movement.

My colleague Rodney Stark has criticized social scientific studies of new religious movements for focusing on idiosyncratic features of the groups they study, rather than collecting systematic data that would be of real comparative value: "Thus, studies of the Children of God (now known as the Family) are almost certain to discuss 'flirty-fishing,' but are unlikely to try to explain why the movement grew rapidly to about 10,000 members and then stagnated."[1]

This study has sought to be both systematic and comparative, and now I will attempt to satisfy Stark's challenge to explain the membership trajectory of The Family.

A qualification is in order first. Careful examination of a single case can identify factors that might, logically, be responsible for a particular set of outcomes, but it is seldom able to test a theory with any great confidence. A single case could provide a counterexample to a sweeping theory, as Malinowski's ethnography of the Trobriand Islanders refuted the supposed universality of the Oedipus complex in Freud's psychoanalytic theory.[2] But proving that a theory is true is not feasible with a single case, and we must be content with a reasonable but tentative analysis.

In a sense, the Family was created by a cultural collision between the holiness movement and the hippie movement of the late 1960s. Thus, in the words of Steven Tipton, people who initially joined the Family may have been merely "getting saved from the sixties."[3] Proverbially, the 1960s were a decade of unusual radicalization among young people that left thousands of them drifting unattached through society in pursuit of impossible goals and open to a particular style of salvation. In this analysis, the Family was so well adapted to the period of its birth that it lost the capacity to recruit new members in significant numbers once the surrounding culture had changed, a few years into the 1970s.

This does not necessarily mean that the birth rate of new religious movements dropped markedly after the 1960s, but rather that the kind of religions created in a particular period or cultural milieu will bear the mark of the environment in which they were born. Bryan Wilson has noted that new religions tend to recruit from relatively narrow constituencies, and the Family's distinctive constituency may simply have vanished, bringing the movement's growth to a halt.[4]

While somewhat plausible, this explanation is rather too facile. Interviews with many people who joined the Family in its early days reveal they were a highly diverse group, and few fit the stereotype of "hippies."[5] Certainly, people like the hippies continue to exist, and it should have been possible for a vigorous missionary campaign to locate enough of them to sustain growth had other factors been propitious.

A different explanation is that the Family stands at too high a degree of tension with the surrounding sociocultural environment, to recruit through conventional social networks. Religious movements need some tension, because they must be strict enough to demand real commitment from members. But if they make extreme demands, then only people who have nothing to lose will be willing to join. This not only greatly reduces the size of the potential recruit pool, but it also means that the few recruits gained are social isolates who lack influence in their communities and thus cannot draw in more recruits.[6]

Thus, high sectarian tension tends to be related to social isolation. In its formative years, the Family underwent a social implosion, in which members lost bonds to outsiders as the bonds between them strengthened markedly.[7] To join the Family requires a recruit to leave his or her former community and live in a high-solidarity communal home. Members of a high tension group tend to build intense, multiple social relationships among themselves. This makes it hard for them to sustain social relationships with outsiders. But the bulk of recruitment to religious movements occurs through social networks. By avoiding conventional employment, by keeping their children out of the schools, by moving frequently from nation to nation, and by introverted practices such as sexual sharing within the group, members of the Family are discouraged from developing ties to the surrounding communities from which they might recruit new members.

Although we have stressed the religious character of the Family, it is also true that membership is a way of life, with distinctive economic and domestic principles. Ever since the first few adventurous years, each home and individual member has had to balance missionary work with the practical tasks of running a household. Historians report that one factor bringing a halt to recruitment to the Shakers, a century and a half ago, was a shift toward living a relatively peaceful, sanctified life rather than exerting the often unrewarded effort required to recruit new members.[8] Thus have many religious movements lost their motivation to expand.

Social scientists have long understood that the birth of a second generation shifts a movement's priorities.[9] For the past two decades, there has been a very real sense in which the children of members have served as the functional equivalent of recruits. Socializing children to be committed and competent adult members may in fact have been far more profitable for their parents than risking the disruption of inviting a stranger into the home. However, it is difficult for a religious movement to have a sufficiently high fertility rate to offset death and defection, let alone to grow rapidly.

There is also a theological factor. The Family does not claim that members alone will be saved at the Endtime. Rather, all those who reject the mark of the beast can be saved, and other real Christians will play their own important roles in the final days. The crucial step in becoming saved is not joining The Family, but simply praying to accept Jesus into one's heart. For their part, this conceptualization allows Family missionaries to feel they have succeeded in winning a soul merely if a person prays, and they need not get discouraged if no new recruits join their communal home.

Thus we have identified six factors that may work against membership growth: loss of the original constituency because of historical change, excessive tension with the surrounding sociocultural environment, isolation from networks of potential recruits because of social implosion, a lifestyle that often distracts members from their missionary work, emphasis on fertility rather than recruitment for the production of new members, and a belief system that fails to emphasize recruitment. The six may reinforce each other, and it is difficult to weigh their relative significances quantitatively.

Although this is all quite plausible, there is a very different way of looking at the history of the Family that may be equally valid. Perhaps we should not emphasize its stagnation but its survival. To be sure, membership has not risen much above ten thousand. But it has not fallen, either. Despite a tumultuous three decades of existence, and the defection of many members, the movement has remained viable and active. This has given it the time to innovate.

The numerical growth of membership is an important measure of success for the social science of religious movements. But so, too, is innovation. Indeed, there may be a trade-off between recruitment and inventiveness. A group that grows rapidly may have no need to explore radical supernatural alternatives. The Family is creative in overcoming adversity, and it has shown a remarkable capacity for constant revolution. The Family is like an expedition, exploring new areas of human experience that may eventually come to be of great value for conventional society.

In recent decades, Western civilization has abandoned many of its traditional constraints on erotic behavior. As we have noted, one apparent result is plummeting birth rates in most countries that may lead before too very much longer to extinction. Perhaps experiments like sexual sharing in the Family will lead to a new spiritualization of erotic experiences in the larger society, that again renders them life-giving rather than selfish.

The materialism of postindustrial society renders spiritual experiences anomalous, yet people need a sense that it is possible to transcend the material world. Thus, the flood of messages that the Family believes it receives from the spirit world is potentially revolutionary. Secularism cannot be defeated by abstract theological speculations that God might possibly exist, but only by palpable evidence that He not only exists but also cares for humans and intervenes in their lives. Thus the personal spiritual experiences that Family members report are a significant resource for restoring faith to a faithless world.

In other areas, the Family seems well prepared to innovate in the future. For example, while making extensive use of modern information technology, the movement warns that computers can be tools of satanic oppression. One of the more remarkable facts about the dawn of the twenty-first century is the lack of a vigorous social movement resisting computerization of human life. Without effective critics to ensure that computers are used for human betterment, bureaucracies may employ the technology to extend their control and thereby stifle freedom. Thus, a computer-savvy movement resisting "the mark of the beast" may contribute to a serious debate on the proper role of computers in society.

Economic, technical, and cultural globalization may be inexorably homogenizing the societies of the world. Just as conservationists are rightly concerned about preserving endangered species and maintaining biodiversity, we should worry about the loss of cultural diversity taking place across the world. The Family shows us that it is possible for a distinct subculture to arise and to participate in globalization without blending into the blandness of transnational corporate society.

Most fundamentally, the Family reminds us that people very much like ourselves may have very different religious beliefs and practices from our own. We have to realize that prejudice against high-tension religious movements is just as unfair and pernicious as racism or anti-Semitism. The primary findings of this study are that members of the Family are sincere religious believers and that persecution of their movement harms innocent human beings.

In following the Law of Love, and by opening their hearts to prophecy, members of the Family have earned a unique right to speak the words of Rom. 8:16: "The Spirit itself beareth witness with our spirit, that we are the children of God."

Notes

Introduction

1. Rodney Stark and William Sims Bainbridge, *A Theory of Religion* (New York: Toronto/Lang, 1987), p. 122; *The Future of Religion* (Berkeley: University of California Press, 1985), pp. 48–66.

2. William Sims Bainbridge, *The Sociology of Religious Movements* (New York: Routledge, 1997), pp. 208–240.

3. Roy Wallis, *Salvation and Protest* (New York: St. Martin's, 1979), pp. 51–90; "Yesterday's Children: Cultural and Structural Change in a New Religious Movement," in *The Social Impact of New Religious Movements*, edited by Bryan Wilson (New York: Rose of Sharon, 1981), pp. 97–133.

Chapter 1. Persecution

1. John L. Brandt, *Great Bible Questions* (New York: Fleming H. Revel, 1926).

2. Virginia Brandt, *The Hem of His Garment* and *Streams that Never Run Dry* (Zurich, Switzerland: World Services, 1981).

3. Samson Warner, *We Are the Children of God!* (Zurich: World Services, 1983), p. 22.

4. Ibid., p. 26.

5. Ibid., p. 30.

6. Ted Patrick and Tom Dulack, *Let Our Children Go!* (New York: Balantine, 1976).

7. James R. Lewis and J. Gordon Melton, editors, *Sex, Slander, and Salvation: Investigating The Family/Children of God* (Stanford, California: Center

175

for Academic Publication, 1994); James T. Richardson and Rex Davis, "Experiential Fundamentalism," *Journal of the American Academy of Religion*, 1983, vol. 51, p. 407.

8. Susan Claire Borowick, "Falsely Accused and Jailed in Argentina," *Persecution Endtime News* (March 1994) 3:1–8; (June 1994) 4:1–12.

Chapter 2. Survey

1. Eileen Barker, "Who'd Be a Moonie?" in *The Social Impact of New Religious Movements*, edited by Bryan Wilson (New York: Rose of Sharon Press, 1981), pp. 59–96; "The Ones Who Got Away," in *Religious Movements*, edited by Rodney Stark (Rose of Sharon Press, 1984); E. Burke Rochford, Jr., "Prabhupada Centennial Survey: A Summary of the Final Report," *ISKCON Communications Journal*, vol. 7 (June 1999), pp. 11–26.

2. James T. Richardson, "Apostates, Whistleblowers, Law, and Social Control, in *The Politics of Religious Apostasy*, edited by David G. Bromley (Westport, Conn.: Praeger, 1998), p. 182.

3. James A. Davis and Tom W. Smith, *General Social Surveys, 1972–1996: Cumulative Codebook* (Chicago: National Opinion Research Center, 1996).

4. William Sims Bainbridge, "Religious Ecology of Deviance," *American Sociological Review*, 1989, vol. 54, pp. 288–295; William Sims Bainbridge and Daniel H. Jackson, "The Rise and Decline of Transcendental Meditation," in *The Sociological Impact of New Religious Movements*, edited by Bryan Wilson (New York: Rose of Sharon Press, 1981), pp. 135–158.

5. Of the 1,025 respondents, 1,014 reported whether they were female or male.

6. At the end of 1997, as the survey data collection came to a close, Peter Amsterdam estimated the mean home size to be 13.3 persons, and 15 is the median across individual respondents, not homes. During this period, there was a strong push to reduce Family homes in size, as more small ones were being established to cover a wider mission field. See Peter Amsterdam, "Victory Review '97!" internal Family publication CM 3159, January 1998, p. 4.

7. Peter Amsterdam, "Victory Review '97!" internal Family publication CM 3159, January 1998, p. 5.

8. *The Love Charter* (Zurich: The Family, 1998).

9. James T. Richardson, "Financing the New Religions," *Journal for the Scientific Study of Religion*, 1982, vol. 21, pp. 255–268; see also Rex, Davis,

and James T. Richardson, "The Organization and Functioning of the Children of God," *Sociological Analysis*, 1976, vol. 37, pp. 334–336; Frederick B. Bird and Frances Westley, "The Economic Strategies of New Religious Movements," *Sociological Analysis*, 1985, vol. 46, pp. 157–170.

10. I described how a different new religious movement did this in my earlier book, *Satan's Power* (Berkeley: University of California Press, 1978) pp. 278–279.

11. "Worldwide Activity Report," June 1998, Family publication FAR 070.

12. Anson D. Shupe and David G. Bromley, *The New Vigilantes: Deprogrammers, Anti-Cultists, and the New Religions*, (Beverly Hills: Sage, 1980).

13. William Sims Bainbridge, *Satan's Power* (Berkeley: University of California Press, 1978), p. 14; "Cultural Genetics," in *Religious Movements* edited by Rodney Stark (New York: Paragon, 1985), p. 157.

Chapter 3. Beliefs

1. Those responding "don't know" have been excluded from the analysis because the alternatives already included an agnostic option, so they may have been unwilling to say what their real feelings were.

2. Rodney Stark and William Sims Bainbridge, *The Future of Religion* (Berkeley: University of California Press, 1985).

3. Ted G. Jelen, "Biblical Literalism and Inerrancy: Does the Difference Make a Difference?" *Sociological Analysis*, 49 (1989), pp. 421–429.

4. David Brandt Berg, "The Name of Jesus!" GP 345, April 16, 1975.

5. Larry D. Shinn, "Conflicting Networks: Guru and Friend in ISKCON," in *Religious Movements* edited by Rodney Stark (New York: Paragon, 1985), pp. 95–114.

6. Rodney Stark and Charles Y. Glock, *American Piety* (Berkeley: University of California Press, 1968) p. 37; Rodney Stark and William Sims Bainbridge, *The Future of Religion* (Berkeley: University of California Press, 1985), p. 55.

7. Clark Wade Roof and Jennifer L. Roof, "Review of the Polls: Images of God among Americans," *Journal for the Scientific Study of Religion*, 23 (June 1984), pp. 201–205.

8. Hart M. Nelsen, Neil H. Cheek, Jr., and Paul Au, "Gender Differences in Images of God," *Journal for the Scientific Study of Religion*, 1985, vol. 24, pp. 396–402.

9. Andrew M. Greeley, "Evidence that a Maternal Image of God Correlates with Liberal Politics," *Sociology and Social Research*, 1988, vol. 72, pp. 150–154.

10. Cf. David Kowalewski, "Cultism, Insurgency, and Vigilantism in the Philippines, *Sociological Analysis*, 1991, vol. 52, pp. 241–253.

11. MO Letter 312, "Benefits of Backsliding," August 9, 1972.

12. Philip Sherwood, editor, *Glimpses of Heaven* (Orange, Calif.: Family Care Foundation, 1997), p. 45.

13. John E. Mueller, "Public Expectations of War During the Cold War," *American Journal of Political Science*, 23 (May 1979), pp. 301–329.

14. Norman Cohn, *The Pursuit of the Millennium* (New York: Harper, 1961); Lance Morrow, "A Cosmic Moment" in *Beyond the Year 2000*, a special issue of *Time*, Fall 1992, vol. 140, no. 27, pp. 6–9.

15. Martin Gardner, *Fads and Fallacies in the Name of Science* (New York: Dover, 1957), pp. 181–182; Alan Rogerson, *Millions Now Living Will Never Die: A Study of Jehovah's Witnesses* (London: Constable, 1969); James A. Beckford, *The Trumpet of Prophecy: A Sociological Study of Jehovah's Witnesses* (New York: John Wiley and Sons, 1975); Melvin D. Curry, *Jehovah's Witnesses: The Millenarian World of the Watch Tower* (New York: Garland, 1992).

16. Richard Scruggs, Steven Zipperstein, Robert Lyon, Victor Gonzalez, Herbert Cousins, and Roderick Beverly, *Report to the Deputy Attorney General on the Events at Waco, Texas, February 28 to April 19, 1993*, redacted version (Washington, D.C.: Department of Justice, 1993); Lawrence E. Sullivan, "Recommendations Concerning Incidents such as the Branch Davidian Standoff in Waco," letter reprinted in *Recommendations of Experts for Improvement in Federal Law Enforcement After Waco*. (Washington, D.C.: Department of Justice and Department of the Treasury, 1993); James D. Tabor and Eugene V. Gallagher, *Why Waco? Cults and the Battle for Religious Freedom in America* (Berkeley: University of California Press, 1995); Stuart A. Wright (ed.), *Armageddon: Critical Perspectives on the Branch Davidian Catastrophe* (Chicago: University of Chicago Press, 1995).

17. Lofland, John and Rodney Stark, "Becoming a World-Saver: A Theory of Conversion to a Deviant Perspective," *American Sociological Review* 1965, vol. 30, pp. 862–875.

18. Shoko Asahara, *The Day of Destruction* [Metsubo No Hi] (Tokyo: AUM 1989); *Doom to Emptiness* [Metsubo Kara Kokue] (Tokyo: AUM, 1989).

19. David Brandt Berg, "70–Year Prophecy," GP 156, March 1, 1972.

20. David Brandt Berg, *The Book of the Future!* (Zurich: World Service, 1984), p. 29.

21. Ibid., p. 137.

22. Ibid., p. 201.

23. Ibid., p. 219.

Chapter 4. Practices

1. Rodney Stark and Charles Y. Glock, *American Piety* (Berkeley, California: University of California Press, 1968), p. 109.

2. The Family, *The Love Charter* (Zurich: The Family, 1995–1998), p. 1.

3. Ibid.

4. Ibid., p. 2.

5. Rodney Stark and William Sims Bainbridge, *The Future of Religion* (Berkeley: University of California Press, 1985), p. 339.

6. Ibid.

7. Andrew Greeley, "The Paranormal Is Normal: A Sociologist Looks at Parapsychology," *The Journal of the American Society for Psychic Research*, 1991, vol. 85, pp. 367–374.

8. William C. McCready and Andrew M. Greeley, *The Ultimate Values of the American Population* (Beverly Hills: Sage, 1976), pp. 129–157.

9. Rodney Stark, "Normal Revelations: A Rational Model of 'Mystical' Experiences," *Religion and the Social Order*, 1991, vol. 1, p. 242.

10. Apollos, edited from the writings of David Brandt Berg, "Communicating with Heavenly Messengers!" (Zurich: The Family, 1996), p. 3.

11. Ironically, Alberta has a long history of religious radicalism. See William E. Mann, *Sect, Cult and Church in Alberta* (Toronto: University of Toronto Press, 1955).

12. Cf. "The Call of India!" MO Letter 177, September 10, 1972.

13. Maria, "Go for the Gold!" *Good News!* GN 657 DO, November 1995.

14. Maria, "Healing Balm for Grieving Parents," *Good News!* GN 645 DO, August 1995, p. 4.

15. Peter Amsterdam, "Victory Review '97!" Family internal publication CM 3159, January 1998, p. 6.

16. Sir Walter Scott, *The Perfect Ones* (Thailand: Aurora Productions, 1998), un-numbered preface page.

Chapter 5. Alienation

1. Allan W. Eister, "A Theory of Cults," *Journal for the Scientific Study of Religion* 1972, 11: 319–333.

2. Miriam Williams, *Heaven's Harlots* (New York: William Morrow, 1998), p. 258.

3. Benjamin Zablocki, *Alienation and Charisma* (New York: Free Press, 1980).

4. Leo Srole, "Social Integration and Certain Corollaries: An Exploratory Study," *American Sociological Review*, 1956, vol. 21, pp. 709–716; Jack Martin and Steven Stack, "The Effect of Religiosity on Alienation: A Multivariate Analysis of Normlessness," *Sociological Focus*, 1983, vol. 16, pp. 65–76.

5. Lawrence K. Hong, "Anomia and Religiosity: Some Evidence for Reconceptualization," *Review of Religious Research* 1981, vol. 22, p. 243.

6. Eugen Schoenfeld, "Integration and Anomia: A Re-Examination," *Humboldt Journal of Social Relations* 1983, vol. 11, pp. 74–85.

7. John Ryan, "Marital Happiness and Anomia," *Journal of Marriage and the Family*, 1981, vol. 43, pp. 643–649; Lawrence A. Lovell-Troy, "Anomia among Employed Wives and Housewives: An Exploratory Analysis," *Journal of Marriage and the Family*, 1983, vol. 45, pp. 301–310.

8. Arthur Couch and Kenneth Kenniston, "Yeasayers and Naysayers: Agreeing Response Set as a Personality Variable," *Journal of Abnormal and Social Psychology*, 1960, vol. 60, pp. 151–174; William Sims Bainbridge, *Social Research Methods and Statistics* (Belmont, Calif.: Wadsworth, 1992), p. 213.

9. Seymour Martin Lipset and William Schneider, *The Confidence Gap* (New York, Free Press: 1983); "The Confidence Gap During the Reagan Years, 1981–1987," *Political Science Quarterly*, 102 (Spring 1987), 1–23.

10. Susannah Feher, "Who Looks to the Stars? Astrology and Its Constituency," *Journal for the Scientific Study of Religion*, 31 (March 1992), pp. 88–93.

11. J. Gordon Melton, "The Revival of Astrology in the United States," in *Religious Movements*, edited by Rodney Stark (New York: Paragon, 1985), pp. 279–299.

12. David Berg, MO Letter 107, "Personal Replies," January 1971.

13. Abbey Jack Neidik and Irene Angelico, *The Love Prophet and the Children of God*, television documentary (Toronto: DLI Productions and TV Ontario, 1998).

14. Kuo-Tsai Liou, Donald D. Sylvia, and Gregory Brunk, "Non-work Factors and Job Satisfaction Revisited," *Human Relations*, 1990, vol. 43, pp. 77–86.

15. For example, see Frank Clemente and William J. Sauer, "Life Satisfaction in the United States," *Social Forces*, 1976, vol. 54, pp. 621–631; Jay A. Mancini, "Social Indicators of Family Life Satisfaction: A Comparison of Husbands and Wives," *International Journal of Sociology of the Family*, 1979, vol. 9, pp. 221–231.

16. Jon P. Alston, George D. Lowe, and Alice Wrigley, "Socioeconomic Correlates for Four Dimensions of Self-Perceived Satisfaction, 1972," *Human Organization*, 1974, vol. 33, pp. 99–102; Harsha N. Mookherjee, "Perceptions of Well-Being by Metropolitan and Nonmetropolitan Populations in the United States," *The Journal of Social Psychology*, 1992, vol. 132, pp. 513–524.

17. Rosabeth Moss Kanter, *Commitment and Community* (Cambridge, Massachusetts: Harvard University Press, 1972).

18. Kenneth F. Ferraro and Cynthia M. Albrecht-Jensen, "Does Religion Influence Adult Health?" *Journal for the Scientific Study of Religion*, 1991, vol. 30, pp. 193–202.

19. Melvin Pollner, "Divine Relations, Social Relations, and Well-Being," *Journal of Health and Social Behavior*, 1989, vol. 30, pp. 92–104.

20. Christopher G. Ellison, "Religious Involvement and Subjective Well-Being," *Journal of Health and Social Behavior*, 1991, vol. 32, pp. 80–89; see also Christopher G. Ellison, David A. Gay, and Thomas A. Glass, "Does Religious Commitment Contribute to Individual Life Satisfaction?" *Social Forces*, 1989, vol. 68, pp. 100–123.

21. Benjamin Zablocki, *Alienation and Charisma* (New York: Free Press, 1980), pp. 8, 258–266.

22. Charles N. Weaver and Robert S. Franz, "Work-Related Attitudes of Entrepreneurs, Public, and Private Employees," *Psychological Reports*, 1992, vol. 70, pp. 387–390.

23. Number of cases for these three items ranges from 1,017 to 1,019 for the Family, and from 901 to 902 for the General Social Survey.

24. Andrew F. Henry and James F. Short, *Suicide and Homicide* (Glencoe, Ill.: Free Press, 1954).

25. Rodney Stark and William Sims Bainbridge, *Religion, Deviance and Social Control* (New York: Routledge, 1996), pp. 31–51.

26. George C. Homans, *The Nature of Social Science* (New York: Harcourt, Brace and World, 1967); *The Human Group* (New York: Harcourt, Brace and World, 1950); *Social Behavior: Its Elementary Forms* (New York: Harcourt Brace Jovanovich, 1974).

27. Daniel Bell, "Religion in the Sixties," *Social Research* 1971, 38: 447–497.

Chapter 6. Sexuality

1. Angela A. Aidala, "Social Change, Gender Roles, and New Religious Movements," *Sociological Analysis*, 1985, vol. 46, pp. 287–314.

2. Paul A. M. Lange, "Being Better but Not Smarter Than Others," *Personality and Social Psychology Bulletin*, 1991, vol. 17, pp. 689–693.

3. *Word Topics* (Thailand: World Services, 1998), pp. 653, 655.

4. "Solid" means statistically significant at or beyond the 0.01 level by several tests, using the raw data with six values for the friend-quality variables rather than percentages based on collapsed categories. Given that we have fully fifteen relationships to test, the 0.05 level of significance did not seem demanding enough, because we would expect 1/20 of such tests to come out positive purely by chance. Marginally significant means achieving the 0.02 level.

5. *The Song of Solomon* 1:2, 4:3–5, 5:4–5, 8:6–7.

6. Lawrence Foster, *Religion and Sexuality* (New York: Oxford University Press, 1981).

7. Frederic M. Thrasher, *The Gang* (Chicago: University of Chicago Press, 1927); Jules Henry, *Jungle People: A Kaingang Tribe of the Highlands of Brazil* (New York: Vintage, 1964).

8. Rosabeth Moss Kanter, *Commitment and Community: Communes and Utopias in Sociological Perspective* (Cambridge: Harvard University Press, 1972).

9. William Sims Bainbridge, "Shaker Demographics 1840–1900," *Journal for the Scientific Study of Religion*, 21 (1982), pp. 352–365; "The Decline of the Shakers," *Communal Societies*, 4 (1984), pp. 19–34; Stephen J. Stein, *The Shaker Experience in America* (New Haven, Connecticut: Yale University Press, 1992).

10. John R. Hall, *Gone from the Promised Land* (New Brunswick, N.J.: Transaction, 1987); David Chidester, *Salvation and Suicide* (Bloomington: Indiana University Press, 1988); Stuart A. Wright (ed.), *Armageddon in Waco* (Chicago: University of Chicago Press, 1995).

11. William Sims Bainbridge, *Satan's Power* (Berkeley, California: University of California Press, 1978).

12. Maren Lockwood Carden, *Oneida* (Baltimore: Johns Hopkins University Press, 1969).

13. Stephen, "God's Love Erased the Pain of a Thousand Wounds," *Flirty Fishing—The Inside Story*, FFT03-DFO, August 1995, pp. 5–6.

14. Paul Williams, *Christianity and Sex* (Zurich: The Family 1995).

15. "Position and Policy Statement: Attitudes, Conduct, Current Beliefs and Teachings Regarding Sex," World Services, The Family, April 1992.

16. Norval D. Glenn and Charles N. Weaver, "Attitudes Toward Premarital, Extra-Marital, and Homosexual Relations in the United States in the 1970's," *Journal of Sex Research*, 1979, vol. 15, pp. 108–118; B. Krishna Singh, "Trends in Attitudes Toward Premarital Sexual Relations," *Journal of Marriage and the Family*, 36 (May 1980), pp. 387–393.

17. Ira L. Reiss, Ronald E. Anderson, and G. C. Sponaugle, "A Multivariate Model of the Determinants of Extramarital Sexual Permissiveness," *Journal of Marriage and the Family*, 42 (May 1980), pp. 395–411; Jon P. Alston, "Attitudes Toward Extramarital and Homosexual Relations," *Journal for the Scientific Study of Religion*, 1974, vol. 13, pp. 479–481.

18. Rodney Stark and William Sims Bainbridge, *Religion, Deviance and Social Control* (New York: Routledge, 1996), p. 93.

19. E. Wilbur Bock, Leonard Beeghley, and Anthony J. Mixon, "Religion, Socioeconomic Status, and Sexual Morality," *Sociological Quarterly*, 1983, vol. 24, pp. 545–559; John K. Cochran and Leonard Beeghley, "The Influence of Religion on Attitudes toward Nonmarital Sexuality," *Journal for the Scientific Study of Religion*, 1991, vol. 30, pp. 45–62.

20. John H. Simpson, "Moral Issues and Status Politics," in *The New Religious Right*, Robert C. Liebman and Robert Wuthnow (eds.) (New York, Aldine, 1983); Carol Mueller, "In Search of a Constituency for the 'New Religious Right,'" *Public Opinion Quarterly*, 46 (1983), pp. 213–229; William Schneider and I. A. Lewis, "The Straight Story on Homosexuality and Gay Rights," *Public Opinion*, 7 (February/March 1984), pp. 16–60; Robin D. Perrin, "American Religion in the Post-Aquarian Age," *Journal for the Scientific Study of Religion*, 28 (1989) 75–89; Randy Fisher, Donna Derison, Chester F. Polley III, Jennifer Cadman, and Dana Johnston, "Religiousness, Religious Orientation, and Attitudes Towards Gays and Lesbians," *Journal of Applied Social Psychology*, 24 (1994), pp. 614–630.

21. William Ray Arney and William H. Tresher, "Trends in Attitudes Toward Abortion, 1972–1975," *Family Planning Perspectives*, 8 (May/June 1976), pp. 117–124; B. Krishna Singh and Peter J. Leahy, "Contextual and Ideological Dimensions of Attitudes Toward Discretionary Abortion," *Demography* 15 (August 1978), pp. 381–388; William Alex McIntosh, Letitia T. Alston, and Jon P. Alston, "The Differential Impact of Religious Preference and Church Attendance on Attitudes Toward Abortion," *Review of Religious*

Research, 20 (Spring 1979), pp. 195–213; John H. Simpson, "Moral Issues and Status Politics," in *The New Religious Right*, Robert C. Liebman and Robert Wuthnow (eds.) (New York, Aldine, 1983); Carol Mueller, "In Search of a Constituency for the 'New Religious Right,'" *Public Opinion Quarterly*, 46 (1983), pp. 213–229; Mary Holland Benin, "Determinants of Opposition to Abortion," *Sociological Perspectives*, 28 (April 1985), pp. 199–216; Ted G. Jelen, "Changes in the Attitudinal Correlations of Opposition to Abortion, 1977–1985," *Journal for the Scientific Study of Religion*, 27 (June 1988), pp. 211–228; Robert F. Szafran and Arthur F. Clagett, "Variable Predictors of Attitudes Toward the Legalization of Abortion," *Social Indicators Research*, 20 (June 1988), pp. 271–290; Everett Carll Ladd, "A Debate on Abortion," *Public Opinion*, 12 (May/June 1989), pp. 3–8; Robin D. Perrin, "American Religion in the Post-Aquarian Age," *Journal for the Scientific Study of Religion*, 28 (1989) 75–89; Eric Woodrum and Beth L. Davison, "Reexamination of Religious Influences on Abortion Attitudes," *Review of Religious Research* 33 (March 1992), pp. 229–243.

22. Mario Renzi, "Ideal Family Size as an Intervening Variable Between Religion and Attitudes Toward Abortion," *Journal for the Scientific Study of Religion*, 14 (March 1975), pp. 23–27; B. Krishna Singh and Peter J. Leahy, "Contextual and Ideological Dimensions of Attitudes Toward Discretionary Abortion," *Demography* 15 (August 1978), pp. 381–388; Ted G. Jelen, "Respect for Life, Sexual Morality, and Opposition to Abortion," *Review of Religious Research*, 25 (March 1984), pp. 220–231; Allan L. McCutcheon, "Sexual Morality, Pro-life Values, and Attitudes Toward Abortion," *Sociological Methods and Research*, 16 (November 1987), pp. 256–275.

23. David Millikan, "Flirty Fishing Interview," in James R. Lewis and J. Gordon Melton, editors, *Sex, Slander, and Salvation: Investigating The Family/ Children of God* (Stanford: Center for Academic Publication, 1994), pp. 263–266.

24. Miriam Williams, *Heaven's Harlots* (New York: William Morrow, 1998), p. 109.

25. S. Kenneth Chi and Sharon K. Houseknecht, "Protestant Fundamentalism and Marital Success," *Sociology and Social Research*, 1985, vol. 69, pp. 351–375.

26. *The Love Charter* (Zurich: The Family, 1998), p. 6.

27. "Living the Lord's Law of Love!—Part 1," *Good News!* GN 804 CM, September 1998, pp. 3, 12–13.

28. "Living the Lord's Law of Love!—Part 2," *Good News!* GN 805 CM, September 1998, p. 11.

29. C. S. Lewis, *The Return of the Seven Keys* (Thailand: Aurora Productions, 1998), p. 106.

30. Ibid., p. 111.

31. Anonymous, *Cool Tips for Hot Sex* (Mexico: World Services, n.d.).

32. Maria, "Go for the Gold!" *Good News!* GN 657 DO, November 1995, p. 16.

Chapter 7. Children

1. Nathan Keyfitz, "The Family that Does not Reproduce Itself." In *Below Replacement Fertility in Industrial Societies*, edited by Kingsley Davis, Mikhail Bernstam and Rita Ricardo-Campbell (Cambridge, UK: Cambridge University Press, 1987).

2. Kingsley Davis, "The Theory of Change and Response in Modern Demographic History," *Population Index* 1963, 29:345–366; William Fielding Ogburn, *Social Change* (New York: Huebsch, 1922).

3. Rodney Stark, *The Rise of Christianity* (Princeton: Princeton University Press, 1996).

4. John Knodel and Etienne van de Walle, "Lessons from the Past: Policy Implications of Historical Fertility Studies," *Population and Development Review* 1979, 5:217–245.

5. Andrew Cherlin, *Marriage, Divorce and Remarriage* (Cambridge: Harvard University Press, 1981); Alice S. Rossi, "Gender and Parenthood," *American Sociological Review* 1984, 49:1–16; Martin King Whyte, *Dating, Mating and Marriage* (New York: Aldine de Gruyter, 1990).

6. Judith Blake, "Family Size and the Quality of Children," *Demography*, 1981, vol. 18, pp. 421–442; *Family Size and Achievement* (Berkeley: University of California Press, 1989).

7. Nancy R. Vogt, *Correlates of Adolescent Sexual Activity in the Family*, unpublished doctoral dissertation (Fuller Theological Seminary, 1998).

8. Based on responses from 1,019 Family members and 1,397 GSS respondents.

9. Based on responses from 1,022 Family members and 1,398 GSS respondents.

10. Christian Vocational College, *Program of Studies* (Glendale, Calif.: Christian Vocational College, 1996), p. iii.

11. Gerhard Lenski, *The Religious Factor* (Garden City, New York: Doubleday, 1961); Duane F. Alwin, "Religion and Parental Child-Rearing Orientations," *American Journal of Sociology*, 1986, vol. 92, pp. 412–440.

12. Emile Durkheim, *Suicide* (New York: Free Press, 1951 [1897]); Max Weber, *The Protestant Ethic and the Spirit of Protestantism* (New York: Scribner's, 1958 [1904–1905]).

13. Duane F. Alwin, "Changes in Qualities Valued in Children in the United States, 1964 to 1984," *Social Science Research*, 1989, vol. 18, pp. 195–236.

14. Andrew Greeley, "Protestant and Catholic," *American Sociological Review*, 1989, vol. 54: 485–502.

15. The number of Family members responding equals 1,014; 1996 GSS, 1,956 American adults responded.

16. William Sims Bainbridge, *The Sociology of Religious Movements* (New York: Routledge, 1997), pp. 54–58.

17. Rodney Stark and William Sims Bainbridge, *A Theory of Religion* (New York: Peter Lang: 1987), p. 270; H. Richard Niebuhr, *The Social Sources of Denominationalism* (New York: Henry Holt, 1929).

18. Charlotte E. Hardman, "The Ethics of Children in Three New Religions," in *Children in New Religions*, edited by Susan J. Palmer and Charlotte E. Hardman (New Brunswick, N.J.: Rutgers University Press, 1999), pp. 239–240.

19. Maria, "Trash Your Trinkets and Head for the Hills!," Maria #434 CM/FM 3186, April 1998.

20. John Humphrey Noyes, *History of American Socialisms* (Philadelphia: Lippincott, 1870); *Male Continence* (New York: Gideon Press, 1975 [1872]); *Essay on Scientific Propagation* (Oneida, N.Y.: Oneida Community, 1875); Pierrepont Noyes, *My Father's House: An Oneida Boyhood* (New York: Farrar and Reinhart, 1937); Maren Lockwood Carden, *Oneida: Utopian Community to Modern Corporation* (Baltimore: Johns Hopkins Press, 1969).

21. Catherine R. Dobbs, *Freedom's Will, the Society of Separatists of Zoar* (New York: William Frederick Press, 1947).

22. Stephen J. Stein, *The Shaker Experience in America* (New Haven: Yale University Press, 1992).

23. Rodney Stark and William Sims Bainbridge, *Religion, Deviance and Social Control* (New York: Routledge, 1996), pp. 172–181.

24. William Sims Bainbridge, "Shaker Demographics," *Journal for the Scientific Study of Religion* 21 (1982), pp. 352–265; "Decline of the Shakers" *Communal Societies* 4 (1984), pp. 19–34.

25. Peter Amsterdam, "Year-end Review of 1998," CM 3224, December 1998; "End of a Millennium!" CM 3291, January 2000.

26. Herman Kahn and Anthony J. Wiener, *The Year 2000* (New York: Macmillan, 1967); Daniel Bell (editor), *Toward the Year 2000* (Boston: Beacon Press, 1969).

27. William Sims Bainbridge, *The Spaceflight Revolution* (New York: Wiley-Interscience, 1976).

28. Robert Houriet, *Getting Back Together* (New York: Avon, 1972); Hugh Gardner, *The Children of Prosperity* (New York: St. Martin's, 1978).

29. Charlotte Hardman, "Keeping the Faith and Leaving the Army: TRF Supporters of the Lord's Endtime Family," in James R. Lewis and J. Gordon Melton, editors, *Sex, Slander, and Salvation* (Stanford: Center for Academic Publication, 1994), pp. 97–112.

30. *The Love Charter* (Zurich: The Family, 1998) pp. 352–354.

31. Maria, "The Shakeup 2000," GN 857 CM/FM, September 1999, p. 2.

32. Ibid., p. 3.

33. Father David quoted by Maria, ibid., p. 31.

34. Peter Amsterdam, "End of a Millennium!" CM 3291, January 2000.

35. Maria, "Our Activated Future!" CM 3298, April, 2000.

Conclusion

1. Rodney Stark, "Why Religious Movements Succeed or Fail: A Revised General Model," *Journal of Contemporary Religion*, 11 (1996), pp. 133–146.

2. Bronislaw Malinowski, *Sex and Repression in Savage Society* (New York: Meridian, 1970 [1927]).

3. Steven M. Tipton, *Getting Saved from the Sixties* (Berkeley: University of California Press, 1982).

4. Bryan R. Wilson, "Factors in the Failure of the New Religious Movements," in David G. Bromley and Phillip E. Hammond, editors, *The Future of New Religious Movements* (Macon, Georgia: Mercer University Press, 1987), pp. 30–45.

5. William Sims Bainbridge, *The Sociology of Religious Movements* (New York: Routledge, 1997), pp. 208–240.

6. Rodney Stark and William Sims Bainbridge, *The Future of Religion* (Berkeley: University of California Press, 1985); *A Theory of Religion* (New York: Toronto/Lang, 1987); *Religion, Deviance and Social Control* (New York: Routledge, 1986).

7. Extended analysis of a social implosion in another new religious movement can be found in William Sims Bainbridge, *Satan's Power* (Berkeley: University of California Press, 1978).

8. John McKelvie Whitworth, *God's Blueprints* (London: Routledge and Kegan Paul, 1975); William Sims Bainbridge, "Shaker Demographics 1840–1900: An Example of the Use of Census Enumeration Schedules," *Journal for the Scientific Study of Religion* 21 (1982), pp. 352–365; "The Decline of the Shakers," Communal Societies 4 (1984), pp. 19–34; "Utopian Communities: Theoretical Issues," in Phillip E. Hammond, editor, *The Sacred in a Secular Age* (Berkeley: University of California Press, 1985), pp. 21–35; Stephen J. Stein, *The Shaker Experience in America* (New Haven: Yale University Press, 1992).

9. H. Richard Niebuhr, *The Social Sources of Denominationalism* (New York: Henry Holt, 1929).

Bibliography

Aidala, Angela A. "Social Change, Gender Roles, and New Religious Movements." *Sociological Analysis* 46 (1985): 287–314.

Alston, Jon P., George D. Lowe, and Alice Wrigley. "Attitudes Toward Extramarital and Homosexual Relations," *Journal for the Scientific Study of Religion* 13 (1974): 479–481.

————. "Socioeconomic Correlates for Four Dimensions of Self-Perceived Satisfaction," *Human Organization* 33 (1974): 99–102.

Alwin, Duane F. "Religion and Parental Child-Rearing Orientation," *American Journal of Sociology* 92 (1986): 412–440.

————. "Changes in Qualities Valued in Children in the United States, 1964 to 1984," *Social Science Research* 18 (1989): 195–236.

Anonymous. *The Family: Making the World a Better Place!* Various locations including Zurich: The Family, 1994.

Arney, William Ray, and William H. Tresher. "Trends in Attitudes Toward Abortion, 1972–1975," *Family Planning Perspectives* 8 (1976): 117–124.

Bainbridge, William Sims. *The Spaceflight Revolution.* New York: Wiley-Interscience, 1976.

————. *Satan's Power.* Berkeley: University of California Press, 1978.

————. Book review of *The New Vigilantes* by Anson D. Shupe and David G. Bromley, Social Forces 60 (1982): 955–957.

————. "Shaker Demographics 1840–1900," *Journal for the Scientific Study of Religion* 21 (1982): 352–365

————. "The Decline of the Shakers," *Communal Societies,* 4 (1984): 19–34.

————. "Cultural Genetics." In *Religious Movements,* edited by Rodney Stark. New York: Paragon, 1985, p. 157–198.

————. "Utopian Communities: Theoretical Issues." In *The Sacred in a Secular Age*, edited by Phillip E. Hammond. Berkeley: University of California Press, 1985, p. 21–35.

————. "Religious Ecology of Deviance," *American Sociological Review* 54 (1989): 288–295.

————. *Survey Research: A Computer-Assisted Introduction*. Belmont, California: Wadsworth, 1989.

————. *Social Research Methods and Statistics*. Belmont, California: Wadsworth, 1992.

————. *The Sociology of Religious Movements*. New York: Routledge, 1997.

————. *Sociology*. New York: Barron's, 1997.

Bainbridge, William Sims, and Daniel H. Jackson. "The Rise and Decline of Transcendental Meditation." In *The Sociological Impact of New Religious Movements*, edited by Bryan Wilson. New York: Rose of Sharon Press, 1981, p. 135–158.

Barker, Eileen. "Who'd Be a Moonie?" In *The Social Impact of New Religious Movements*, edited by Bryan Wilson. New York: Rose of Sharon Press, 1981, p. 59–96.

————. "The Ones Who Got Away." In *Religious Movements*, edited by Rodney Stark. Rose of Sharon Press, 1984.

Bell, Daniel (ed.). *Toward the Year 2000*. Boston: Beacon Press, 1969.

Bell, Daniel. "Religion in the Sixties," *Social Research* 38 (1971): 447–497.

Benin, Mary Holland. "Determinants of Opposition to Abortion," *Sociological Perspectives* 28 (1985): 199–216.

Berg, David Brandt. *The Book of the Future!* Zurich: World Service, 1984.

Bird, Frederick B., and Frances Westley. "The Economic Strategies of New Religious Movements," *Sociological Analysis* 46 (1985): 157–170.

Blake, Judith. "Family Size and the Quality of Children," *Demography* 18 (1981): 421–442.

————. *Family Size and Achievement*. Berkeley: University of California Press, 1989.

Bock, E. Wilbur, Leonard Beeghley, and Anthony J. Mixon. "Religion, Socioeconomic Status, and Sexual Morality," *Sociological Quarterly* 24 (1983): 545–559.

Borowick, Susan Claire. "Falsely Accused and Jailed in Argentina," *Persecution Endtime News*, two parts: (March) 3 (1994): 1–8; (June) 4:1–12.

Brandt, John L. *Great Bible Questions*. New York: Fleming H. Revel. 1926.

Brandt, Virginia. *The Hem of His Garment and Streams that Never Run Dry*. Zurich: World Services, 1981.

Bromley, David G. (ed.). *The Politics of Religious Apostasy.* Westport, Conn.: Praeger, 1998.

Carden, Maren Lockwood. *Oneida.* Baltimore: Johns Hopkins University Press, 1969.

Chi, S. Kenneth, and Sharon K. Houseknecht. "Protestant Fundamentalism and Marital Success," *Sociology and Social Research* 69 (1985): 351–375.

Chancellor, James D. *Life in the Family: An Oral History of the Children of God.* Syracuse, N.Y.: Syracuse University Press, 2000.

Chidester, David. *Salvation and Suicide.* Bloomington: Indiana University Press, 1988.

Clemente, Frank, and William J. Sauer. 1976 "Life Satisfaction in the United States," *Social Forces* 54 (1976): 621–631.

Cochran, John K., and Leonard Beeghley. "The Influence of Religion on Attitudes toward Nonmarital Sexuality, *Journal for the Scientific Study of Religion* 30 (1991): 45–62.

Cohn, Norman. *The Pursuit of the Millennium.* New York: Harper and Row, 1961.

Couch, Arthur, and Kenneth Kenniston. "Yeasayers and Naysayers: Agreeing Response Set as a Personality Variable," *Journal of Abnormal and Social Psychology* 60 (1960): 151–174.

Davis, James A., and Tom W. Smith. *General Social Surveys, 1972–1996: Cumulative Codebook.* Chicago: National Opinion Research Center, 1996.

Davis, Rex, and James T. Richardson. "The Organization and Functioning of the Children of God," *Sociological Analysis* 37 (1976): 321–339.

Durkheim, Emile. *The Division of Labor in Society.* New York: Free Press, 1893. Reprint 1964.

———. *Suicide.* New York, Free Press, 1897. Reprint 1951.

Eister, Allan W. "A Theory of Cults," *Journal for the Scientific Study of Religion* 11 (1972): 319–333.

Ellison, Christopher G. "Religious Involvement and Subjective Well-Being," *Journal of Health and Social Behavior* 32 (1991): 80–89

Ellison, Christopher G., David A. Gay, and Thomas A. Glass. "Does Religious Commitment Contribute to Individual Life Satisfaction?" *Social Forces* 68 (1989): 100–123.

Ellison, Christopher G., and Darren E. Sherkat. "Conservative Protestantism and Support for Corporal Punishment," *American Sociological Review* 58 (1993): 131–144.

Feher, Susannah. "Who Looks to the Stars?" Astrology and Its Constituency," *Journal for the Scientific Study of Religion* 31 (1992): 88–93.

Ferraro, Kenneth F., and Cynthia M. Albrecht-Jensen. "Does Religion Influence Adult Health?" *Journal for the Scientific Study of Religion* 30 (1991): 193–202.

Fisher, Randy, Donna Derison, Chester F. Polley III, Jennifer Cadman, and Dana Johnston. "Religiousness, Religious Orientation, and Attitudes Towards Gays and Lesbians," *Journal of Applied Social Psychology* 24 (1994): 614–630.

Foster, Lawrence. *Religion and Sexuality.* New York: Oxford University Press, 1981.

Gardner, Hugh. *The Children of Prosperity.* New York: St. Martin's, 1978.

Glenn, Norval D., and Charles N. Weaver. "Attitudes Toward Premarital, Extra-Marital, and Homosexual Relations in the United States in the 1970's," *Journal of Sex Research* 15 (1979): 108–118;

Greeley, Andrew M. *The Sociology of the Paranormal: A Reconnaissance.* Beverly Hills: Sage, 1975.

———. "Evidence that a Maternal Image of God Correlates with Liberal Politics," *Sociology and Social Research* 72 (1988): 150–154.

———. "Protestant and Catholic: Is The Analogical Imagination Extinct?" *American Sociological Review* 54 (1989): 485–502.

———. "The Paranormal Is Normal: A Sociologist Looks at Parapsychology," *The Journal of the American Society for Psychic Research* 85 (1991): 367–374.

Hall, John R. *Gone from the Promised Land.* New Brunswick, N.J.: Transaction, 1987.

Hardman, Charlotte E. "Keeping the Faith and Leaving the Army: TRF Supporters of the Lord's Endtime Family." In *Sex, Slander, and Salvation,* edited by James R. Lewis and J. Gordon Melton. Stanford: Calif.: Center for Academic Publication, 1994.

———. "The Ethics of Children in Three New Religions." In *Children in New Religions,* edited by Susan J. Palmer and Charlotte E. Hardman. New Brunswick, N.J.: Rutgers University Press, 1999, pp. 227–243.

Henry, Andrew F., and James F. Short. *Suicide and Homicide.* Glencoe, Ill.: Free Press, 1954.

Homans, George C. *The Human Group.* New York: Harcourt, Brace and World, 1950.

———. *The Nature of Social Science.* New York: Harcourt, Brace and World, 1967.

———. *Social Behavior: Its Elementary Forms.* New York: Harcourt Brace Jovanovich, 1974.

Hong, Lawrence K. "Anomia and Religiosity: Some Evidence for Reconceptualization," *Review of Religious Research* 22: 233–244, 1981.

Houriet, Robert. *Getting Back Together*. New York: Avon, 1972.

Jelen, Ted G. "Respect for Life, Sexual Morality, and Opposition to Abortion," *Review of Religious Research* 25 (1984): 220–231.

———. "Changes in the Attitudinal Correlations of Opposition to Abortion, 1977–1985," *Journal for the Scientific Study of Religion* 27 (1988): 211–228.

———. "Biblical Literalism and Inerrancy: Does the Difference Make a Difference?" *Sociological Analysis* 49 (1989): 421–429.

Kahn, Herman, and Anthony J. Wiener. *The Year 2000*. New York: Macmillan, 1967.

Kanter, Rosabeth Moss. *Commitment and Community*. Cambridge: Harvard University Press, 1972.

Kowalewski, David. "Cultism, Insurgency, and Vigilantism in the Philippines," *Sociological Analysis* 52 (1991): 241–253.

Ladd, Everett Carll. "A Debate on Abortion," *Public Opinion* 12 (1989): 3–8.

Lange, Paul A. M. "Being Better but Not Smarter Than Others," *Personality and Social Psychology Bulletin* 17 (1991): 689–693.

Lewis, C. S. *The Return of the Seven Keys*. Thailand: Aurora Productions, 1998.

Lewis, I. M. *Ecstatic Religion*. Baltimore: Penguin, 1971.

Lewis, James R, and J. Gordon Melton (eds.). *Sex, Slander, and Salvation: Investigating The Family/Children of God*. Stanford, Calif.: Center for Academic Publication, 1994.

Lenski, Gerhard. *The Religious Factor*. Garden City, New York: Doubleday, 1961.

Liou, Kuo-Tsai, Donald D. Sylvia, and Gregory Brunk. "Non-work Factors and Job Satisfaction Revisited," *Human Relations* 43 (1990): 77–86.

Lipset, Seymour Martin, and William Schneider. *The Confidence Gap*. New York, Free Press, 1983.

———. "The Confidence Gap During the Reagan Years, 1981–1987," *Political Science Quarterly* 102 (1987): 1–23.

Lofland, John, and Rodney Stark. "Becoming a World-Saver: A Theory of Conversion to a Deviant Perspective," *American Sociological Review* 30 (1965): 862–875.

Lovell-Troy, Lawrence A. "Anomia among Employed Wives and Housewives: An Exploratory Analysis," *Journal of Marriage and the Family* 45 (1983): 301–310.

Malinowski, Bronislaw. *Sex and Repression in Savage Society.* New York: Meridian, 1927. Reprint 1970.

Mancini, Jay A. "Social Indicators of Family Life Satisfaction: A Comparison of Husbands and Wives," *International Journal of Sociology of the Family* 9 (1979): 221–231.

Mann, William E. *Sect, Cult and Church in Alberta.* Toronto: University of Toronto Press, 1955.

Martin, Jack, and Steven Stack. "The Effect of Religiosity on Alienation: A Multivariate Analysis of Normlessness," *Sociological Focus* 16 (1983): 65–76.

McCready, William C., and Andrew M. Greeley. *The Ultimate Values of the American Population.* Beverly Hills, California: Sage, 1976.

McCutcheon, Allan L. "Sexual Morality, Pro-life Values, and Attitudes Toward Abortion," *Sociological Methods and Research* 16 (1987): 256–275.

McIntosh, William Alex, Letitia T. Alston, and Jon P. Alston. "The Differential Impact of Religious Preference and Church Attendance on Attitudes Toward Abortion," *Review of Religious Research* 20 (1979): 195–213.

Melton, J. Gordon. "The Revival of Astrology in the United States." In *Religious Movements,* edited by Rodney Stark. New York: Paragon, 1985, pp. 279–299.

———. *Encyclopedia of American Religions.* Detroit: Gale Research, 1993.

Mookherjee, Harsha N. "Perceptions of Well-Being by Metropolitan and Nonmetropolitan Populations in the United States," *The Journal of Social Psychology* 132 (1992): 513–524.

Mueller, Carol. "In Search of a Constituency for the 'New Religious Right,'" *Public Opinion Quarterly* 46 (1983): 213–229.

Mueller, John E. "Public Expectations of War During the Cold War," *American Journal of Political Science* 23 (1979): 301–329.

Nelsen, Hart M., Neil H. Cheek, Jr., and Paul Au. "Gender Differences in Images of God," *Journal for the Scientific Study of Religion* 24 (1985): 396–402.

Niebuhr, H. Richard. *The Social Sources of Denominationalism.* New York: Henry Holt, 1929.

Nordhoff, Charles. *The Communistic Societies of the United States.* London: John Murray, 1875.

Noyes, John Humphrey. *History of American Socialisms.* Philadelphia: Lippincott, 1870.

Ogburn, William Fielding. *Social Change.* New York: Huebsch, 1922.

Patrick, Ted, and Tom Dulack. *Let Our Children Go!* New York: Balantine, 1976.

Perrin, Robin D. "American Religion in the Post-Aquarian Age," *Journal for the Scientific Study of Religion* 28 (1989): 75–89.

Pfeifer, Jeffrey E. 1992 "The Psychological Framing of Cults: Schematic Representations and Cult Evaluations," *Journal of Applied Social Psychology* 22 (1992): 531–544.

Pollner, Melvin. "Divine Relations, Social Relations, and Well-Being," *Journal of Health and Social Behavior* 30 (1989): 92–104.

Reiss, Ira L., Ronald E. Anderson, and G. C. Sponaugle. "A Multivariate Model of the Determinants of Extramarital Sexual Permissiveness," *Journal of Marriage and the Family* 42 (1980): 395–411.

Renzi, Mario. "Ideal Family Size as an Intervening Variable Between Religion and Attitudes Toward Abortion," *Journal for the Scientific Study of Religion* 14 (1975): 23–27.

Richardson, James T. "Financing the New Religions: Comparative and Theoretical Considerations," *Journal for the Scientific Study of Religion* 21 (1982): 255–268.

Richardson, James T., and Rex Davis. "Experiential Fundamentalism," *Journal of the American Academy of Religion* 51 (1983): 397–425.

Roof, Clark Wade, and Jennifer L. Roof. "Review of the Polls: Images of God among Americans," *Journal for the Scientific Study of Religion* 23 (1984): 201–205.

Ryan, John. "Marital Happiness and Anomia," *Journal of Marriage and the Family* 43 (1981): 643–649.

Schneider, William, and I. A. Lewis. "The Straight Story on Homosexuality and Gay Rights," *Public Opinion* 7 (1984): 16–60.

Schoenfeld, Eugen. "Integration and Anomia: A Re-Examination," *Humboldt Journal of Social Relations* 11 (1983): 74–85.

Scott, Sir Walter. *The Perfect Ones.* Thailand: Aurora Productions, 1998.

Shinn, Larry D. "Conflicting Networks: Guru and Friend in ISKCON." In *Religious Movements,* edited by Rodney Stark. New York: Paragon, 1985, pp. 95–114.

Shupe, Anson D., and David G. Bromley. *The New Vigilantes: Deprogrammers, Anti-Cultists, and the New Religions.* Beverly Hills: Sage, 1980.

Simpson, John H. "Moral Issues and Status Politics." In *The New Religious Right,* edited by Robert C. Liebman and Robert Wuthnow. New York: Aldine, 1983.

Singh, B. Krishna. "Trends in Attitudes Toward Premarital Sexual Relations," *Journal of Marriage and the Family* 36 (1980): 387–393.

Singh, B. Krishna, and Peter J. Leahy. "Contextual and Ideological Dimensions of Attitudes Toward Discretionary Abortion," *Demography* 15 (1978): 381–388.

Srole, Leo. "Social Integration and Certain Corollaries: An Exploratory Study," *American Sociological Review* 21 (1956): 709–716.

Stark, Rodney. "Normal Revelations: A Rational Model of 'Mystical' Experiences," *Religion and the Social Order* 1 (1991): 239–251.

———. *The Rise of Christianity*. Princeton: Princeton University Press, 1996.

———. "Why Religious Movements Succeed or Fail: A Revised General Model," *Journal of Contemporary Religion* 11 (1996): 133–146.

Stark, Rodney, and Charles Y. Glock. *American Piety*. Berkeley: University of California Press, 1968.

Stark, Rodney, and William Sims Bainbridge. *The Future of Religion*. Berkeley: University of California Press, 1985.

———. *A Theory of Religion*. New York/Toronto: Lang, 1987. Reprint. New Brunswick, N.J.: Rutgers University Press, 1996.

———. *Religion, Deviance and Social Control*. New York: Routledge, 1996.

Stein, Stephen J. *The Shaker Experience in America*. New Haven: Yale University Press, 1992.

Szafran, Robert F. and Arthur F. Clagett. "Variable Predictors of Attitudes Toward the Legalization of Abortion," *Social Indicators Research* 20 (1988): 271–290.

Tipton, Steven M. *Getting Saved from the Sixties*. Berkeley: University of California Press, 1982.

Van Zandt, David E. *Living in the Children of God*. Princeton: Princeton University Press, 1991.

Vogt, Nancy R. *Correlates of Adolescent Sexual Activity in the Family*. Unpublished doctoral dissertation, Fuller Theological Seminary, 1998.

Wallis, Roy. "Millennialism and Community: Observations on the Children of God." In *Salvation and Protest*. New York: St. Martin's, 1979, pp. 51–90.

———. "Yesterday's Children: Cultural and Structural Change in a New Religious Movement." In *The Social Impact of New Religious Movements*, edited by Bryan Wilson. New York: Rose of Sharon, 1981, pp. 97–133.

Wangerin, Ruth. *The Children of God*. Westport, Conn.: Bergin and Garvey, 1993.

Warner, Samson. *We Are the Children of God!* Zurich: World Services, 1993.

Weaver, Charles N., and Robert S. Franz. "Work-Related Attitudes of Entrepreneurs, Public, and Private Employees," *Psychological Reports* 70 (1992): 387–390.

Weber, Max. *The Protestant Ethic and the Spirit of Protestantism.* New York: Scribner's 1904–1905. Reprint 1958.

Whitworth, John McKelvie. *God's Blueprints.* London: Routledge and Kegan Paul, 1975.

Williams, Miriam. *Heaven's Harlots: My Fifteen Years in a Sex Cult.* New York: William Morrow, 1998.

Wilson, Bryan R. "Factors in the Failure of the New Religious Movements." In *The Future of New Religious Movements,* edited by David G. Bromley and Phillip E. Hammond. Macon, Ga: Mercer University Press, 1987, pp. 30–45.

Woodrum, Eric, and Beth L. Davison. "Reexamination of Religious Influences on Abortion Attitudes," *Review of Religious Research* 33 (1992): 229–243.

Zablocki, Benjamin. *Alienation and Charisma.* New York: Free Press, 1980.

Index